Building Communities
A History of the Eruv in America

North American Jewish Studies
Series Editor
Ira Robinson (Concordia University)

Other Titles in this Series

Catalog of the Gerald K. Stone Collection of Judaica: A Bibliographical Resource for Canadian Jewish Studies
Gerald K. Stone

Strange Journey: John R. Friedeberg Seeley and the Quest for Mental Health
Paul Roberts Bentley

A Story of Jewish Experience in Mississippi
Leon Waldoff

Anti-Shechita Prosecutions in the Anglo-American World, 1855–1913: "A major attack on Jewish freedoms"
David Fraser

Conversations with Colleagues: On Becoming an American Jewish Historian
Edited by Jeffrey S. Gurock

History, Memory, and Jewish Identity
Edited by Ira Robinson, Naftali S. Cohn, and Lorenzo DiTommaso

Jews and American Public Life: Essays on American Jewish History and Politics
David G. Dalin

This Was America, 1865–1965: Unequal Citizens in the Segregated Republic
Gerd Korman

For more information on this series, please visit:
academicstudiespress.com/northamericanjewishstudies

Building Communities
A History of the Eruv in America

Adam Mintz

BOSTON
2023

Library of Congress Cataloging-in-Publication Data

Names: Mintz, Adam, author.
Title: Building communities : a history of the eruv in America / Adam Mintz.
Description: Boston : Academic Studies Press, 2023. | Series: North American Jewish studies | Includes bibliographical references and index.
Identifiers: LCCN 2022049258 (print) | LCCN 2022049259 (ebook) | ISBN 9798887190822 (hardback) | ISBN 9798887190839 (paperback) | ISBN 9798887190846 (adobe pdf) | ISBN 9798887190853 (epub)
Subjects: LCSH: Eruv--History. | Orthodox Judaism--United States.
Classification: LCC BM685 .M528 2023 (print) | LCC BM685 (ebook) | DDC 296.8/320973--dc23/eng/20221013
LC record available at https://lccn.loc.gov/2022049258
LC ebook record available at https://lccn.loc.gov/2022049259

ISBN 9798887190822 (hardback)
ISBN 9798887190839 (paperback)
ISBN 9798887190846 (adobe pdf)
ISBN 9798887190853 (epub)

Book design by Lapiz Digital Services.
Cover design by Ivan Grave.

Published by Academic Studies Press in 2023.
1577 Beacon Street
Brookline, MA 02446, USA
press@academicstudiespress.com
www.academicstudiespress.com

Contents

Acknowledgements

In 2012, I was awarded a fellowship at the Tikvah Center for Law and Jewish Civilization. The annual theme of the fellowship was "Reconsidering the Public and Private Spheres in Law and Jewish Civilization." In seminars, workshops, and conversations around afternoon tea, the topic of *eruv* was discussed in the context of the relationship between the public and private spheres. The difficulty of appreciating how an "invisible string" could demarcate a private sphere in Jewish law was brought home to me when I showed a precocious fifteen-year-old son of one of the other fellows the eruv string that was tied to two lampposts on Sixth Avenue in Manhattan. As we stood on opposite sides of the string, I tried to explain that I was standing in a public space, while he was standing in a private area. The expression on his face allowed me to recognize the fragility and uniqueness of this halakhic argument.

The challenges inherent in studying *eruvin* and building a community eruv have fascinated me since my days in the Yeshiva University *beit midrash*. My halakhic interest in eruvin was integrated with the historical and cultural importance of the topic through the suggestion and mentorship of Professor Lawrence Schiffman at the Skirball Department of Hebrew and Judaic Studies at New York University. Professor Schiffman's mastery of the halakhic and practical aspects of eruvin never ceased to amaze me, and his tales about how he supervised the building of one of the first suburban eruvin in America testified to his vast experience in this area.

I wrote my dissertation about the history of eruvin in America while I served as Associate Rabbi at Congregation Kehilath Jeshurun and Senior Rabbi at Lincoln Square Synagogue, both in Manhattan. The appreciation of the value of my doctorate expressed by both congregations encouraged me as I balanced my pastoral and academic responsibilities. More recently, the congregants at Kehilat Rayim Ahuvim and my colleagues and students at Maharat have encouraged me as I completed both my doctoral work and the manuscript of this volume. Following the completion of my doctorate, on the occasion of the publication of a Festschrift in his honor, Professor Schiffman reminded me that there was a spot on his bookshelf waiting for my published dissertation.

The preparation of the manuscript for this volume would have been impossible without the editorial and scholarly assistance of Eve Levavi Feinstein. During many of our discussions of the intricacies of eruvin, I felt as if I was back in the beit midrash or the lounge in the Skirball Department at NYU. Eve both improved and strengthened the contents of the manuscript, translating an academic work into a more accessible volume.

Along the way, there have been many people who have offered advice and friendship. Teachers and mentors, colleagues and friends, students and congregants have all contributed to make this volume come to life. As always, there is one person without whom there would have been no dissertation or book. Rabbi Shmuel Pultman, who for years quietly collected historical and halakhic material on every aspect of the eruv in an attempt to prove the validly of community and city eruvin, mentored and guided me from the beginning of my journey in eruvin. He was always available to answer questions, to strengthen my arguments, and to correct mistakes.

My congregants have been especially gracious in supporting and encouraging my work. They smile each time I give a historical lecture or halakhic *shiur* on eruvin, and I hope that they have come to share my fascination with this topic and its implications for the history of Orthodoxy in America. I am especially appreciative of the Lewis family, having shared many years of davening and Torah Study with Dorothy and Bob Lewis. Tragically, Dorothy passed away in September 2021, and the family has dedicated this book to her memory.

I conclude with an appreciation of my family. My father and mother taught us the value of books and education, and my father's rabbinic and legal training never let me get away with an argument or *d'var Torah* that was not clear and well-articulated. My father passed away in the year before this book was published, but his steadfast commitment to Jewish life in America is evident on every page.

For my children, Noam, Lily, Ariel, Ashley, and Shoshana, the topic of eruvin still elicits a smile. At least now, it is a smile of completion and satisfaction. Finally, I am grateful to my wife Sharon, whose love of Jewish books and Jewish learning has created in our home an atmosphere of passionate engagement with our culture and tradition. This book is dedicated to her.

Introduction

According to the Mishnah, thirty-nine types of labor are prohibited on the Sabbath, including carrying an object from one domain to another. However, the rabbis in Roman Palestine introduced a procedure by which such carrying would be permissible, called an *eruv* (plural *eruvin*). Three elements are necessary to permit carrying in a public or semi-public area: The property must be enclosed by a physical boundary, a joint partnership must be created between the property's residents through the sharing of a food product, and if non-Jews live within the property, their property must be leased by the Jewish residents.

Each of these requirements created certain challenges for rabbinic authorities as Jewish communities expanded beyond the traditional courtyards of Roman Palestine. The Mishnah describes the symbolic enclosing of a courtyard through the utilization of crossbeams and end posts at its entrance, but these structures no longer sufficed as Jews moved outside self-enclosed areas and into larger neighborhoods. This change of circumstance required the rabbis to utilize natural or existing boundaries such as city walls and bodies of water to create enclosures around these neighborhoods and later around the cities in which Jews lived.

The requirements that Jews within the enclosure form a joint partnership and that they lease the property of non-Jews also created challenges as Jews increasingly shared living areas with non-Jews or with Jews who did not accept the principle of eruvin. Furthermore, once Jews began to reside in larger cites, they were a minority within the area that was to be enclosed by the eruv, and they often had to deal with local governmental authorities who might not be sympathetic to the idea of creating an eruv.

Yet, in spite of these challenges, eruvin were created by Jewish communities throughout the world. In Europe and the Middle East, rabbis spearheaded the creation of eruvin in small Jewish neighborhoods and larger urban settings. As the medieval walls of many European cities were taken down in the nineteenth century, rabbis replaced these eruv boundaries with other natural or man-made borders. The invention of the telegraph, which had wires and poles that resembled the crossbeams and end posts of the courtyards of Roman Palestine, presented new potential eruv boundaries in the modern city. However, this option also raised many new halakhic issues that were matters of heated dispute among the leading rabbis of the time.

As Jews immigrated in increasing numbers from Europe to North America at the end of the nineteenth century, rabbis were faced with the question of how to transplant the European tradition of community eruvin into American cities. Prior to 1970, the only city eruvin in North America were those in St. Louis, Toronto, and the East Side of Manhattan, followed by an eruv encompassing the entire borough of Manhattan. These eruvin were established by rabbis of Eastern European background who initially based their arguments for the validity of their eruvin on the precedents set by the rabbis of earlier generations, especially those of their native countries in Europe.

At the same time, however, the discussions around these American eruvin reflected the new realities that these rabbis found in the cities in which they resided. Members of their Orthodox synagogues did not observe the laws of the Sabbath with the same punctiliousness with which the rabbis were familiar. The question of how to address these "non-observant Orthodox" was critical for American rabbis, who debated the desirability of creating eruvin for communities in which the prohibition of carrying was often not observed.

Another challenge facing the rabbis who established the earliest North American eruvin was the lack of a relationship with local governmental officials, which made it impossible for them to erect their own eruv structures or to lease the areas encompassed by their eruvin from government authorities. Over time, a growing and strengthening relationship with broader society, including local political officials, allowed a more established Jewish community to create eruvin that met a more stringent standard.

The challenges facing the Eastern European Orthodox immigrant rabbis to America were daunting. The famed Rabbi Israel Meir Ha-Kohen, known as the

Ḥafeẓ Hayyim, wrote in 1893 that "whoever wanted to have true merit before the Lord should strengthen himself and not live in those faraway lands." He went on to say that if someone was forced to travel to these places, he should leave his children behind.[1]

This view was shared by Rabbi Jacob David Wilowsky, founder of a prominent yeshiva in Slutsk, Belarus, and known by the acronym Ridbaz. In 1900, he traveled to the United States for six months to raise money to complete his commentary on the Jerusalem Talmud. During his stay, he addressed a gathering of the Union of Orthodox Congregations in New York and was quoted as condemning anyone who came to America. "For here, Judaism . . . is trodden underfoot. It was not only home that the Jews left behind them in Europe, it was their Torah, their Talmud, their Yeshebahs (sic), their Chochomim (sic)."[2] Nevertheless, in 1903, Rabbi Wilowsky immigrated to Chicago, where he lived for two years before becoming disillusioned and moving to Safed.[3]

Although this negative view of America was not shared by all the Eastern European rabbis, the ambivalence toward Judaism, and especially halakhic Judaism, in America was fundamental to the thinking of the early American Orthodox rabbis, who relied on the rabbinic opinions of the rabbis of Eastern Europe and did not take seriously the precedent or the opinions of the rabbinic leaders in America.[4]

---

1 Israel Meir ha-Kohen, *Nidḥei Yisra'el* (Warsaw, 1893), epilogue. For a thorough review of the rabbinic voices in opposition to emigration to America and the popular anti-emigration sentiment expressed in the Hebrew and Yiddish newspapers in Eastern Europe, see Arthur Hertzberg, "'Treifene Medina': Learned Opposition to Emigration to the United States," in *Proceedings of the Eighth World Congress of Jewish Studies: Panel Sessions Jewish History* (Jerusalem, 1984), 1–30. The view that saw the immigration to America as a move to the promised land, a view that was most often expressed by those who sought freedom from pressure to be observant in Eastern Europe, is surveyed in Israel Bartal, "Amerika shel ma'alah: Arẓot ha-Berit ke-idi'al u-khe-mofet le-Yehudei mizraḥ Eiropah be-me'ah ha-19," in *Be-ikvot Kolumbus: Amerikah, 1492–1992*, ed. Miri Eliav-Feldon (Jerusalem, 1996), 511–522.

2 Jacob David Wilowsky, "Union of Orthodox Congregations," *American Hebrew* 68, no. 7 (January 4, 1901): 236.

3 For a biography of Ridbaz, see Aaron Rothkoff, "The American Sojourns of Ridbaz: Religious Problems within the Immigrant Community," *American Jewish Historical Quarterly* 57, no. 4 (June 1968): 557–572; and Abraham J. Karp, "The Ridwas: Rabbi Jacob David Wilowsky; 1845–1913," in *Perspectives on Jews and Judaism: Essays in Honor of Wolfe Kelman* (New York, 1978), 215–237.

4 The premier example of an immigrant American Orthodox rabbi who viewed life in America and American democracy in a positive light is Rabbi Chaim Hirschenson, who served as rabbi in Hoboken, New Jersey from 1903 to 1935. See Eliezer Schweid, *Democracy and Halakhah* (Lanham, MD, 1994), 47–75; and Chaim Hirschenson, *Sefer malki ba-kodesh*, ed. David Zohar (Jerusalem, 2006).

The attitude of the rabbinic community toward Judaism in America was slow to change. Yet a change can be seen in a sermon delivered by Rabbi Moshe Feinstein in commemoration of the one hundred fiftieth anniversary of the United States Constitution in 1939, two years after he immigrated to the United States. He said:

> And so, the government of the United States, which already 150 years ago established its law that it will not uphold or favor any faith but will allow anyone to do as they see fit, and the government will serve only to assure that no one harms another, they are thus following the will of Almighty God, and they therefore succeeded and grew during this time. And, we are obligated to pray for them that Almighty God shall have them succeed in whatever they undertake.[5]

Rabbi Feinstein's public statement of approval for the American model of separation of religion and state was not an endorsement of American secularism. Yet, in the years leading up to World War II, there was a feeling among Orthodox rabbis that America could serve as a haven for those who were forced to leave Europe due to the rise of Hitler and that the arrival of leading rabbinic authorities in America would allow Jews to recreate the Torah community of Eastern Europe in the United States.[6] With the destruction of European Jewry in the Holocaust, the shift of Judaism's center from Europe to America became a reality. In the discussions surrounding the creation of the Manhattan eruv between 1949 and 1962, rabbis on all sides of the dispute accepted the establishment of the religious community in America and began to acknowledge an American tradition of eruvin.

This book traces the history of North American eruvin from the early efforts by immigrant rabbis to those of the more established Orthodox community of subsequent decades. As we will see, the story of American eruvin is the story of the American Orthodox community, which developed from a non-observant laity led by immigrant rabbis with little independent power into a religiously engaged and observant community with strong ties to local government, which ultimately forged its own halakhic tradition.

---

5 Moshe Feinstein, *Darash Mosheh* (New York, 1988), *derush* 10, p. 416. Translation in Chaim I. Waxman, "From Treifene Medina to Goldene Medina: Changing Perspectives on the United States among American Haredi," in *Why is America Different? American Jewry on Its 350th Anniversary*, ed. Steven T. Katz (Lanham, MD, 2009), 117.

6 Waxman, "Treifene Medina," 118.

Primary Sources

Extensive halakhic material was published both in favor of and in opposition to the creation of the North American eruvin discussed in this study. The St. Louis eruv controversy led Rabbi Zekhariah Rosenfeld, the creator of that eruv, and Rabbi Shalom Elchanan Jaffe, an opponent, to pen lengthy treatises defending their views. These treatises provide insight into the halakhic reasoning of each of these rabbis, the social considerations that they addressed, and the relationship between them.

Rabbi Joshua Seigel, the creator of the eruv on the East Side of Manhattan, likewise authored a defense of his eruv in a treatise written for members of the Jewish community who had requested that he look into building one. Three responsa opposing Rabbi Seigel's eruv were also published, which, in addition to offering halakhic arguments, lamented the fact that many Jews on the East Side were carrying on the Sabbath.

Rabbi Yehudah Leib Graubart's articulation of the halakhic basis for the creation of the Toronto eruv was included in his collection of responsa, entitled *Havalim ba-ne'imim*. Later material on the expansion of the Toronto eruv can be found in rabbinic journals and in an unpublished manuscript written Rabbi Abraham Price, which he privately distributed to members of his community.

The dispute over the eruv surrounding the entirety of Manhattan played out over thirteen years, from 1949 to 1962. It took the form of written responsa, journal articles, and personal letters. Some of this material has been published, and other, unpublished material has been obtained from the Library of Yeshiva University and the archives of The Jewish Center.

An important source for the study of the halakhic and social aspects of the disputes over the North American eruvin can be found in the approbations that were appended by each of the rabbis to their works. These approbations, which came from Eastern European rabbis, supported the American rabbis' arguments and provided them with credibility. Rabbi Jaffe's treatises included several approbations from rabbis in Israel who supported his argument against the creation of an eruv in St. Louis. Rabbi Seigel's treatise in support of creating an eruv on the East Side of Manhattan included an approbation by Rabbi Shalom Mordekhai Schwadron of Brezhin Poland, which became a subject of dispute, with some rabbis challenging both its content and its authenticity. There has been no systematic treatment of any of this material in either scholarly or popular literature to date.

Secondary Literature

Not surprisingly, because of the complexities surrounding the creation of eruvin, this topic has spawned many volumes of rabbinic literature. These include guidebooks for the creation and maintenance of community eruvin, several of which were penned in the last decades of the twentieth century. In the past several decades, however, the topic of eruvin has also caught the attention of scholars and artists, sociologists and politicians. Historians have begun to study the development of the eruv from the courtyards of Roman Palestine to the urban eruvin of the modern period. How did the walls and gates of the early period evolve into the virtually invisible lines of the modern period? How can the history of the eruv inform an understanding of the history of Jews in cities and towns throughout Europe and the Muslim world? And how can the history of the eruv in the twentieth century contribute to an appreciation of the development of Orthodoxy in America and modern-day Europe? Several historians, most prominently Charlotte Elisheva Fonrobert and Boaz Hutterer, have grappled with these issues and attempted to weave the eruv into the fabric of the history of Jewish communities and cultures.[7] For artists, the ability to imagine "virtually invisible" lines as solid walls has created endless opportunities to delve into the worlds of the imaginary and the real and the relationship between them.[8] Yet the history of eruvin in America has not been studied in depth.

The story of Orthodoxy in America has been reviewed and written about by scholars and rabbis. Jeffrey Gurock analyzed the challenges that faced first- and second-generation immigrant rabbis as they addressed the American Orthodox community. The tension between what Gurock describes as the "resistors" and the "accommodators"—those who attempted to maintain the traditions of the past and those who were willing to accommodate the different religious behaviors and outlooks they encountered in America—set the agenda for all

---

7 Charlotte Elisheva Fonrobert, "From Separatism to Urbanism: The Dead Sea Scrolls and the Origins of the Rabbinic Eruv," *Dead Sea Discoveries* 11, no. 1 (2004): 43–71; and Boaz Hutterer, "Eruv ḥaẓerot be-merḥav ha-eroni: Hishtasheluto ha-hilkhatit mi-tekufat ha-Mishnah ve-ha-Talmud ve-ad teḥilat ha-meah ha-20" ["The 'Courtyard Eruv' in the Urban Space: Its Development From the Time of the Mishnah and the Talmud to the Twentieth Century"] (PhD diss., Bar-Ilan University, Tel Aviv, 2013).

8 See Adam Mintz, ed., *It's a Thin Line: Eruv from Talmudic to Modern Culture* (New York, 2014) for a collection of historical, halakhic, and artistic articles and depictions of the eruv.

subsequent studies of American Orthodoxy.[9] Yet the study of the American Orthodox has not, for the most part, focused on the halakhic literature written by these rabbis. How did these rabbis adapt their halakhic decision-making to the American Orthodox community?[10]

The example of Rabbi Hayyim Hirschensohn, who arrived in America in 1903, caught the interest of several scholars. Rabbi Hirschensohn wrote that halakhic decisions must address the needs of the American community and, most importantly, that the American Orthodox rabbinate needed to find ways to be more lenient. As he wrote, "it is just as easy to be lenient as it is to be strict" in halakhic rulings.[11]

Kimmy Caplan has written a thorough and insightful history of the immigrant Orthodox preacher, or pulpit rabbi, in America, exploring the challenges and tensions that these rabbis faced in attempting to transplant their Eastern European traditions and mores into American soil.[12] Caplan's work falls into the genre of microhistory, the study of a narrow field for the purpose of shedding light on a larger phenomenon, in this case the broader history of American Orthodoxy. The present volume takes a similar approach but applies it to the study of the immigrant Orthodox halakhist, or legal decisor. Halakhists were forced to grapple with the questions of whether halakhah exhibited enough flexibility to be adapted to their new society and, if it did, whether to utilize this flexibility to accommodate the more lax American community or to opt for a more rigid stance in the hope of strengthening American Orthodoxy. All this

---

9 Jeffrey Gurock, "Resisters and Accommodators: Varieties of Orthodox Rabbis in America, 1886–1983," *American Jewish Archives* (November 1983): 100–187. Reprinted in *The American Rabbinate: A Century of Continuity and Change, 1883–1983* (New York, 1985), 10–97.

10 For some important initial works on "American Halakhah" see Jonathan D. Sarna, "How Matzah Became Square: Manischewitz and the Development of Machine-Made Matzah in the United States," in *Chosen Capital: The Jewish Encounter with American Capitalism*, ed. Rebecca Kobrin (Ithaca, NY, 2012), 277–288; and the first three chapters in Zev Eleff, *Authentically Orthodox: A Tradition-Bound Faith in American Life* (Detroit, 2020), 29–80.

11 For several treatments of this topic, see Jeffrey S. Gurock, *Orthodox Jews in America* (Bloomington, IN, 2009); Adam Mintz, "Is Coca-Cola Kosher? Rabbi Tobias Geffen and the History of American Orthodoxy," in *Rav Chesed: Essays in Honor of Rabbi Dr. Haskel Lookstein*, ed. Rafael Medoff (Jersey City, 2009), vol. 2, 75–90; Marc Shapiro, "Another Example of Minhag America," *Judaism* 39, no. 2 (Spring 1990): 148–154; and David Tamar, *Jewish Commitment in a Modern World: Rabbi Hayyim Hirschensohn and His Attitude to Modernity* [Hebrew] (Jerusalem, 2003), reviewed by Marc Shapiro, *Edah Journal* 5, no. 1 (Tamuz 5765), http://www.edah.org/backend/JournalArticle/5_1_Shapiro.pdf.

12 Kimmy Caplan, "Ortodokẓiah ba-olam he-ḥadash: Rabbanim u-derashot be-Amerika, 1881–1924," *American Jewish History* 90, no. 1 (2002): 74–76.

occurred in a context in which rabbis were attempting to establish their own authority in a foreign and sometimes hostile environment.

As background to its study of the North American eruvin, this book will discuss the talmudic sources for the concept of eruvin and the responsa on medieval and early modern eruvin that created precedent for those in America. Academic scholarship on this material is limited. The only treatments to date are those of Charlotte Elisheva Fonrobert and Boaz Hutterer, cited above. Primary source material on city eruvin from the medieval and early modern periods is found in the responsa literature and other halakhic works, but no books on the topic were published until the nineteenth century, when disputes over the creation of eruvin in Cracow and Odessa were chronicled in treaties written by local rabbinic authorities. Rabbi Yosef Gavriel Bechhofer's *The Contemporary Eruv: Eruvin in Modern Metropolitan Areas* (Jerusalem, 1998) has been updated and published in its fourth edition in 2020, and Rabbi Chaim Jachter's *Walking the Line: Hilchot Eruvin from the Sources to the Streets* (2020) contains some historical material about the early American eruvin. However, these works were written as guidebooks for the creation of modern eruvin and should not be considered historical works.

An extremely valuable resource on eruvin is the blog *Eruv Online*, which has been available since 2005.[13] It contains incredible information about the history of eruvin generally and the debates surrounding American eruvin specifically. It was initially posted anonymously, as community eruvin were a divisive topic in several communities in the New York Metropolitan area. However, it is now safe to give credit where credit is due and to acknowledge Rabbi Shmuel Pultman as an expert on both the halakhic and historical material on eruvin.

These sources, both primary and secondary, will provide the foundation for the analysis of the laws of eruv and its application for the history of the eruv in North America.

---

13 Shmuel Pultman, *Eruv Online*, http://eruvonline.blogspot.com/.

1

History of the Eruv

The Talmud contains an entire tractate discussing the laws of *eruvin*, yet the *eruv* went through generations of evolution as the rabbis attempted to apply the talmudic principles to changing realities. In this chapter, we will explore the development of many of the halakhic principles first introduced in the Talmud and how they were applied in different neighborhoods and cities throughout the post-talmudic, medieval, and early modern periods. In order to appreciate the debates surrounding the eruvin of North America in the twentieth century, it is crucial to understand the challenges that faced rabbis as they built eruvin in cities and towns throughout the Jewish world.

Rabbinic Sources

The sanctity of the Sabbath is a cornerstone of Judaism. It is one of the Ten Commandments, and there are numerous other references throughout the Torah to God's demand that the Jewish People observe the Sabbath.[1] The Sabbath is a day on which the Jewish people—including their children, slaves,

1 References to the Sabbath occur in Gen 2:2–3; Exod 16:22–28, 20:8–11, 23:12, 24:21, 35:2–3; Num 15:32–36; Deut 5:12–15.

servants, and animals and the foreigners who live with them—are forbidden to work. However, the Torah never makes clear what constitutes "work," and establishing the parameters of work was a major concern of early rabbis.

The definition of "work" appears in the Mishnah in the form of a list of thirty-nine prohibited activities (Shabbat 7:2). One of these activities is *hoẓa'ah,* carrying on the Sabbath in the public domain (*reshut ha-rabbim*) or from one public or private domain into another. However, the Mishnah also introduces a legal device to circumvent the prohibition of *hoẓa'ah,* which it calls *eruv ḥaẓerot.* An *eruv ḥaẓerot* (or simply *eruv*) effectively encloses an area in which Jews live, allowing it to be classified as a single private domain (*reshut ha-yaḥid*), in which carrying is permissible.

While in later parlance, the term "eruv" came to refer primarily to the physical enclosure that demarcates the area, in rabbinic terminology, *eruv ḥaẓerot* ("courtyard" eruv) refers primarily to the sharing of food, which, along with the physical enclosure, allows the area to be treated as a private domain. While this chapter will focus primarily on physical enclosures and the leasing of property, which were key to the legal disputes discussed throughout the rest of this book, it is important to note the centrality of food sharing to the rabbinic concept.

Definition of Domains

Although the Mishnah lists *hoẓa'ah,* carrying from one domain to another, as one of the thirty-nine categories of work prohibited on the Sabbath (Shabbat 7:2), it does not explain what constitutes a "domain" (*reshut*). This is clarified in a baraita in Shabbat (6a):

> There are four domains in respect to the Sabbath: a private domain (*reshut ha-yaḥid*), a public domain (*reshut ha-rabbim*), a *karmelit,*[2] and a place of exemption (*makom petur*). And what is a private domain? A trench ten [handbreadths (*tefaḥim*)] deep and four wide, and likewise the top of a wall ten [handbreadths] high and four broad—that is a private domain. And what is a public domain? A major road (*seratya*), a great public square (*pelatya*), and open alleys (*mevo'ot ha-mefulashim*)—that is a public domain. One may not carry out from this private domain to the public one, nor carry in from this public domain to the private one. And if one does carry out or in unwittingly, one is

2 This term will be explained subsequently.

> liable for a sin offering; if deliberately, one is punished by *karet* [excision] or stoned. But the sea, an open field, a stone block in front of the stores, or a *karmelit* ranks neither as a public nor as a private domain: one must not carry [objects] about within it, but if one does, one is not liable; and one must not carry out [an object] into the public domain or from the public domain into it, nor carry [an object] from it into the private domain or from the private domain into it; yet if one does carry out or in, one is not liable. As for courtyards with many owners (*ḥaẓer shel rabbim*) and closed alleys (*mevo'ot she'einan mefulashim*), if an eruv is made, they are permitted [to carry within them]; if an eruv is not made, they are forbidden [to carry within them].[3]

This baraita identifies four basic types of domains.

1. Private domain (*reshut ha-yaḥid*). The baraita explains that a private domain is any space that is four handbreadths long and four handbreadths wide and has sides or partitions that are ten handbreadths high. The examples given are a trench that is ten handbreadths deep and an area surrounded by a wall that is ten handbreadths high. Surprisingly, this text does not describe a typical private domain, which would be a house or courtyard surrounded by walls, but the Gemara takes it for granted that an individual house or a private courtyard (*ḥaẓer shel yaḥid*) falls into this category.

2. Public domain (*reshut ha-rabbim*). The baraita's examples of public domains are a major road (*seratya*), a great public square (*pelatya*), and open alleys (*mevo'ot ha-mefulashim*). A "public square" was a marketplace through which people, carts, and camels passed, using the major roads (*seratya*) for ingress and egress.[4] Leading off from the square were open alleyways that were often filled with shops and booths. These alleyways often had a concentration of

---

3 Shabbat 6a. A similar tradition is found in t. Shab. 1:1–5. (All references to Tosefta will be taken from Saul Liberman, *Tosefta* [New York, 1962]. This edition utilizes the Vienna manuscript of Tosefta.) The tosefta begins, "there are four domains" but goes on to identify only the public and private domains. The baraita also introduced four domains and did not identify the *makom patur*. Both formulations point to the fact that the public and private domains are the two domains on the basis of which the other domains are identified. For a discussion of the relationship between the baraita and the tosefta, which preceded it chronologically, see Saul Lieberman, *Tosefta ki-feshutah* (New York, 1962), Shab. 1–4; and Shmuel and Zeev Safrai, *Mishnat Ereẓ Yisrael: Masekhet Eruvin* (Jerusalem, 2009), 2–5. See also y. Shab. 1:1 for a variant of the baraita and tosefta.

4 Daniel Sperber, *The City in Roman Palestine* (New York, 1998), 9.

specialized craftsmen, organized in a guild framework.[5] The gemara in Shabbat 99a asserts that the width of the road on which the Jews in the wilderness transported the boards for the tabernacle was sixteen cubits wide. Therefore, the rabbis say that a public domain is an area that is at least sixteen cubits wide.[6]

3. *Karmelit.* The baraita identifies several types of spaces that have the status of a *karmelit,* which is "neither a public nor a private domain":[7] the sea, an open field, and a *stoa,* a covered walkway on which merchants sold their wares but which was not easily accessible.[8] These spaces are technically open to the public but are not easily reachable for travel and are not surrounded by walls.[9]

4. Place of exemption (*makom patur*). The term "place of exemption" is defined in Shabbat 7b as an area that does not meet the criteria of either a public domain or a private domain but has a width of less than four handbreadths and therefore is not considered a *karmelit.*[10]

Carrying from a private domain to a public domain or from a public domain to a private one is forbidden and punishable by the death penalty if done deliberately. (An accidental transgression necessitates as sin offering.) Since a *karmelit* (or a "place of exemption") is neither public nor private, the rules for a public domain apply, but transgressing them carries no penalty.

The baraita does not explicitly state that carrying within a public domain is prohibited, but this seems to be implied by the rules for the *karmelit.* (The prohibition is stated explicitly in the gemara in Shabbat 96b.) The rules for a "place of exemption" are also not stated explicitly, but later halakhah gives them the same status as a *karmelit.*

The baraita also mentions two additional types of domains.

---

5 Ibid., 11.

6 There is another source that identifies a public domain as sixteen cubits wide. M. B. Bat. 6:7 says: "A public domain is sixteen cubits wide." For the relationship between this mishnah and the rabbinic statement in b. Shab. 99a, see Rav Nissim Gaon on b. Shab. 99a. Sperber argues that this width does not match the width of major roads in Roman times. However, he explains that the rabbis and the Greeks had different methods of measuring, which may account for the discrepancy in the measurements they give for the widths of the major roads (Sperber, *The City in Roman Palestine,* 103–104).

7 The "in-between" status of the *karmelit* is reflected in the possible derivations of the word. The Yerushalmi (Shab. 1:1) argues that *karmelit* is composed of the words *rakh,* "soft," and *male,* "full," reflecting the in-between status of grain that is still moist and soft but ripe to be harvested. Rambam in his *Commentary to the Mishnah,* Shab. 1:1, argued that *karmelit* is derived from *ke-armelit,* "like a widow," who is in-between as she is neither married nor a virgin.

8 Sperber, *The City in Roman Palestine,* 11–12.

9 See *Tosefta ki-feshutah,* Shab. 3.

10 B. Shab. 7b.

1. Courtyard with many owners (*ḥaẓer shel rabbim*). In his study of Palestinian houses during the Roman period, Yizhar Hirschfeld explains that courtyards were situated in common areas in front of homes and served a variety of purposes for those who lived around them. In many cases, multiple families used the same courtyard.[11] Eating and drinking, washing and food preparation, cooking and baking, raising and slaughtering of fowl, production and storage of goods for household use and sometimes even the sale of market goods, visiting among neighbors, and sometimes sleeping all took place in the courtyard.[12] The common ownership of the courtyard was an important element in the creation of small communities, and, generally, a wall would be built around the courtyard to separate it from other courtyards that may have adjoined it.[13]

2. Closed alleyway (*mavoi she-eino mefulash*). Closed alleys were common in Roman times. In contrast to an open alleyway (*mavoi mefulash*), which opened into to a public domain at both ends, a closed alleyway opened at one end into a public domain but was closed at the other end, similar to the modern-day cul-de-sac. In both cases, walls bordered the adjoining courtyards to separate them from the more public *mavoi* area.[14]

It is with respect to these two final categories that the baraita introduces the concept of eruv. Within these areas, which are partly enclosed, carrying is permitted with an eruv but forbidden without one.

The gemara in Shabbat 96b provides a biblical derivation for the prohibition of carrying from one domain to another:

> Where is carrying out [from a private domain to a public domain or vice versa] written? Said Rabbi Yoḥanan, "The Torah states, 'And Moses instructed, and a proclamation went out throughout the camp [to stop the donations to the tabernacle]' [Exod 36:6]. Now, where was Moses standing? In the camp of the Levites,

---

11 See Yizhar Hirschfeld, *The Palestine Dwelling in the Roman Byzantine Period* (Jerusalem, 1995), 21–107. Baker argues that is impossible to know for certain whether the residents in the houses in a courtyard were members of the same extended family, and, therefore, there may have been some blurring of lines between the need for privacy in the *ḥaẓer* and the sharing that took place between neighbors. See Cynthia M. Baker, *Rebuilding the House of Israel: Architectures of Gender in Jewish Antiquity* (Stanford, CA, 2002), 35–42 and 114–122. The fact that the small *ḥaẓer* was shared by different families may be reflected in the baraita's term *ḥaẓer shel rabbim*.
12 See, for example, m. B. Bat. 3:5. For a list of items that were generally found in the courtyard with a discussion of the archaeological discoveries and their relevance to the talmudic descriptions, see Hirschfeld, *Palestinian Dwelling*, 272–288.
13 See m. Ma'as. 3:5 and the discussion in Hirschfeld, *Palestinian Dwelling*, 272–273.
14 Hirschfeld, *Palestinian Dwelling*, 273.

> which was a public domain. And he said to the Israelites, 'Do not carry from your private domain to this public domain.'"

The gemara goes on to address the prohibition of carrying within a public domain: "From where is it known that one who carries four cubits (*amot*) in the public domain is liable? All instances of carrying four cubits in a public domain are prohibited by tradition."

Unlike carrying from one domain to another, which is given a biblical source, the prohibition of carrying within the public domain is merely attributed to "tradition." The gemara also makes this prohibition more specific: Carrying within the public domain is forbidden for more than a distance of four cubits.

Which Domains Can Be Enclosed by an Eruv?

The baraita in Shabbat 7a describes the role of an eruv only in the cases of a courtyard with many owners and a closed alleyway, and it seems to imply that an eruv cannot be used to enclose a public domain. Another baraita, cited in Eruvin 6a, offers guidelines for constructing an eruv within a public domain, but the Gemara restricts these guidelines to an open alleyway, excluding the other types of public domains (open roads and public squares).

At the same time, the Gemara raises the issue of creating an eruv around an entire city: "As Rabbah bar Bar Ḥannah said in the name of Rabbi Yoḥanan, 'The city of Jerusalem, were its doors [gates] not closed at night, one would be liable there for carrying in a public.'"[15] According to this gemara, even an area as large as Jerusalem does not have the status of a public domain if it is surrounded by walls and its gates are not closed at night.

None of these texts directly address the issue of building an eruv around a *karmelit*. However, it would seem that a courtyard with many owners and a closed alleyway have the same in-between status as a *karmelit*. They are not private domains, since numerous people live in houses adjoining these spaces. Yet they are also not public domains, since they are not spaces of public access. The ability to create eruvin in in-between spaces such as a *ḥaẓer, mavoi*, or *karmelit* is the subject of most of the medieval rabbinic discussion regarding the institution of eruvin.

Construction of the Eruv

To create an eruv around a particular space, the area must be physically enclosed so that it resembles a private domain, in which carrying on the Sabbath is

---

15 B. Eruv. 6b.

permitted. The Talmud introduces different methods of enclosing different types of spaces to create an area in which carrying is permitted.[16]

1. Closed alleyway (*mavoi she'eino mefulash*). A typical closed alleyway requires a partition on the side of the alley that opens into the public domain. The Mishnah writes: "Concerning the preparation of an alleyway [for the purpose of establishing an eruv], the school of Shammai says: A side post (*leḥi*) and a crossbeam (*korah*) [are required]. The school of Hillel says: A side post or a crossbeam [is required]."[17]

2. Courtyard (*ḥaẓer*). Although the Mishnah addresses the manner in which the opening of an alleyway can be closed to create an eruv partition, it does not discuss the closing of the entrance to a courtyard. The Gemara quotes a baraita concerning this issue: "[Carrying in] a courtyard becomes permitted by placing one board [at the side of the entrance]. Rabbi said: By placing two boards [one on either side of the entrance]."[18] This baraita appears to require a more substantial eruv partition for a courtyard than for a closed alleyway, where a side post of any width is acceptable.

3. Open alleyway (*mavoi ha-mefulash*). The Gemara introduces several other forms of partitions that are more substantial than the side post and the crossbeam. Regarding the issue of how to enclose an open alleyway, the baraita presents several views. The first view is that one is required to build a *tẓurat ha-petaḥ*, a symbolic doorway, by placing a crossbeam between two end poles on one end, in addition to having a side post and crossbeam on the other end. Ḥannaniah, however, argues that, according to the school of Shammai, one must close off each end of the alleyway with a door that must be locked when leaving the area, whereas, according to the school of Hillel, one needs to erect a door on one end and a side post and crossbeam on the other end, but the door need not be locked.[19] Although the baraita in Shabbat 6a identifies an open alleyway as a public domain, the Gemara records a dispute over whether this property requires a wall with door partition as is required in a public domain or whether a combination of symbolic doorway and a side post and crossbeam is sufficient.

The status of the symbolic doorway can be seen in the following talmudic discussion. The Gemara states,

---

16 See Hutterer, "Eruv ḥaẓerot be-merḥav ha-eroni," 18–30.

17 M. Eruv. 1:2. Safrai suggested that the dispute between the school of Shammai and the school of Hillel may have been based on an earlier source that read *leḥi ve-korah* and that they debated whether the *vav* denotes "and" or "or." See Safrai, *Eruvin*, 27.

18 B. Eruv. 12a.

19 B. Eruv. 6a–b. See m. Eruv. 1:2 and Safrai, *Eruvin*, 27–31.

> Rav Hisda said: If one made a symbolic doorway from the side (*ẓurat ha-petaḥ min ha-ẓad*) so that the crossbeam extends from the side of the posts, he has accomplished nothing. And Rav Hisda also said: The symbolic doorway must be strong enough to support a door, even if only a door made of straw. Resh Lakish cited in the name of Rav Yannai: A symbolic doorway must have hinges [so that it looks like a door].[20]

It is evident from this amoraic discussion that although the *ẓurat ha-petaḥ* is merely a symbolic doorway, it is critical that it maintains certain aspects of a regular doorway to be considered a valid eruv partition.

The Gemara explains that there are also natural boundaries that can serve as eruv partitions for open alleyways. Regarding the use of a river or lake as an eruv partition, the gemara in Eruvin 8a relates the following story:

> There was an incident concerning a certain alleyway whose one side terminated at the sea . . . and the matter came before Rabbi, but he would not permit or prohibit this partition. He did not prohibit it because partitions existed. But he did not permit it because the sea might bring up sediment [thus depriving the partitions of the necessary height and incline].

The gemara concludes, "Maremar separated the alleyway of the town of Sura from the sea with nets because he was afraid that the sea would bring up sediment." It is evident from this story that the sea is an acceptable eruv partition as long as it creates the proper height and incline. The only concern is that sediment could nullify the sea as an eruv boundary, since it would diminish the height of the sea wall and potentially impact the necessary incline required for an eruv enclosure.

The mishnah in Eruvin 22a introduces a disagreement between Rabbi Judah and the sages concerning the possibility of public traffic nullifying an eruv partition. "Rabbi Judah says, if the path of the public domain cuts between the posts [surrounding a well], one must divert the path to the side. The sages say it is not necessary."[21] The Gemara discusses this issue with respect to a natural eruv partition: "If a mound rises to a height of ten handbreadths within a distance

---

20 B. Eruv. 11b.

21 M. Eruv. 2:1 addresses the issue of a public well that was utilized by groups of farmers who would camp around the well and would draw water even on the Sabbath. The mishnah describes the way in which an eruv can be created around these wells. See Safrai, *Eruvin*, 56–57.

of four cubits and the public travel over it, is one who carries liable or not?" The Gemara explains that this is dependent on the disagreement between Rabbi Judah and the sages. According to Rabbi Judah, the traffic would nullify the eruv. According to the sages, public traffic never disrupts an eruv, and in this case, the enclosed area would not be considered a public domain.

Charlotte Fonrobert has argued that the introduction of these symbolic and actual partitions served to create an early model of Jewish neighborhoods, as the eruv partitions separated the Jewish space from neighboring areas. The creation of these eruv communities served to strengthen the Jewish community around the ritual observance of the Sabbath.[22]

Food Sharing

Although the building of partitions serves to enclose these in-between properties, the rabbis insisted that a community that was going to be unified through an eruv must engage in a symbolic act of sharing food. In this manner, the "eruv community" would be bound together by structural boundaries and by a shared communal meal. The Talmud takes great effort to define who may be included in this "eruv community" and what type of symbolic act is required to bring this group together.[23]

The Mishnah distinguishes between the way joint ownership is created in an alleyway and the way it is created in a courtyard. This joint ownership needed for an alleyway is described as follows:

> How is *shittuf* (unification) in the alleyway effected? One [of the residents] places a jar of food there and declares, "This belongs to all the residents of the alleyway," and he may confer possession upon them through his adult son or daughter, through his Hebrew manservant or through his wife; but he may not confer possession either through his son or through his daughter if they are minors or through his Canaanite [i.e., non-Jewish] bondman or bondwoman, because their hand is as his hand.[24]

---

22 Charlotte Elisheva Fonrobert, "Neighborhood as Ritual Space: The Case of the Rabbinic Eruv," *Archiv fur Religionsgeschichte* 10 (2008): 252–257.

23 See Hutterer, "Eruv ḥaẓerot be-merḥav ha-eroni," 65–67.

24 M. Eruv. 7:6.

In order to effect this "unification," all the people living in the alleyway must be co-owners of a common food object. This is accomplished through the transfer of the vessel of food from one resident to all the other residents.[25]

The Mishnah does not explicitly address the issue of creating joint ownership in the courtyard, but the Tosefta brings up the question and says: "You may make a unification in an alleyway, and if they did not make an eruv, one can make an eruv. One may make an eruv in a courtyard, but one may not make a unification in a courtyard."[26] According to this opinion in the Tosefta, there is a fundamental difference between the way joint ownership is created in an alleyway and how it is created in a courtyard. In an alleyway, the residents may utilize the process of *shittuf*, or "unification," in which one resident transfers the food on behalf of all the other residents. Alternatively, the residents may utilize the process of eruv, in which each resident donates a food item to the collective group. However, in a courtyard, one may only utilize the process of eruv and may not use the *shittuf* process.[27]

Safrai explains that the distinction between the way joint ownership is effectuated in an alleyway and how it is done a courtyard was based on the evolution of the practice of eruv. Initially, an eruv was limited to a family or group of families living in a courtyard. For such people, actual sharing by each family in the courtyard was required. As the courtyard expanded to include all the residents of an alleyway, the sharing of food became more symbolic, as the people in different courtyards would not literally share each other's food. Therefore, the process evolved into a *shittuf*, in which one resident could symbolically create a joint ownership of the vessel of food on behalf of all the inhabitants of the alleyway.[28] Although the Mishnah differentiates between eruv

25 This is stated explicitly in m. Eruv. 7:11. T. Eruv. 6:8 quotes the view of Rabbi Meir, who did not apply the principle of *zakhin le-adam* regarding *shittuf* because people ordinarily do not want others to share in their property.

26 T. Eruv. 6:6. The Sages permit a *shittuf* procedure even in a courtyard.

27 See Lieberman, *Tosefta ki-feshutah*, Eruv., 420–421, who argued that this tosefta is repeated in b. Eruv. 71b, which states: "One can make an eruv in a courtyard with bread. However, one may not make an eruv with wine in a courtyard. One may make a *shittuf* in a *mavoi* with wine, and if one likes, one may make the *shittuf* with bread." Lieberman states that the words "wine" and "bread" are synonymous with *eruv* and *shittuf*. Albeck argues that the dispute concerning whether *shittuf* is valid in a courtyard is also the debate between the opinions in m. Eruv. 7:11 concerning whether one is allowed to create joint food ownership in a courtyard without the explicit consent of each of the residents. See Chanoch Albeck, *Shishah sidrei Mishnah: Mo'ed* (Jerusalem, 1958), 439–440.

28 See Safrai, *Eruvin*, 10. A similar analysis is offered by Albeck, *Mo'ed*, 437–438. According to the opinion of the Sages in the tosefta, once the joint ownership was transformed into a symbolic act, the symbolic transfer of ownership was extended to the courtyard.

and *shittuf*, halakhic literature uses *eruv* as a blanket term for food sharing, even as the *shittuf* process became predominant.

Leasing of Property

The creation of the eruv community requires the participation of all members of the community in the sharing of the food object. This raises the question of whether the residents of the courtyard or alleyway are permitted to carry if a non-Jew or "someone who does not accept the principle of the eruv" lives in the courtyard.[29] The Mishnah states that the mere presence of a non-Jew in the courtyard invalidates the eruv for all the residents. The Mishnah does not offer a remedy for this situation. Yet, the Tosefta says, "And, concerning a non-Jew, [the eruv is invalid] until he [the Jew] leases [*ad sha'ah she-yaskir*] his [the non-Jew's] portion."[30]

In discussing the leasing of the property of the non-Jew in the courtyard, the Gemara quotes a disagreement between Rav Ḥisda and Rav Sheshet about whether a formal lease is required between the Jew and the non-Jew or a token lease is sufficient, with Rav Ḥisda arguing that a formal lease is required and Rav Sheshet arguing that a formal lease is not required. The Gemara suggests that a formal lease requires the transference of at least a *perutah*, a coin of minimal value, and that it allows the lessee to fill the courtyard with benches and chairs, while a token lease would not give the lessee this right.[31] This disagreement about the lease of the property of the non-Jew in the courtyard for the sake of creating an eruv points to the fact that the term *sekhirut*, "lease," is not being used in terms of property rights. Rather, the rabbis have introduced this category of *sekhirat reshut* to achieve the creation of an eruv community that does not include non-Jews. For this reason, the term "lease" will be used throughout this work with the understanding that it refers to this specific lease regarding eruvin and does not impact the property rights of the Jew or non-Jew in the courtyard.

Rules of Decision-Making

Although the Gemara rarely provides guidelines to determine which opinion to follow in a talmudic debate, it does provide an important guideline in the laws of eruvin. Regarding a dispute among the Tannaim, the Bavli says the following:

---

29 See Hutterer, "Eruv ḥaẓerot be-merḥav ha-eroni," 60–65.

30 T. Eruv. 5:18.

31 B. Eruv. 62a.

"Rabbi Joshua ben Levi states: the halakhah follows the one who rules more leniently regarding issues of eruvin."[32] The Yerushalmi tells the following story: "There was an incidence of a woman who donated a portion of food for the eruv on behalf of her mother-in-law without the knowledge of the mother-in-law. The matter came before Rabbi Ishmael, and he wanted to disallow this food donation [and require the explicit consent of the mother-in-law]. Rabbi Ḥiyah said: I heard from your father [Rabbi Yosi] that wherever you can be lenient regarding eruvin, you should be lenient."[33]

An Eruv around a City or Town in the Mishnaic Period

While the Mishnah is filled with discussions concerning the creation of eruvin around courtyards and closed alleyways, there is only one mention in the Mishnah of an eruv that was built around a city.[34] The Mishnah records:

> If a town belonging to an individual is converted into one belonging to many people, one eruv may be provided for all the town; but if a town belonging to many is converted into one belonging to an individual, no single eruv may be provided for all the town unless a section of it of the size of the town of Ḥadashah in Judea, which contains fifty residents, is excluded, according to Rabbi Judah. Rabbi Simeon ruled: Three courtyards, each of which contains two houses, [must be excluded].[35]

Safrai explains that the "town of the individual" in this mishnah is a Roman villa, in a piece of land owned by a wealthy individual on which his workers and servants lived. The conversion of the town into one "belonging to many people" refers to a situation in which the inhabitants of the villa became independent owners of their homes and were no longer tenants of the landowner. According to Safrai, the mishnah teaches that since an eruv is permitted in a villa, once the villa is transformed into a "town of many," the eruv is still permitted. However, if the "town of many" is converted into a villa, a single eruv is not permitted, since it was not permitted in the original town. The exception is a situation in which a portion of the town is left out of the eruv, in which case the eruv is

---

32 B. Eruv. 46a. See also y. Eruv. 1:1.

33 Y. Eruv. 7:10.

34 See Hutterer, "Eruv ḥaẓerot be-merḥav ha-eroni," 48–52.

35 M. Eruv. 5:6 and the corresponding gemara, b. Eruv. 59a–b.

permissible, since the excluded area serves as a reminder that generally eruvin are not permitted in this type of town.[36]'

Eruvin in Babylonian Cities and Towns in the Talmudic Period

The Gemara makes several references to eruvin in cities in Babylonia.[37] The Gemara records: "Rabbah bar Avuhah made *eruvei ḥaẓerot* ['courtyard' eruvin] for the entire city of Maḥoza, neighborhood by neighborhood, because of the ditches [that held food for the oxen]."[38] Rashi explains that Maḥoza was not surrounded by a wall but was enclosed by partitions that were erected to protect the ditches of animal fodder from damage. Since there was a requirement that eruv partitions be built for the sake of enclosing homes, these partitions did not suffice. Therefore, Rabbah created eruvin for each neighborhood in Maḥoza by building appropriate eruv boundaries.[39] Maḥoza, the Jewish suburban community across the Tigris River from Ctesiphon, the winter capital of the Parthians, was among the most highly acculturated and cosmopolitan Jewish communities in Babylonia. Rabbah insured that carrying would be permitted throughout the city by erecting eruv partitions in each neighborhood.

The Gemara also discusses an eruv in the city of Pumbedita, which was situated on the Euphrates River about 100 kilometers west of Maḥoza. Commenting on the mishnah that says that an "town of many" that becomes a "town of an individual" can only be enclosed by an eruv if a small portion of the city remains outside the eruv, the Gemara remarks: "There was a storehouse of straw owned by Mar bar Pophidata from Pumbedita, and he designated it [as the excluded section within the eruv in Pumbedita]."[40] While it is not stated explicitly, the Gemara takes for granted that there was an eruv encompassing

---

36 See Safrai, *Eruvin,* 167–172. The traditional medieval talmudic commentators interpret this mishnah as referring to a public domain as defined according to the laws of eruvin. See Rashi and Tosafot on Eruvin 59a, s.v. *ir shel yaḥid.* This reflects a reinterpretation of the mishnah to conform it to the traditional definition of a public domain.

37 See Hutterer, "Eruv ḥaẓerot be-merḥav ha-eroni," 52–55.

38 B. Eruv. 26a, 60a.

39 Rashi on Eruvin 26a, s.v. *arsiyata* and *mi-shum.* See Yaakov Elman, "Middle Persian Culture and Babylonian Sages: Accommodation and Resistance in the Shaping of Rabbinic Legal Tradition," in *The Cambridge Companion to the Talmud and Rabbinic Literature,* ed. Charlotte Elisheva Fonrobert and Martin S. Jaffee (New York, 2007), 165–197.

40 The mishnah is in Eruv. 59a. Rashi, s.v. *ve-shel,* explains that a city that remains a "town of many" can also be encompassed by an eruv and that the mishnah is merely presenting the more unusual case of as "town of many" that is transformed into a "town of an individual." The gemara can be found in b. Eruv. 60a.

the entire city and that the exclusion of the storehouse from the eruv allowed the eruv to be effective.

However, there is a passage of gemara that suggests that there was no eruv encompassin the entire city of Pumbedita:

> Rabbah bar Rav Hannan asked Abaye: How is it that in an alley in which two great men like our rabbis [that is, Abaye and his uncle Rabbah] reside has neither a *shittuf* nor an eruv?
>
> "What can we do?" said Abaye. "For the master [Rabbah] [to collect the contribution of the residents] would not be seemly, I am busy with my studies, and the other residents do not care. And if I were to transfer possession of a loaf in a basket to them, since if they demand it of me I could not afford to give it to them [since I am poor], the *shittuf* would be nullified.[41]

Although the place is not mentioned, the gemara is apparently referring to Pumbedita, since Rabbah was the head of the Pumbedita academy at the end of the third century and beginning of the fourth century CE and Abaye was his nephew and an Amora in Pumbedita. It is evident from this story that that there was no eruv encompassing the entire city, necessitating the creation of an eruv in the alleyway. Abaye claims that at least the people living in his alleyway did not care whether or not there was an eruv around that alleyway. Yaakov Elman has studied the cities of Pumbedita and Maḥoza and concluded that this indifference to rabbinic enactments was prevalent in Pumbedita.[42]

Although this story may have taken place at a time when Pumbedita did not have a city eruv, it is also possible that the city eruv described in the Gemara never encompassed the entire city.

Geonic Sources

The Geonic period began in Babylonia in the second half of the sixth century CE. By the time of rise of the Abbasid Dynasty in 750, the reign of Islam extended

---

41 B. Eruv. 68a.

42 See Yaakov Elman, "The Socioeconomics of Babylonian Heresy," in *Jewish Law Association Studies* 17 (2007)*: Studies in Mediaeval Halakhah in Honor of Stephen M. Passamaneck*, ed. Alyssa Gray and Bernard Jackson, 94–96; and Yaakov Elman, "Ma'aseh bi-shtei ayarot: Maḥoza u-Pumbedita ke-meyaẓgot shtei tarbuyot hilkhatiyot," in *Torah li-shmah: Meḥkarim be-mada'ei ha-Yahadut likhvod Professor Shama Yehudah Friedman*, ed. David Golinkin et al. (Jerusalem, 2007), 3–38.

from Spain and North Africa in the west to the Indian subcontinent in the east. International trade and banking flourished, and the Jews played a leading role in both these areas. The Babylonian Jewish leaders were positioned to influence Jews worldwide.[43]

Simhah Assaf has argued that the Geonim accomplished two things intellectually that had a lasting impact on the Jewish world of learning. First, although the Talmud was well known in the academies in Babylonia, the Geonim were successful at making the Talmud accessible to the wider Jewish population through their numerous commentaries. Second, they transformed the Talmud, which had been edited in the sixth century as an encyclopedia of Judaism, into the authoritative code of the Jewish people. Both of these aspects of the Geonic contribution were significant in the area of eruvin, the laws surrounding which were complex and often obscure and had practical application that required clarification.[44]

Definition of a Public Domain

The baraita defined a public domain as a major road, a great public square, or an open alley. The gemara in Shabbat 99a added that a public domain is sixteen cubits wide, since the road on which the Jews transported the boards for the tabernacle in the wilderness was sixteen cubits wide. The *Halakhot gedolot,* written by Rabbi Simeon Qayyara in the last quarter of the ninth century,[45] adds a criterion that is not found in the Talmud: "The definition of a public domain is a place which six hundred thousand men traverse every day just like the Israelite encampment in the desert."[46] Although the authenticity of this statement has been called into

---

43 For background on the Geonic period and the intellectual and cultural life of the time, see Robert Brody, *The Geonim of Babylonia and the Shaping of Medieval Jewish Culture* (New Haven, 1998) and the literature cited therein.

44 These two aspects of the Geonic contribution are best articulated in Simhah Assaf, *Tekufat ha-ge'onim ve-sifrutah: Harẓa'ot ve-shi'urim* (Jerusalem, 1955), 137–153.

45 For a discussion of the debate concerning the attribution of *Halakhot gedolot* to Rabbi Simeon Qayyara and the dating of the work, which is also debated by scholars, see Neil Danzig, *Mavo le-sefer Halakhot pesukot im tashlum Halakhot pesukut* (New York, 1999), 175–186. Danzig points out that Rabbi Simeon is never referred to as a gaon (179, n. 21).

46 This line is only found in the Berlin manuscript of the *Halakhot gedolot,* edited by Esriel Hildesheimer (Berlin, 1888), 131. For a discussion of the different versions of the *Halakhot gedolot,* see Ezriel Hildesheimer, ed., *Halakhot gedolot* (Jerusalem, 1972), vol. 1, 15–27. (The 1972 edition, which is based on the Milan manuscript, was edited by Ezriel Hildesheimer, the grandson of Esriel Hildesheimer.) Ezriel Hildesheimer identified the Berlin manuscript as the Spanish version, since it was utilized by the Spanish talmudic scholars. See Ezriel Hildesheimer, *Halakhot gedolot,* vol. 1, 22 for a discussion on the different views on this issue. For an analysis of why this definition of a public domain does not appear in any of the other

question,[47] the same criterion is found in other Geonic sources.[48] *Sefer ha-itim,* written by the late eleventh- and early twelfth-century Spanish Talmudist Rabbi Judah ben Barzillai, says: "In the responsum of the Gaon . . . What is a public domain? An area that has six hundred thousand people that has neither walls nor gates."[49] It goes on to state that "a state or a city that does not have six hundred thousand people or that has six hundred thousand but its gates are locked at night does not become a public domain."[50] The same definition is found in the name of Rav Sar Shalom Gaon, who was the head of the academy in Sura from 847/51 to 857[51] and predated the author of the *Halakhot gedolot.*[52]

Construction of the Eruv

Most of the laws about physical demarcation given by the Geonim are identical to those given in the Gemara.[53] There is, however, a statement by the author

---

versions of the *Halakhot gedolot,* see Israel Ta-Shma, *Halakhah, minhag u-meẓi'ut be-Ashkenaz 1100–1350* (Jerusalem, 1996), 143.

47 Israel Ta-Shma expresses some doubt about the authenticity of this statement for two reasons: first, it appears in only one manuscript of the *Halakhot gedolot,* the Berlin manuscript, and, second, it does not seem to follow from the preceding law in the *Halakhot gedolot,* which states: "So it is said in the name of Rav Judah, the head of the academy from Nehar Pekod: Boẓra is a public domain during the day. However, at night, since it is filled with broken pottery, it is considered a *karmelit*" (Ezriel Hildesheimer, *Halakhot gedolot,* vol. 2, 265). In this statement, Rav Judah is defining the difference between a public domain and a *karmelit* based on how easy or difficult it is to travel on the roads. There is no attempt to define the different domains based on the number of people in each domain (Ta-Shma, *Halakhah, minhag u-meẓi'ut,* 143). However, in support of the attribution of this definition of a public domain to Rav Judah, an unpublished manuscript of *Halakhot gedolot,* Vatican MS (Biblioteca Apostolica ebr. 304), also contains this definition of a public domain attributed to Rav Judah of Nehar Pekod. See "The Reprinting of the Berlin Edition of the Behag," Eruv Online, June 22, 2009, http://eruvonline.blogspot.com/2009/06/reprinting-of-berlin-edition-of-behag.html for a facsimile of this manuscript.

48 See Hutterer, "Eruv ḥaẓerot be-merḥav ha-eroni," 77–80.

49 Judah ben Barzillai, *Sefer ha-itim* (Cracow, 1903), 306. *Sefer ha-itim* also quotes the tradition of Rav Judah of Nehar Pekod (Ben Barzillai, *Sefer ha-itim,* 310). *Sefer ha-itim* refers to six hundred thousand people (*benei adam*), while *Halakhot gedolot* refers to six hundred thousand men (*gavrei*). Who counts toward this figure of six hundred thousand would become a matter of dispute in modern eruvin, as discussed in the following chapters.

50 Ben Barzillai, *Sefer ha-itim,* 113.

51 The dates that each Gaon served can be found in Brody, *The Geonim of Babylonia,* 344–345.

52 Refael Shmuel Ha-Kohen Weinberg, ed., *Teshuvot Rav Sar Shalom Gaon* (Jerusalem, 1975), no. 34 and accompanying footnotes. The same language, attributed to Rav Sar Shalom, is also found in *Ḥemdah genuzah* (Jerusalem, 1967), no. 70 and, without an attribution, in the collection of Geonic responsa *Sefer sha'arei teshuvah,* edited by Yeruham Fishel ben Zvi Hirsch Ha-Levi, no. 209.

53 See Hutterer, "Eruv ḥaẓerot be-merḥav ha-eroni," 80–82.

of the *Halakhot gedolot* that provides a formulation of the necessary eruv partitions that was not stated explicitly in the talmudic sources. Rabbi Simeon Qayyara writes: "If the city is surrounded by a wall or is enclosed by rivers or is surrounded by a hill or other natural partition that inclines at least ten handbreadths, this is an acceptable eruv partition, and all that is required is an *eruv ḥaẓerot* [of food-sharing]."[54] Although each of these types of eruv partitions is discussed in the Talmud, the formulation in the *Halakhot gedolot* is the first time that man-made and natural eruv partitions are listed together. The author of the *Halakhot gedolot* thus established a standard for determining acceptable eruv boundaries that would be utilized throughout the centuries.

The Creation of Eruvin in Cities

Two Geonic sources relate to the creation of eruvin around entire cities. A responsum from Rav Natronai Gaon addresses the sages of the city of Lucena (Alisana) in southern Spain, whose residents inquired about creating eruvin around the city's wells:

> I have a serious question on this matter [of making an eruv]. Great sages such as yourselves, men of Torah, meticulous in areas of Jewish law, do you need to create an eruv around the wells? Thank God, there are no non-Jews in Alisana who would prevent the creation of the eruv. Why do you not make an *eruv ḥaẓerot* [around the entire city]?[55]

---

54 See Ezriel Hildesheimer, *Halakhot gedolot*, 260. The text is also found in the *Tashlum Halakhot pesukot* printed at the end of Danzig, *Mavo le-sefer Halakhot pesukot*, 555–556. Danzig argues that the material that is found in both the *Halakhot pesukot* and *Halakhot gedolot* originated in the *Halakhot pesukot* of Rav Yehudai Gaon in the mid-eighth century and was later incorporated into the *Halakhot gedolot*. See Danzig, *Mavo le-sefer Halakhot pesukot*, 214–216.

55 Yoel Ha-Kohen Miller, ed., *Teshuvot ge'onei mizraḥ u-ma'arav* (Berlin, 1888), no. 26; and Ben Barzillai, *Sefer ha-itim*, 148. Lucena, or Alisana as it was called by the Jews, was a center of Jewish life and scholarship from the ninth through eleventh centuries. There is historical evidence that a majority of the population was Jewish. Yet, the claim of Rav Natronai Gaon that "there are no non-Jews in Alisana" is matter of dispute. See the notes of A. Harkabi to Tzvi Graetz, *Sefer divrei yemei Yisrael* (Warsaw, 1984), vol. 4, 25 (note section at end of volume), which cite both Arab and Jewish writers who argue that Lucena was entirely Jewish during this period. This was clearly the view of Rav Natronai Gaon, inasmuch as the residence of even one non-Jew would have required the leasing of the city from him. In a related responsum concerning *eruvei teḥumin* in Lucena, Rav Natronai Gaon wrote, "Since Alisana is a place of Jews with many Jewish residents, may God add to them one thousand times, and there is not even one non-Jew there." See W. Warnheim, ed., *Kevuẓat ḥakhamim* (Jerusalem, 1970), 110–111; also found in B. M. Levin, ed., *Oẓar ha-ge'onim* (Jerusalem, 1931), vol. 3, 24–25. For

The author of the *Halakhot gedolot* goes further, suggesting that creating an eruv around a city is actually mandatory: "A city is required to make an eruv, whether with ropes or with a symbolic doorway."[56]

The move from neighborhood eruvin to city eruvin reflects the development of cities in Muslim countries following the Muslim conquests in the seventh and eighth centuries. Non-Muslims, including Jews, Christians, and Zoroastrians, lived in these cities together with Muslims and participated in the cosmopolitan life. Many Jews left the life of farming for crafts that were more appropriate for city life.[57] Although there is some evidence of Jewish neighborhoods in several Muslim cities, Noam Stillman argues that for the most part, Jews lived together with non-Jews.[58] As the number of Jews in cities quickly increased, the need for city eruvin increased. While the actual building of these eruvin may have lagged behind the rabbinic advice, the statements of Rav Natronai Gaon and the author of the *Halakhot gedolot* reflect the changing reality in Muslim countries.

Lease of Property

Although Rav Natronai Gaon addressed the situation of Lucena, a city "without any non-Jews," the issue of creating an eruv where there were non-Jewish residents raised serious problems for the Geonim.[59] As previously shown and as reflected in the talmudic stories, the cities in Babylonia had both Jewish and non-Jewish residents. However, until the period of the Geonim, the eruvin were created around courtyards and alleyways. Therefore, the relationship with the non-Jew, whose residence invalidated the eruv, was confined to very few Jewish

---

the history of Lucena, see Joseph Rivlin, *Shetarei kehillot Alisana min ha-me'ah ha-aḥat esreh* (Ramat Gan, 1995), 27–30.

56 This version appears in the Berlin ms. (Esriel Hildescheimer, *Halakhot gedolot,* 127) as well as in the edition edited by Avrohom Shimon Troyb, *Halakhot gedolot* (Warsaw, 1974), 54. The Milan ms. (Ezriel Hildesheimer, *Halakhot gedolot,* 260), however, reads: "If a city needs to make an eruv, they should make it with ropes or a symbolic doorway." This version retains the voluntary nature of the city eruv. The version from the Berlin ms. is quoted by Isaac ben Moshe, *Or zarua* (Jerusalem, 2009), vol. 2, Hilkhot eruvin, no. 164.

57 For the history of Islamic cities during the Muslim conquest, see S. M. Stern, "The Constitution of the Islamic City," in *The Islamic City: A Colloquium,* ed. A. H. Hourani and S. M. Stern (Philadelphia, 1970), 25; and Noam Stillman, "Ha-Yehudim be-historiyah ha-ironot shel ha-Islam bi-ymei ha-beinayim," in *Masa'it Mosheh: Mekhkarim be-tarbut Yisrael ve-arav mugashim le-Mosheh Gil,* ed. Ezra Fleisher, Mordekhai Akiva Friedman, and Yoel Kramer (Jerusalem, 1998), 246–255.

58 There was a Jewish neighborhood in Baghdad and possibly also in Jerusalem. However, these were the exceptions rather than the rule. See Stillman, "Ha-Yehudim be-historiyah ha-ironot," 252–254.

59 See Hutterer, "Eruv ḥaẓerot be-merḥav ha-eroni," 86–88.

families. In the period of the Geonim, on the other hand, when eruvin were being created in cities, the issue of a non-Jewish resident created an additional problem. The author of the *Halakhot gedolot* describes a "place of non-Jews," in which he advises that the Jews lease the property from each non-Jewish resident. If, however, a non-Jew refuses to lease his space, the *Halakhot gedolot* advises that the Jews follow the recommendation of Rava in Pumbedita that a Jewish resident place his vessels in the home of one of the non-Jews, thereby becoming his tenant, at which point the other Jews can include the non-Jew in the eruv through his Jewish tenant.[60]

Medieval Commentators

As Jewish communities moved to Northern Europe and Christian Spain, the medieval commentators continued to expound on the conceptual and practical aspects of the eruv. These discussions were often influenced by the realia of the different cities and towns in which Jews lived.

Definition of a Public Domain

Rashi's comment on the talmudic definition of a public domain incorporates the Geonic criterion that the space have six hundred thousand people:

> It means that it is sixteen cubits wide and is a city that has six hundred thousand [people] and is not enclosed by a wall; for the public domain requires roads that are open from one gate of the city to the other similar to the encampment of the Jews in the desert.[61]

According to Rashi, there are three criteria for an area to be considered a public domain: first, it must contain a road that is at least sixteen cubits wide; second,

---

60 Ezriel Hildesheimer, *Halakhot gedolot*, vol 1, 261.

61 Rashi on b. Eruv. 6a, s.v. *reshut ha-rabbim*. Rashi repeats the need for six hundred thousand to create a public domain in his definition of the difference between a "city of an individual" and a "city of many." See Rashi on b. Eruv. 69a, s.v. *ir shel yaḥid*. His opinion can also be found in his comments on b. Eruv. 6b, s.v. *Yerushalayim*; b. Eruv. 26a, s.v. *Arsayta*; and b. Eruv. 47a, s.v. *shalosh ḥaẓerot*.

it must have a population of at least six hundred thousand people; and finally, its streets must run from one gate of the city to the opposite gate.[62]

Rabbi Moshe ben Nahman (Ramban) questions Rashi's definition. He writes: "I do not know the source of Rashi's definition, for it is not mentioned anywhere in the Talmud. However, it is found in the *Halakhot gedolot,* and therefore, it is based on great sages." Nevertheless, Ramban disagrees with Rashi's explanation, as the baraita on Shabbat 6a does not mention the need for six hundred thousand people in its definition of a public domain. Ramban maintains that a public domain is simply a space that is at least sixteen cubits wide and has neither a wall nor a roof.[63] Rambam similarly codifies the definition of a public domain as follows: "What is a public domain? . . . As long as its road is sixteen cubits wide and it does not have a roof."[64]

Construction of the Eruv

The medieval commentators addressed the construction of the eruv partitions in light of the realities of the physical layout of their cities and towns.[65] The gemara in Eruvin contains a debate regarding the definition of an alleyway: Rav says that an alleyway adjoins two courtyards, each with two houses, whereas Shmuel says that only one courtyard with one house is necessary to constitute an alleyway.[66] The *Raavyah* comments on this gemara: "This is true in those days when the courtyards were in front of the house and one entered the public domain through the courtyard. However, where the houses open directly into the alleyway and the courtyards are behind the houses, it is sufficient to have houses opening into the courtyard in order to create the alleyway [and it is not necessary that each house have a courtyard]."[67] According to the *Raavyah,* the introduction of "backyards" changed the laws of eruvin and served to redefine an alleyway.

Rabbi Isaac ben Sheshet, the Spanish and North African talmudist of the second half of the fourteenth century, was asked about establishing an eruv in a city that was walled and did not have a road of sixteen cubits but had one

---

62 See Hutterer, "Eruv ḥaẓerot be-merḥav ha-eroni," 92–94.

63 Rabbi Moshe ben Nahman, *Ḥiddushei ha-Ramban,* ed. Moshe Hirschler (Jerusalem, 1973), Eruv. 59a. Ritba agrees with Ramban. See Ritba on b. Eruv. 59a, s.v. *Matnitin ir shel rabbim.* For a possible answer to Ramban's question about Rashi's explanation, see Menachem Mendel Kasher, *Torah sheleimah* (New York, 1953), vol. 15, 165–166.

64 Rabbi Moshe ben Maimon, *Mishneh Torah,* Hilkhot Shabbat, 14:1.

65 See Hutterer, "Eruv ḥaẓerot be-merḥav ha-eroni," 101–110, 143–147.

66 B. Eruv. 73b–74a.

67 *Raavyah,* Hilkhot eruvin, 1:400.

entranceway to the city without a gate. There was a disagreement among the scholars in the city over whether the city was considered a *karmelit* and therefore could be partitioned with a side bar and crossbeam, or a public domain, in which case it would require a symbolic doorway to enclose the one opening in the entranceway. Rabbi Isaac ben Sheshet responded that even though in certain cases in the Gemara a *karmelit* is equated with a public domain, unless the Gemara explicitly makes the connection, any area that does not satisfy the criteria of a public domain has the status of a *karmelit* and does not require a symbolic doorway.[68] Unlike other legal authorities, such as the author of the *Terumat ha-deshen,* who claimed that any area with the status of a shared courtyard required a symbolic doorway, Rabbi Isaac ben Sheshet concluded that the city was a *karmelit* and allowed for the creation of a partition through the use of a side post and crossbeam.

The Rishonim also addressed the use of natural eruv partitions, though they disagreed about the Gemara's concern about utilizing the sea wall as an eruv partition "lest it build up sediment"[69] because of a textual variant in the Gemara. Rashi agreed with the printed version of the Gemara and quoted, "Maremar separated the alleyway of Sura from the sea with nets as he explained, 'lest the sea bring up sediment.'"[70] Rabbeinu Hananel, however, had a different version of the text: "Maremar created nets in Sura, and he was not concerned that the sea would build up sediment."[71] Ibn Adret, in his commentary on the Gemara, pointed out that Maremar's actions only make sense if one assumes that he was concerned with the buildup of sediment.[72] However, Rambam followed the version of Rabbeinu Hananel and wrote, "There is no concern that the sea will build up sediment."[73]

Regarding the disagreement between Rabbi Judah and the Sages over whether public traffic invalidates an eruv, Rambam wrote explicitly, "Even if the public passes through the eruv partitions, the partitions are still valid."[74] The author of the *Raavyah* represented the German tradition and also followed the view of the sages that public traffic does not invalidate eruv partitions.[75]

---

68 Isaac ben Sheshet, *She'elot u-teshuvot Rivash* (New York, 1974), no. 405.

69 B. Eruv. 8a.

70 Rashi on b. Eruv. 8a, s.v. *amar shema.*

71 Rabbeinu Hananel on b. Eruv. 8a.

72 Yaakov Dovid Ilan, ed., *Ḥiddushei ha-Rashba massekhet Eruvin* (Jerusalem, 1989), b. Eruv. 8a, s.v. *hakhi garsinan.*

73 *Mishneh Torah,* Hilkhot Shabbat, 17:5. See also *Maggid Mishneh,* Hilkhot Shabbat, 17:5, s.v. *mavoi.*

74 *Mishneh Torah,* Hilkhot Shabbat, 17:33; and see *Maggid Mishneh.*

75 *Raavyah,* Hilkhot eruvin, 1:270.

Lease of Property

As the issue of creating the eruv community expanded from the courtyard and alleyway to the city eruv, the question arose of how to lease the city from its non-Jewish residents. Some of the Rishonim argued that the Jews needed to lease the city from each non-Jewish resident. Mordekhai ben Hillel wrote: "Rabbi Meir [of Rothenberg] decreed that it is not sufficient to lease the space from the governing official in the city. Rather, [the Jewish community] must lease from each individual non-Jewish resident."[76] Rabbi Jacob ben Asher, in his *Tur*, concured with this view and wrote: "It is not sufficient to lease from a governing official in the city."[77] Ibn Adret was asked: "Is it sufficient to lease from the governing official in the town who receives a stipend each year from each household, or do you have to lease from each individual non-Jewish resident?" He responded that if the governing official has the right to expel people from their homes, one can lease directly from him. Otherwise, they must lease from each individual non-Jewish resident.[78] Isaac ben Sheshet added another consideration. He wrote: "There is an additional reason to allow for leasing the space from the head of the city, for it is known that the head of the city has the right to change the public roads and to force the non-Jews to travel on a different road."[79] According to Rabbi Isaac ben Sheshet, even if the government official does not have authority over the houses of the city, since he has authority over the streets, the Jews can lease the city from him.

Rules of Decision-Making

These disagreements bring up an important consideration among the Rishonim. Although the Gemara states that "The halakhah follows the lenient opinion regarding eruvin," Rabbi Meir of Rothenberg offered two qualifications. First, he argued that this principle only applies to a disagreement among Tannaim. In a disagreement among Amoraim, the law does not necessarily follow the lenient view. Furthermore, he suggested that the law only follows the lenient view regarding food sharing but that when there is an issue regarding a partition, it does not necessarily follow the lenient view.[80] The Rivash explained

---

76 Mordekhai on Eruvin, no. 509. See *Teshuvot Rabbi Meir ben Barukh*, vol. 1, *Pesakim u-minhagim*, no. 286. The view is also found in *Sefer kol bo* (Jerusalem, 1997), no. 33.

77 Tur, *Oraḥ ḥayyim*, 391.

78 *Teshuvot ha-Rashba* (Jerusalem, 1997), vol. 1, no. 626.

79 Ben Sheshet, *She'elot u-teshuvot Rivash*, no. 427.

80 This version of Rabbi Meir of Rothenberg's opinion is found in Rosh on b. Eruv. 2:4.

the distinction between the food sharing and the partitions as follows: Food sharing is a rabbinic institution, so the law can be lenient. However, partitions relate to the biblical prohibition of *hoẓa'ah*, so the law is not lenient in such a dispute.[81] There were, however, Rishonim who maintained this principle even regarding a dispute between Amoraim and issues regarding partitions.[82] There is also an alternate tradition that claims that Rabbi Meir of Rothenberg applied this principle of leniency to questions of both food sharing and partitions.[83] The application of this principle was significant to future generations, as it served as a useful vehicle to allow flexibility in applying the rules of the Gemara and Rishonim to practical scenarios in neighborhoods and cities.

Shulḥan Arukh

The *Shulḥan arukh*, composed by Rabbi Joseph Caro of Spain in 1565 and later glossed by Rabbi Moses Isserles of Poland, served to organize and codify the centuries of legal discussion and analysis in the Talmud and the works of the Rishonim. The *Shulḥan arukh*'s discussion of the laws of eruvin, in both Caro's text and the glosses, established the foundation for the creation of city eruvin in the premodern and modern periods.

Definition of a Public Domain

Rabbi Joseph Caro presented two opinions on the definition of a public domain. The first is that a public domain is a street or market that is at least sixteen cubits wide and is not surrounded by walls. According to this opinion, even if the area is walled, it is considered a public domain if the streets run from one end to the other. The second view is that an area is only a public domain if six hundred thousand people traverse it every day. The *Shulḥan arukh* does not endorse one of these views over the other.

---

81 Ben Sheshet, *She'elot u-teshuvot Rivash*, no. 405. See also Ritba on b. Eruv. 89a, s.v. *ve-ha*; and Ibn Adret, *Avodat ha-kodesh* (Warsaw, 1876), 2:1, who concur with this view.

82 Tosafot on Eruv. 65b, s.v. *ikli'u*, as explained by Meir ha-Kohen, *Haggahot Maimoniyyot*, Hilkhot Shabbat, chapter 16, no. 7. The *Haggahot Maimoniyyot* also claims that there is a version of the works of Rabbi Meir of Rothenberg in which he argues that this principle applies regarding disputes among Amoraim. See Rabbi Eliyahu of Vilna, *Oraḥ ḥayyim*, 358:5, who argues that Rabbi Meir of Rothenberg, in addition to other Rishonim, applies this principle to amoraic disputes.

83 Mordekhai on Eruvin, no. 482.

The *Shulḥan arukh*'s failure to decide between these views is problematic, because Rabbi Caro wrote that an eruv can be constructed around any domain other than a public domain through the erection of symbolic doorways but that, in a public domain, the eruv is not valid unless the area is surrounded by partitions that include gates that either are or can be locked at night.[84] This issue is addressed by the commentaries on the *Shulḥan arukh*. Both Rabbi Abraham Gombiner, author of the *Magen Avraham*, and David Ha-Levi Segal, author of the *Turei zahav* (*Taz*), early seventeenth-century commentators, explain that even though there are many rabbis who argue that a public domain does not require six hundred thousand people, the majority of the rabbinic authorities and the custom of the people was to define a public domain as an area that has at least six hundred thousand people traversing through it every day.[85] The *Taz* adds, "The strict one should be strict for himself but should not criticize those who follow the present-day custom to be lenient."[86] These opinions and the *Taz*'s view that a stringent person should not criticize those who are more lenient reflect the fact that this was a practical issue that arose in the construction of eruvin at the time. While there were few, if any, cities that had populations of six hundred thousand, many cities and even small towns had streets that were at least sixteen cubits wide. According to the strict opinion referred to by the *Taz*, any city with a street that was sixteen cubits wide would require gates to establish an eruv. According to the lenient view, those cities would be able to establish eruvin through the construction of symbolic doorways. It was only the rare city with a population of six hundred thousand that would require gates to create an eruv.

Lease of Property

In keeping with earlier sources, the *Shulḥan arukh* states that if two or more Jews live in a courtyard with a non-Jew, the Jews must lease the non-Jew's property. The lease can be done for less than a *perutah* worth of value, an insignificant amount, and the lease can be done without specifying the reasons for the lease.[87] The *Shulḥan arukh* also states that the lease is required only when the non-Jewish and Jewish residents share access to a common courtyard, such as a case in which the non-Jew must pass through the courtyard of the Jew to enter the

---

84 Rabbi Eliyahu of Vilna, *Oraḥ ḥayyim*, 364:2.

85 Avraham Gombiner, *Magen Avraham*, Oraḥ ḥayyim, 345:7; and David Ha-Levi Segal, *Taz*, Oraḥ ḥayyim, 345:6.

86 *Taz*, Oraḥ ḥayyim, 345:6.

87 *Taz*, Oraḥ ḥayyim, 382:2–11.

public domain. However, if the non-Jew does not have access to the courtyards of the Jews, such as a case in which they each enter the public domain directly from their own houses, a lease is not required.[88]

Rabbi Caro concluded the laws of lease of space from non-Jews in the following manner:

> You are required to lease from each courtyard of the non-Jew, and it is not sufficient to lease from the head of the city. This is describing a case where the governing official does not own the houses of the city and does not have the right to use the houses even in a time of war. However, in a city where all the activities of the city are conducted under the auspices of the governing official or his assistant, then lease from this official or his assistant is permitted, for he has permission to place people and weapons in the houses during a time of war even without the knowledge or consent of the residents.[89]

Eruvin in the Early Modern and Modern Periods

In the sixteenth through nineteenth centuries, Jewish communities continued to create city eruvin based on the guidelines given by the Talmud and its commentators as well as the *Shulḥan arukh*, adapting these laws to the realities of the cities in which they lived.

Sixteenth through Eighteenth Centuries: Eruv Boundaries

We have reports of several city eruvin that were in existence in the sixteenth, seventeenth, and eighteenth centuries.[90] Rabbi Joseph ibn Lev, a sixteenth-century rabbi who lived in Salonika and Constantinople, discussed the eruvin in both of these cities. Both cities were walled, and he concluded that, in a walled city, there is no need for any additional eruv partitions.[91] Rabbi Yom Tov Zahalon, a rabbinic authority from Safed who lived at the end of the sixteenth

---

88 *Taz*, Oraḥ ḥayyim, 382:3.
89 *Shulḥan arukh*, Oraḥ ḥayyim, 371:1.
90 See Hutterer, "Eruv ḥaẓerot be-merḥav ha-eroni," 159–167.
91 Joseph ibn Lev, *She'elot u-teshuvot Mahari ibn Lev* (Frankfurt, 1726), vol. 3, 74.

and the beginning of the seventeenth centuries, described the need for an enclosure in Safed due to the destruction of the city walls by intruders. Rabbi Zahalon explained that symbolic doorways should be erected throughout the city and argued that Safed did not require a walled enclosure since its population did not exceed six hundred thousand.[92]

In the late seventeenth and in the eighteenth centuries, there are several references to city eruvin in cities that were not surrounded by walls.[93] The first mention of an eruv of this type during the period is the eruv in The Hague, which was first inhabited by Portuguese Jews in the last decades of the seventeenth century.[94] The Hague was surrounded by canals, and there was a rabbinic discussion about whether the canal walls served as eruv boundaries. In 1692, a responsum was written by the rabbinical court of Amsterdam, consisting of three leaders of the Portuguese Jewish community of Amsterdam, explaining that it was permissible to carry within The Hague because it was completely surrounded by canals and waterways in which the water was higher than ten handbreadths.

The utilization of natural boundaries to create an eruv raised questions. Hakham Zevi Ashkenazi, head of the rabbinical court in Altona, near Hamburg, was asked whether the sea walls surrounding Great Britain would allow the entire island of England to be considered enclosed by an eruv. In a responsum written in 1694, he explained that the sea walls could not serve as eruv boundaries because people traveled in and out of England.[95]

Sixteenth through Eighteenth Centuries: Leasing of Property

Leasing property from non-Jews continued to be an issue in the creation of city eruvin. The *Shulḥan arukh* had argued that property could be leased from a government official, but rabbis of later generations struggled to apply the *Shulḥan arukh*'s definition of a governmental official to their situations. In 1656, Hakham

---

92 Yom Tov ben Moses Zahalon, *She'elot u-teshuvot Mahariẓ* (Venice, 1694), no. 251. See the discussion of this responsum in Jacob Saul Elyashar, *She'elot u-teshuvot simḥah le-ish* (Jerusalem, 1888), no. 3.

93 Rabbi Hayim Algazi, rabbi of Rhodes in the late seventeenth century, defended the sharing of food that was practiced in Rhodes. Rhodes was a walled city, and, therefore, there was no need for an enclosure. See Hayim Algazi, *Sefer banei ḥayyei* (Constantinople, 1707), 16a. For the history of the Jews of Rhodes, see Marc D. Angel, *The Jews of Rhodes: The History of a Sephardic Community* (New York, 1978).

94 Hutterer, "Eruv ḥaẓerot be-merḥav ha-eroni," 195–197.

95 Zevi Ashkenazi, *She'elot u-teshuvot Ḥakham Ẓevi* (Jerusalem, 2004), no. 37. See Hutterer, "Eruv ḥaẓerot be-merḥav ha-eroni," 240–254.

Ashkenazi addressed the question of whether Altona could be leased from the *Burgermeister*, the leading local official appointed by the emperor. The *Shulḥan arukh* stated that the official from whom a city was leased had to be able to place people and weapons in homes during war. Hakham Ashkenazi argued that there was no basis for the limitation of this right to wartime and suggested that the author of the *Shulḥan arukh* was referring to a situation in which the authority had permission to engage in war without consulting with the townspeople. The Burgermeister, however, did not have the right to engage in war without the permission of the people of Hamburg. In addition, the Rivash required that the city be leased from someone with the ability to redirect traffic on the city streets, which was not true of the Burgermeister. Finally, Hakham Ashkenazi wrote that the ability to collect taxes did not carry with it the authority to lease the city to the Jews.[96]

In a responsum written in 1683, Rabbi Samuel Aboab addressed concerns regarding the eruv in Genoa. He explained that the eruv in Genoa had been accepted "for generations." However, he argued that people should no longer rely on this eruv because the "protectores," who were appointed exclusively to deal with Jewish affairs and from whom the Jews leased the area, did not have the authority to alter the houses and streets or to place people in homes without the permission of the homeowners. Therefore, the situation in Genoa did not meet the requirements of the *Shulḥan arukh*.[97]

In the middle of the eighteenth century, Rabbi Ezekiel Landau of Prague addressed the status of a lease if there was a military presence in the city. Would the lease still be effective given that the city official had no authority over the soldiers of the emperor? He responded that if the soldiers were stationed in homes of residents of the city, the lease would still be effective because the authority of the city official applied to those residents and their houses. However, if the soldiers had to sleep in their own barracks, the lease would have to be received from an official of the emperor.[98]

These sources highlight the fact that the history of city eruvin was linked with the history of the relationship between Jews and local officials. It is particularly noteworthy that both Rabbi Aboab and Rabbi Ashkenazi were willing to reject city eruvin in Genoa and Hamburg that had been in use for generations and that

---

96 Ashkenazi, *Ḥakham Ẓevi*, no. 6. For a description of the role of the Burgermeister and a discussion of the relationship of the Jews and the Burgermeister in Hamburg during this period, see Joachim Whaley, *Religious Toleration and Social Change in Hamburg, 1529–1819* (Cambridge, MA, 1985), 8–44.

97 Samuel Aboab, *Sefer devar Shemu'el* (Venice, 1702), no. 257.

98 Ezekiel Landau, *Nodah bi-Yehudah*, 2nd ed. (Jerusalem, 1990), no. 32.

Rabbi Landau declared that the lease had to be redone. While the tradition had been to encourage the creation of eruvin, the potential violation led these rabbis to be strict in some cases.

Nineteenth Century: The Importance of Creating an Eruv

The emancipation of Jews, combined with the gradual demolition of the walls of European cities and towns, created new opportunities for Jews but greater challenges for the establishment of community eruvin.[99] Given that many, if not most, observant Jews had been used to living in towns with eruvin, it is not surprising that Rabbi Moses Sofer, the great rabbinic authority of the early nineteenth century and the head of the rabbinical seminary in Pressburg, was asked in 1827 by the rabbi of Wurzburg to provide rabbinic proofs that it was appropriate for every community to have an eruv. Rabbi Sofer wrote:

> This fact does not require proof, as it is logical. The logic obligates the establishment of eruvin, as it is known that the observance of the Sabbath is one of the leading commandments, and one who does not observe the Sabbath is a heretic and a rejecter of the entire Torah. The prohibition of carrying from one domain to another is one of the categories of labor for which you are considered a rejecter of the entire Torah. . . . Therefore, every logical person will realize that it is impossible for every Jew to protect his children, the women, and the weak of character for the entire Sabbath day without leaving the house with small items or the children with their food in their hands. In addition, this causes pain for the adult men who are unable to carry their *siddur* [prayer book] and their *tallit* [prayer shawl]. Therefore, logic dictates that it is proper and obligatory to fix the courtyards with an eruv to permit carrying.[100]

Rabbi Sofer followed the tradition dating back to the author of the *Halakhot gedolot* and Rabbeinu Asher stressing the importance of creating community eruvin. However, Rabbi Sofer's argument was the most direct argument of his time in support of the creation of community eruvin, and he cited the necessity of eruvin given the impossibility of all Jews observing the Sabbath properly.

---

99 See Hutterer, "Eruv ḥaẓerot be-merḥav ha-eroni," 325–329.
100 Moses Sofer, *She'elot u-teshuvot Ḥatam Sofer* (Bratislava, 1841), vol. 1, no. 99.

During this same period, there was a strong movement in Hasidic communities in Poland to build community eruvin. The Baal Shem Tov is quoted as saying, "Ritual slaughter, eruv, and *mikveh* [ritual bathing] are the three foundations by which the world will stand."[101] This tradition led many Hasidic leaders to encourage their Hasidim to build eruvin in their communities. For example, in the mid-nineteenth century, there was no eruv in the Hungarian town of Sighet. The Hasidic Rebbe in the town, Rabbi Yekutiel Yehudah Teitelbaum, responded to a fire that destroyed all the property of an influential member of the community by explaining to his congregation that the cause of the fire was the fact that people were violating the prohibition of *hoẓa'ah* on the Sabbath. He therefore promised anyone who would build an eruv in Sighet a successful life, and the rabbi offered to give up his share in the world to come if someone built this eruv. However, an eruv was not built during Rabbi Teitelbaum's lifetime due to opposition within the community.[102]

Nineteenth Century: Defining a Public Domain

As more city walls were demolished in the first decades of the nineteenth century, the debate over the definition of a public domain, which had high stakes for whether eruvin could be built in most Jewish cities and towns, was rekindled.[103] The debate played out between Rabbi Jacob Brukhin, the rabbi of Karlin in Lithuania and a student of Rabbi Chaim of Volozhin, and Rabbi Ephraim Zalman Margolioth, the rabbi of Brod in Poland and the leading halakhic authority for Polish Jewry. In an exchange of lengthy responsa about the definition of a public domain, Rabbi Brukhin wrote to Rabbi Margolioth in Brod:

> A question concerning the custom nowadays to permit carrying in all cities through the use of a symbolic doorway with a post on one side, etc. This is done even in cities which have open roadways and streets and markets that are sixteen cubits wide and, furthermore, the king's path (highway) passes through

---

101 *Sefer Ba'al Shem Tov al ha-Torah* (Jerusalem, 1992), 338.

102 See Yekutiel Yehudah Teitelbaum, *Sefer gedulat Yehoshua*, ed. Moshe Arye Low (New York, 1986), vol. 1, 20. The editor adds that he did not include the name of the opponent to the building of the eruv in order to protect his family's reputation. For the abundant literature on the history of Hasidim and community eruvin, see Shmuel Pultman, *Me-az u-mi-kedem* (New York, 2008).

103 See Hutterer, "Eruv ḥaẓerot be-merḥav ha-eroni," 319–325.

> these cities. Are they correct [in building eruvin on these cities] or not?

Rabbi Brukhin answered his own question: "It appears clear that they are not acting properly, and I consider their actions to be mistaken.[104] Rabbi Brukhin rejected the opinions of the *Magen Avraham* and the *Taz* and concluded that the majority of Rishonim did not think that a public domain required the daily passage of six hundred thousand people and that any city with a street sixteen cubits wide was considered a public domain.[105]

Rabbi Margolioth responded to Rabbi Brukhin with his own lengthy responsum.[106] After conducting his own tally of the opinions of the Rishonim on the issue, he wrote: "No one has the authority to condemn a custom that was established by the great rabbis of France and Germany, from whom we descend and from whose water [Torah] we drink."[107] He wrote that it was impossible to tally the numbers of rabbis who were lenient and stringent, since it was impossible to know which of their writings were still in manuscript form and had not been published. Therefore, according to Rabbi Margolioth, most of the cities and towns in which the Jews lived should not be considered public domains.[108]

The debate regarding the definition of a public domain continued into the twentieth century. Initially, it divided the Jews of Galicia, who followed the *Beit Efraim,* and the Lithuanian Jews, who followed the *Mishkenot Ya'akov,* but over the centuries, it incorporated all rabbis and communities that dealt with the question of city eruvin.[109] In these centuries in Eastern Europe, the cities and towns did not have populations of six hundred thousand, but they often contained streets sixteen cubits wide. All the eruvin that were built in these cities were built according to the conclusion of Rabbi Margolioth, as Rabbi Brukhin would not have permitted them.[110]

---

104 Jacob Brukhin, *Mishkenot Ya'akov* (Jerusalem, 1960), Oraḥ ḥayyim, no. 120, p. 105.

105 Brukhin, *Mishkenot Ya'akov*, Oraḥ ḥayyim, no. 120, p. 105.

106 Ephraim Zalman Margolioth, *She'elot u-teshuvot beit Efraim* (Warsaw, 1884), Oraḥ ḥayyim, no. 26.

107 Margolioth, *Beit Efraim*, 98.

108 Ibid., 98–99.

109 For a collection of traditions and sources that address the continuation of the debate between the *Mishkenot Ya'akov* and the *Beit Efraim* and which authorities followed each opinion, see Pultman, *Me-az u-mi-kedem*.

110 For a list of the many cities and towns that have eruvin in Eastern Europe, see Pultman, *Me-az u-mi-kedem*; and "List of Cities," Israel613.com, www.israel613.com/books/KKE12_LISTALL-E.pdf.

Nineteenth Century: Construction of the Eruv

While Rabbi Sofer and the Hasidic leaders were emphatic in their insistence that community eruvin be built, the halakhic questions remained. Many cities did not have proper natural boundaries, and so the rabbis of the nineteenth century began to explore other forms of eruv boundaries. According to the Talmud, a Jewish neighborhood that does not have the status of a public domain can be enclosed with symbolic doorways. However, there was a serious problem with building symbolic doorways, because these structures could only be built with the permission of the city authorities. Although this permission varied from city to city, in Pressburg, Rabbi Sofer wrote:

> Thank God the kings and their assistants and officers in the places where the Jews reside have allowed the Jews to practice their religion freely. Specifically, they allow the Jews to establish eruvin in their courtyards, even in the courtyards where the members of the royalty reside. . . . And, where will you find a larger city than our city Pressburg, the metropolis of our country? Several times the king and his advisors stop here, and it is presently the seat of the government, and all the government officials gather here. There is one place that requires a symbolic doorway with two poles and a string between them . . . and they do not prohibit them at all.[111]

Rabbi Sofer concluded his letter to the rabbi of Wurzburg with the wish that he, too, would be able to convince the bishop of his city to allow the Jews to construct an eruv.

While Rabbi Sofer described the cooperation that he received from the Austro-Hungarian authorities in building symbolic doorways, this permission was not given in all locations. Rabbi Gershon Leiner, a great nineteenth-century rabbinic scholar and member of the Izbica Hasidic dynasty in Poland, wrote a pamphlet in which he asked: "Can we rely on the construction of gateways that have been introduced in our times in order to carry on the Sabbath since the age old tradition of building symbolic doorways is impossible today?"[112] Rabbi Leiner was evidently referring to the fact that the governmental authorities did not allow the building of symbolic doorways in his town of Izbica.

---

111 Sofer, *She'elot u-teshuvot Ḥatam Sofer*, vol. 1, no. 99.
112 Gershon Leiner, *Ma'amar daltot sha'ar ha-ir* (Warsaw, 1892), 9.

One improvement in the ability of the Jewish community to create eruvin where symbolic doorways were not permitted came from technological innovation. In the mid-nineteenth century, the invention of the electrical telegraph led to the building of telegraph poles throughout the cities and countryside of Europe and the United States.[113] For some rabbinic authorities, telegraph poles and wires provided the perfect solution to their problem because they lined cities and towns and could be utilized as symbolic doorways. However, some questioned whether these poles with wires running between them constituted acceptable eruv partitions given that the wires did not go directly on top of the poles, potentially making them *ẓurot ha-petaḥ min ha-ẓad* ("symbolic doorways from the side"). Rabbi Joseph Nathanson, rabbi in Lemberg and one of the leading Galician rabbinic scholars in the middle of the nineteenth century, argued that telegraph poles could be utilized as eruv boundaries because the Gemara did not invalidate a "symbolic doorway from the side" unless it was created for the sake of an eruv.[114] However, Rabbi Shneur Zalman Fradkin of Lublin wrote a lengthy responsum arguing that a symbolic doorway from the side is always invalid if the cord is connected to the side of the end posts.[115] This disagreement played a critical role in the creation of early eruvin because the telegraph pole was often the simplest eruv boundary, and there was often no alternative way to create an eruv in a city or town.[116]

Conclusion

The concept of the eruv was developed by the rabbis to allow Jewish communities to circumvent the prohibition of *hoẓa'ah*, carrying between domains, on the Sabbath. In the mind of the rabbis, carrying on the Sabbath was only permitted within a private domain. For this reason, the rabbinic

---

113 For a history of the telegraph and the construction of telegraph poles in the nineteenth century, see Tom Standage, *The Victorian Internet: The Remarkable Story of the Telegraph and the Nineteenth Century On-Line Pioneers* (New York, 1998).

114 Joseph Nathanson, *Sho'el u-meshiv*, 1st ed. (New York, 1980), vol. 2, no. 88.

115 Shnayer Zalman Fradkin, *Torat ḥesed* (Warsaw, 1883), Oraḥ ḥayyim, no. 9, section 4. See also Avraham Eliyahu Feingold, *Tikkun eruvin* (Lublin, 1891), 43, who also disagreed with Rabbi Nathanson.

116 For an excellent review of all the opinions regarding the use of telegraph poles, see Elimelekh Lange, *Hilkhot eruvin* (Jerusalem, 1973), 52–53 and n. 67. The issue of the acceptability of telegraph poles as eruv boundaries was also addressed in Western Europe. See Mordechai Breuer, *Modernity within Tradition: The Social History of Orthodox Jewry in Imperial Germany* (New York, 1992), 261, especially n. 246.

material attempts to create symbolic private domains, allowing the residents of those domains to carry on the Sabbath.

The transformation of semi-private domains into private domains for the sake of circumventing the prohibition of *hoẓa'ah* involves two considerations: first, the creation of physical boundaries around the semi-private domain so that it can be considered a private domain, and second, the establishment of a community within the enclosed area that is limited to Jews committed to the principle of eruv. During the rabbinic period in Palestine, the requirement to create an enclosed property in which all the Jews accepted the principle of eruv was based on a typical Jewish neighborhood, which was centered around a courtyard and required only the sealing off of the entranceway to create the necessary enclosed area. However, as the Jewish neighborhood expanded and a need arose to enclose several courtyards that all opened into an alleyway, the eruv became a more symbolic enclosure with symbolic walls enclosing the alleyway and separating it from the public domain. In addition, the possibility that these courtyards included non-Jewish residents or Jewish residents who did not accept the principle of eruv required a symbolic arrangement that would, in essence, allow these people to remain in the courtyard but remove them from the status of residents with respect to the eruv. This requirement necessitated the creation of a rabbinic construct that allowed for the leasing of the property of the non-Jewish residents or the relinquishing of the property of the Jewish residents who rejected the eruv. Each of these arrangements allowed for the exclusion of those who did not fit into the eruv community while at the same time recognizing that they were residents of the courtyard.

As Jewish communities expanded from small courtyards to larger neighborhoods and then to entire cities, the principles established in the Talmud had to be applied to these new urban realities. Although each new neighborhood or city required a unique application of these rules, the principles established in the talmudic material served as the guidelines for the creation of all eruvin. The Geonic and medieval commentators turned the concept of eruv that had been discussed at length in the Talmud into a reality that served their communities. For the first time, we have discussions about the creation of eruvin around large neighborhoods and cities. By the medieval period, eruvin were found in a number of the larger cities in both Ashkenaz and Spain. While the enclosure of most medieval cities by walls for protection made the creation of eruvin much simpler, many of the talmudic issues still needed to be developed and adapted to particular situations during this period.

As Jewish communities expanded in the early modern period, the talmudic principles of eruvin once again needed to be applied to changing realities. The tension that was often present between a feeling of obligation to halakhah and the needs of different Jewish communities necessitated creativity on the part of rabbinic scholars. The details of how cities were leased varied with the authority of their rulers, and the nature of eruv boundaries was dependent on the specific location and geography of each city. The nineteenth-century invention of the telegraph created new challenges as the rabbinic authorities struggled to determine whether these telegraph poles and wires met the standards defined by the Talmud fifteen hundred years earlier. Yet during this period, the rallying cry of Rabbi Moses Sofer that eruvin must be created in each community seemed to lie at the foundation of all halakhic discussions. Although not all rabbis encouraged or allowed eruvin to be built in cities, there was a basic idea that eruvin benefited Jewish communities.

The debates regarding eruvin in the large cities of Eastern Europe played a central role in the debates that would transpire in North America. As Jews moved out of restricted neighborhoods in the nineteenth century, the need to create eruvin that would enclose entire cities became a source of debate among the members of the rabbinic community. Rules and principles that had been applied throughout the centuries in small Jewish neighborhoods were being extended to apply to the largest cities in Eastern Europe. Rabbinic authorities debated whether eruvin could be constructed around these cities as well as whether it was advisable to create such eruvin.

As the Eastern European rabbis began to immigrate to North America, they came with not only an understanding of the rabbinic sources concerning eruvin but also an appreciation of the tension that city eruvin had caused in Eastern Europe. They were also aware that despite this tension and debate, many eruvin had been built and that Jews in European cities and towns relied on these eruvin to carry objects on the Sabbath.

While some immigrant rabbis attempted to recreate aspects of this Eastern European Jewish experience in America, they were also confronted with a new set of realities particular to their time and place. These realities kindled a new set of debates, which will be explored in the following chapters.

2

The St. Louis Eruv

The first documented *eruv* in North America was established in the last decade of the nineteenth century in St. Louis, Missouri. The existence of an eruv normally not only fulfills the legal requirements to allow carrying on the Sabbath but also symbolizes the existence of a unified Jewish community in the area it encloses. Perhaps ironically, the St. Louis eruv did the opposite. In dividing public and private domains, the eruv also came to divide the nascent Jewish community and its leaders.

A notable feature of the St. Louis eruv is that it was composed entirely of preexisting natural and artificial boundaries, including rivers and telegraph lines. Because the Jewish community had no relationship with local government, it was impossible to erect wires or other structures to augment these existing boundaries. To create the eruv, Rabbi Zekhariah Yosef Rosenfeld simply argued that the enclosure already existed. This argument became the basis of a prolonged dispute between Rabbi Rosenfeld and the other rabbi serving in St. Louis at the time, Rabbi Shalom Elchanan Jaffe.

Background to the Eruv Dispute

The St. Louis Jewish community was young, but it was not small. The end of the nineteenth century and the first decades of the twentieth century brought a large influx of immigrant Jews to St. Louis. From 1880 to 1920, over fifty thousand Jews from the Russian Pale of Settlement, the Kingdom of Poland, Hapsburg Galicia, and Romania settled in St. Louis.[1] The first of these Eastern European Jewish immigrants were not happy with the religious situation that they found in St. Louis. One newcomer commented, "Unfortunately, we came to a city where there was not a single sacred place to offer prayers. . . . Many who have come before us had one objective in view—money-seeking."[2] Faced with the lack of a *minyan* (a group of at least ten Jewish men coming together for prayers), a group of Latvian Jews met and organized one informally. Although the exact date of the founding of this minyan is unknown, by October 1881, it had completed its constitution and became known as Beth Hamedrosh Hagodol. By 1890, the congregation had enough funds to purchase a modest building from the German Evangelical Protestant Congregation of the Church of the Holy Ghost. Although its membership did not exceed about twenty-five people, a Chevra Mishnah Gemora was established for the daily study of Talmud, and a Hebrew school, the first in St. Louis, was founded in 1893.[3]

Several other small synagogues were created by these immigrants. All these synagogues were built in the neighborhood known as the Jewish Ghetto, a crowded rectangular area in the north side of St. Louis.[4] Most of them met in rented space and occupied no more than one room with a makeshift cabinet to house the Torah scrolls that had been brought from Eastern Europe. There is little documentation about the early history of these small synagogues, although we know that one of them, Sheerith Sfard, became an important religious and cultural center. It hosted cantorial concerts, guest lectures, and other social events for these immigrants.[5]

---

1 Averam B. Bender, "*History of the Beth Hamedrosh Hagodol Congregation of St. Louis*, 1879–1969," in *The Bulletin of the Missouri Historical Society* (October 1970): 68–69.

2 Bender, "*Beth Hamedrosh Hagodol,*" 69. For the history of the Jews in St. Louis prior to 1880, see Walter Ehrlich, *Zion in the Valley: The Jewish Community of St. Louis* (Columbia, MI, 1997), vol. 1.

3 Bender, "*Beth Hamedrosh Hagodol,*" 69–72.

4 This neighborhood was bounded on the east by the Mississippi River, on the west by Grand Street, on the north by Cass Avenue, and on the south by Delmar Avenue. See Ehrich, *Zion in the Valley*, vol. 2, 29.

5 Ehrlich, *Zion in the Valley*, vol. 1, 311–313. Ira Robinson claimed that the title "Sfard" reflected the Hasidic nature of the congregation, since the Hasidim followed the Sephardic rite in their services, and he traced this title throughout North America to highlight the gradual increase of Hasidism in North America during the period of the great migration to North America. Sheerith Sfard was not a Hasidic congregation, but it may have been started by Russian Jews who were uncomfortable in the St. Louis congregation, which followed an Ashkenazi liturgy. See Ira Robinson, "Anshe Sfard: The Creation of the First Hasidic Congregations in North America," *American Jewish Archives* 62, no. 1–2 (2005): 53–66.

During the last decade of the nineteenth century, Rabbi Shalom Elchanan Jaffe and Rabbi Zekhariah Yosef Rosenfeld served contemporaneously as rabbis of the two branches of Sheerith Sfard, both of which were located on North Ninth St.[6] Their relationship—which was one of immediate mutual antagonism—is best exemplified by two disputes between them regarding the establishment of a *mikveh* (ritual bath) and an eruv in the city.

Rabbi Jaffe was born in 1858 in Vabalninkas, in the province of Vilnius Gubernia. At the age of fourteen, he went to study at the famed yeshiva in Volozhin, and he received his rabbinical ordination at age nineteen from such leading Lithuanian rabbis as Rabbi Isaac Elchanan Spektor, Rabbi Naphtali Zvi Yehudah Berlin, and Rabbi Rephael Shapiro.[7] In 1879, he became the rabbi of Upyna, in the province of Kovno, and from 1884 to 1847 he served as rabbi of Zeimelis, in the province of Vilnius.[8] In a portent of things to come, he became embroiled in a dispute during his time in Zeimelis, and in 1887[9] he departed for the United States.[10] By November 1887, he was apparently accorded the title of chief rabbi of the St. Louis Orthodox Jewish community[11] and served as rabbi of Congregation Sheerith Sfard. His stint in St. Louis was also tumultuous,[12] and he returned to Russia to serve as rabbi in his hometown of Vabalninkas.[13] By 1891, he had returned to St. Louis,[14] and later that year he was appointed rabbi of Beth Hamedrosh Hagodol.[15] His second experience in St. Louis was equally tumultuous, and in 1895 he left Beth Hamedrosh Hagodol.[16] By 1897,

---

6 Bender, "*Beth Hamedrosh Hagodol,*" 76.

7 Benzion Eisenstadt, *Le-toldot Yisrael Be-Amerikah* (New York, 1917), 60; and Judah David Eisenstein, *Oẓar zikhronotai* (New York, 1930), 158.

8 *Hameliẓ,* November 21, 1884, 1417.

9 Rabbi Eliyahu David Rabinowitz-Teomim, *Seder Eliyahu* (Jerusalem, 1983), 90. In this autobiography, Rabbi Rabinowitz-Teomim, a rabbinic authority in Lithuania who moved to Jerusalem in 1901 to lead the Ashkenazic community there, mentioned that, between the years 1885 and 1886, he was called to Zeimelis to settle a dispute between Rabbi Jaffe and Rabbi Sholom Dov Sprints.

10 The ship's manifest for the *Suvia,* September 7, 1887, line 146 listed Scholem Jaffe.

11 *The Jewish Free Press,* November 4, 1887. Rabbi Jaffe never signed any document as chief rabbi. This newspaper report is the only published reference according him the title, which may reflect the fact that there was no official mechanism to designate a chief rabbi, so the title could be claimed by or accorded to virtually any rabbi. Rabbi Jaffe signed his works "*Av Beit Din* of St. Louis." See, for example, Elchanan Jaffe, *Sho'el ka-inyan* (Jerusalem, 1895), 23.

12 *Voice,* January 27, 1888.

13 Eisenstadt, *Le-toldot Yisra'el be-Amerikah,* 60.

14 *Voice,* January 16, 1891.

15 *Gould's St. Louis Directory, 1891,* 1513.

16 Bender, "*Beth Hamedrosh Hagodol,*" 76.

he was rabbi of a splinter minyan of Sheerith Sfard,[17] but he left later that year to become rabbi of Congregation Beth Hamidrash in Brooklyn.[18] Although his stay in Brooklyn was marred by yet another feud,[19] he remained in New York until his death in 1923.[20]

The other rabbi in St. Louis in the last decade of the nineteenth century was Rabbi Zekhariah Yosef Rosenfeld. Rabbi Rosenfeld was born in Turisk, in the province of Volhynia, in 1847.[21] He served as a rabbi in Kovel, also in Volhynia,[22] and in his hometown of Turisk, where he was respected for his Torah scholarship and his knowledge of medicine.[23] He left Turisk in 1893[24] and, after spending a short time in New York and Baltimore,[25] was elected rabbi of the Agudat Ha-Kehilot, the United Congregations, of St. Louis.[26] In that capacity, he was rabbi of several synagogues, including Bnai Yaakov, Bnai Binyamin, Tifereth Israel, and Beth Abraham, taking a permanent position at Sheerith Sfard, where he served from 1897 until his death in 1915.[27]

During the period in which Rabbis Jaffe and Rosenfeld both served in St. Louis, Rabbi Jaffe built a mikveh, which was criticized by Rabbi Rosenfeld, and Rabbi Rosenfeld built an eruv, which was criticized by Rabbi Jaffe. In the absence of contemporaneous documentation, it is impossible to know which of the two launched the first attack on the other's institution or the exact date on

---

17 *Gould's St. Louis Directory, 1897,* 854 and 2262. By 1900, this splinter minyan had disappeared. See *Gould's St. Louis Directory, 1900,* 2459.

18 Bender, "*Beth Hamedrosh Hagodol,*" 76.

19 Rabbi Jaffe fought with Rabbi Shabsi Rosenberg, rabbi of Beth Hamidrash Hagadol Keser Torah in Brooklyn. See Rabbi Jaffe's obituary in *Morgen zhurnal,* November 16, 1923, 2.

20 See the obituaries in *Morgen zhurnal,* November 16, 1923, 2; and *New York Tribune,* November 17, 1923.

21 Samuel Noach Gottlieb, *Ohalei Shem* (Pinsk, 1912), 308, *American Jewish Year Book* 5 (1903–1904): 91 (hereafter referred to as *AJYB*). While the article gives 1850 as his date of birth, his tombstone states that he was born in 1847.

22 *Modern View,* September 10, 1915, 44.

23 *Turisk Yizkor Book,* 16, 179.

24 The ship's manifest for the *Weimar,* August 22, 1893, line 410, lists a Josef Rosenfeld. Josef was Rabbi Rosenfeld's middle name. In view of the fact that the 1900 Census stated that his year of immigration was 1893, it seems likely that he sailed on the *Weimar.*

25 *AJYB* 5 (1903–1904): 91.

26 The exact date of his arrival in St. Louis is unknown. He signed the letter at the beginning of *Tikvat Zekhariah,* vol. 2 on February 24, 1894. See Zekhariah Rosenfeld, *Tikvat Zekhariah,* vol. 1 (St. Louis, 1896), 7. Yet, he is still listed in the *Baltimore City Directory* in 1895. He may have commuted between Baltimore and St. Louis. By 1896, he is only listed in the St. Louis city directory (see *Gould's St. Louis Directory, 1896,* 1360).

27 *AJYB* 2 (1900–1901): 310; 9 (1907–1908): 234; 2 (1900–1901): 310; 5 (1903–1904): 91; 9 (1907–1908): 234; 9 (1907–1908): 233; 2 (1900–1901): 309; 5 (1903–1904): 91; and 9 (1907–1908): 234. His obituary appeared in *St. Louis Globe-Democrat,* September 10, 1915; and *St. Louis Post-Dispatch,* September 10, 1915.

which the eruv feud began. However, we do know that Rabbi Jaffe published an anti-eruv document in his volume *Sho'el ka-inyan* in January 1894. Although it is difficult to fix a precise date when the two began their clash over the eruv, it evidently occurred within a few months of Rabbi Rosenfeld's arrival in St. Louis at the end of 1893. The feud that ensued was about the technicalities of the laws of *eruvin,* but it was also a struggle over the fundamental questions of what it meant to be an immigrant Jew in urban America. How should religious leaders in America respond to growing secularism? Was the use of halakhic leniencies appropriate in America? Who were figures of religious authority in America?

The issue of the eruv became a formal debate in 1896, when Rabbi Rosenfeld published the second volume of his halakhic work *Tikvat Zekhariah,* in which he defended the eruv against the arguments made by Rabbi Jaffe in *Sho'el ka-inyan.*[28] However, Rabbi Rosenfeld did not refer to Rabbi Jaffe by name or to *Sho'el ka-inyan* itself in this volume.[29] In that same year, 1896, Rabbi Jaffe wrote yet another polemic against the eruv, entitled *Teshuvah ka-halakhah,* which rehearsed, in a different format, all of the points he had made two years prior in *Sho'el ka-inyan.*[30] *Teshuvah ka-halakhah* commenced with a harsh ad hominem introduction attacking Rabbi Rosenfeld. Rabbi Jaffe wrote, "Anyone who has Jewish blood flowing through his arteries will not be able to restrain himself due to the fact that Rabbi Rosenfeld has disparaged those rabbis who are not comfortable with his eruv. . . . We see that his only intention is to find favor with the masses."[31] *Teshuvah ka-halakhah* added very little material that was not already found in *Sho'el ka-inyan.* With the exception of the personal attack on Rabbi Rosenfeld, all that this volume did was organize Rabbi Jaffe's argument by referencing each paragraph to the corresponding page in Rabbi Rosenfeld's *Tikvat Zekhariah.*

The remainder of this chapter will trace the back-and-forth arguments between Rabbis Jaffe and Rosenfeld over the various social and halakhic issues that the St. Louis eruv raised.

---

28 Zekhariah Rosenfeld, *Tikvat Zekhariah,* vol. 1 (Chicago, 1896). *Tikvat Zekhariah* translates to *Hope of Zekhariah.* The titles of Rabbi Jaffe's books, *Sho'el ka-inyan* (*Asks What is Relevant*) and *Teshuvah ka-halakhah* (*Response according to the Law*) refer to Avot 5:7: "There are seven characteristics . . . in a wise man: . . . He asks what is relevant (*sho'el ka-inyan*) and he answers to the point (or: according to the law, *meshiv ke-halakhah*)."

29 Rosenfeld, *Tikvat Zekhariah,* vol. 2 (Chicago, 1896).

30 Shalom Elchanan Jaffe, *Teshuvah ka-halakhah ve-divrei shalom* (Jerusalem, 1896).

31 Jaffe, *Teshuvah ka-halakhah,* 16.

Building an Eruv for Sabbath Violators

Although legal arguments occupy the majority of their volumes, both Rabbi Jaffe and Rabbi Rosenfeld also explained their positions based on their views of the American Orthodox community. Rabbi Rosenfeld began his volume with a comment about the situation of Orthodoxy in America at the time. He wrote:

> I arrived in this nation, and I witnessed even many of the religious Jews carrying on the Sabbath. A religious Jew is not embarrassed to carry his *tallit* [prayer shawl] in public and to wear it in the synagogue. I said to myself, what should I do for the sake of my people to remove this terrible sin? If I raise my voice like the shofar to decry the severity of the prohibition, I know that my words will not make an impact because people have already become accustomed to carrying on the Sabbath. In addition, the preachers in this country have already set the standard of raising their voices, stamping their feet, clapping their hands, and shaking every limb in their bodies to criticize the actions of the people. Yet they have been unsuccessful, and their words have been ignored. If I get upset and embarrass the sinner, I will have nothing to my credit other than my anger. . . . I therefore have decided to return to the words of the law and to look for a way in which the Jewish tradition would allow for carrying on the Sabbath. . . . When I was appointed rabbi in St. Louis, I continued my search, and I found a correct and acceptable way to permit carrying on the Sabbath.[32]

Rabbi Rosenfeld took a critical view of the American Orthodox community, claiming that they not only looked for leniencies but actually carried on the Sabbath. However, he believed that an eruv could be created in St. Louis and would be much more effective at curbing Sabbath violation than public criticism and rebuke.

Rabbi Jaffe began *Sho'el ka-inyan* with the following introduction:

> Recently a rabbi has come to St. Louis and has permitted carrying on the Sabbath with made-up arguments that have no basis at all. Worse than that, he has built an entire structure on

32 Rosenfeld, *Tikvat Zekhariah*, vol. 2, 3–4.

> these arguments, one that permits carrying on the Sabbath in all American cities. Furthermore, violators are rampant in this generation, and those in America hang on to his coattails and argue that "it is preferable to be permissive." And this matter can easily become a plague in the cities of America, for what will prevent other rabbis from permitting that which is prohibited merely to gain the favor of the masses? Furthermore, some have claimed that this rabbi will allow them to keep their stores open on the Sabbath through the sale of the store to one of their non-Jewish employees. Indeed, some people who are concerned about the money that they are losing on the Sabbath are asking me to permit their stores to remain open just as this rabbi has done. The Sabbath is thereby violated even by those who consider themselves religious, and the essence of the Sabbath will be forgotten.[33]

Rabbi Jaffe went on to explain that he wrote this volume to alert the Jewish community to the defective nature of Rabbi Rosenfeld's arguments.

In this introduction, Rabbi Jaffe made several criticisms of the American Orthodox community. First, he argued that they were always seeking leniencies and would therefore "hang onto the coattails" of rabbis such as Rabbi Rosenfeld. Furthermore, he expressed concern that the St. Louis eruv would start a wave of eruv building in North America, all based on the incorrect leniencies expressed by Rabbi Rosenfeld. In these arguments, Rabbi Jaffe combined a criticism of the American Orthodox community with a desire to save it from Sabbath violation.

In the introduction to *Teshuvah ka-halakhah,* Rabbi Jaffe elaborated on his view concerning the status of the eruv and the general Jewish religious climate in America:

> And he [Rabbi Rosenfeld] added a sin upon his sin by publishing a volume permitting carrying on the Sabbath entitled *Tikvat Zekhariah,* in which he hoped that the people would listen to his suggestion. I will tell the truth to the rabbis and scholars. Had he had tried to permit this act and published a book allowing it in Europe, a place where no serpents exist nor rabbis who are not scholars, I would not have bothered to publish my work against him, for who would have listened to him? However, in

33 Jaffe, *Sho'el ka-inyan,* 1.

> America, where we have been exiled to a place of "evil waters," where people wait with open eyes for rabbis to permit activities and praise the words of those who are lenient, the risk is great. Most of the people here are not scholars and are involved in the necessities of the day. . . . The rabbi who has given permission carries on the Sabbath in public, and he has instructed one of the righteous slaughterers to carry so that people will learn that it is permissible.[34]

Once again, Rabbi Jaffe spoke critically of the American Orthodox community, comparing it unfavorably with the Orthodox community in Eastern Europe. In addition, in Rabbi Jaffe's eyes, the fact that Rabbi Rosenfeld required one of the religious officials of the community to rely on the eruv meant that this eruv was creating serious religious divisions within the community. If the slaughterer carried on the Sabbath in St. Louis, his reliability regarding producing kosher meat would be affected.

These introductions provide background to the disparate views of Rabbis Jaffe and Rosenfeld concerning American Orthodoxy at the time. The lack of observance and the desire for leniencies on the part of the community presented rabbis with a dilemma over whether to accommodate or continue to battle. It is notable, however, that while Rabbi Jaffe opposed the St. Louis eruv, he did not deny the benefits of building eruvin in America. He opposed Rabbi Rosenfeld's eruv because he believed that it did not meet the necessary legal standards, but he did not argue that an acceptable eruv would be inappropriate for the American Orthodox community in general.

However, the view that eruvin should not be built in America was expressed by Rabbi Eliezer Grayewsky, the Jerusalem rabbi who published Rabbi Jaffe's volumes on the St. Louis eruv. Rabbi Grayewsky also wrote notes on Rabbi Jaffe's *Sho'el ka-inyan* and *Teshuvah ka-halakhah*. At the conclusion of his notes, he wrote:

> All that Rabbi Shalom Elchanan wrote is correct. . . . Yet, I do not know why the permitting rabbi entered this problematic area to permit this violation for which the punishment is stoning. Is it for the sake of the Sabbath violators who sit all Saturday in their stores and sell and write as if it were a weekday? Do they need the eruv? Is it for the sake of those who are Sabbath observers?

34 Jaffe, *Teshuvah ka-halakhah*, 10–11.

> It is a sin to permit these people to carry on the Sabbath with forced arguments, and this will create a basis for a great breach throughout America. For if we follow his argument, we should permit carrying throughout the world due to the fact that the world is surrounded by the Atlantic Ocean.[35]

Rabbi Grayewsky argued that it was inappropriate to create an eruv to prevent a sin by those who purposely violate the Sabbath and that an eruv for those who observe the Sabbath must not be based on leniencies. Although it is possible that Rabbi Grayewsky did not properly understand the religious situation in America, his opposition to the building of an eruv in a situation where the eruv would prevent individuals who were otherwise Sabbath violators from violating the Sabbath stands in stark contrast even to Rabbi Jaffe, who rejected Rabbi Rosenfeld's eruv but accepted the importance of community eruvin when constructed according to halakhah.

The Importance of Creating an Eruv

Rabbi Rosenfeld prefaced his halakhic arguments with a discussion of the importance of creating community eruvin. He began by quoting the view of Rabbi Moses Sofer in Pressburg, who wrote to the rabbi in Wurzburg that it was incumbent on the rabbi of a community to arrange for the creation of an eruv in the community to prevent Sabbath violation. Rabbi Sofer wrote that because it was impossible to prevent women and children—who are weak-minded and will inevitably carry on the Sabbath—from walking outside on the Sabbath, there is no alternative to the creation of an eruv in each community.[36] Rabbi Rosenfeld added that if the rabbi receives a salary, it is his special responsibility to create an eruv in his community.[37]

Rabbi Rosenfeld also quoted the letter that Rabbi Asher wrote to Rabbi Yaakov ben Moshe regarding the importance of creating an eruv in the local community of Fredes.[38] Based on this responsum, Rabbi Rosenfeld concluded this section, "We see how upset Rabbeinu Asher became, and he criticized this man, Yaakov ben Moshe, for leading people to violate the Sabbath. Therefore,

---

35 Ibid., 30.
36 Moses Sofer, *She'elot u-teshuvot Ḥatam Sofer* (Bratislava, 1841), vol. 1, no. 99.
37 Rosenfeld, *Tikvat Zekhariah*, vol. 2, 1.
38 Asher ben Jehiel, *She'elot u-teshuvot le-Rabbeinu Asher* (Jerusalem, 1994), 110–112.

I find myself obligated to travel around St. Louis and explore the possibility of creating an eruv that will allow Jews to carry on the Sabbath."[39]

Rabbi Jaffe responded to Rabbi Rosenfeld's claim that it is incumbent on a community rabbi to create an eruv by reinterpreting the sources that Rabbi Rosenfeld quoted. First, Rabbi Jaffe explained that Rabbi Sofer was addressing a situation in which the Jews of Wurzburg did not want to create an eruv and were willing to prevent the women and children from going outside on the Sabbath. In that situation, Rabbi Sofer wrote to the rabbi that it was incumbent upon him to create a community eruv and not to rely on the Jews of the town to prevent carrying on the Sabbath. Second, he argued that the eruv that Rabbeinu Asher was defending met a stricter halakhic standard than Rabbi Rosenfeld's and that he would not have validated the eruv in St. Louis.

Defining the Public Domain

The first halakhic issue that both rabbis discussed is whether St. Louis should be considered a *reshut ha-rabbim*, a "public domain," necessitating the surrounding of the city with real walls to create an acceptable eruv. In their discussions of the legal definition of *reshut ha-rabbim*, Rabbis Rosenfeld and Jaffe grappled with and argued over how to apply the idea of "public space" to their foreign reality.

At the beginning of volume two of *Tikvat Zekhariah*, Rabbi Rosenfeld clarified his view on the definition of a public domain, claiming that most rabbinic authorities take the view that a public domain exists only where the population of the area exceeds six hundred thousand. He explained, based on the opinion of Rabbeinu Nissim, that for an area to be classified as a public domain, six hundred thousand people must gather in one place each day, as was the case during the Israelites' journey in the wilderness, where the entire population gathered in the Levite camp. If there were one street in which everyone gathered, Rabbi Rosenfeld argued, then the entire city would be considered a public domain, by analogy to the Israelite camps, in which people only congregated in the Levite camp, yet the entire Jewish encampment was considered a public domain.[40]

In an addendum to *Tikvat Zekhariah*, Rabbi Rosenfeld elaborated on the question of whether St. Louis was a public domain. First, he stateed that the population of St. Louis was approximately five hundred thousand, so it did not

---

39 Rosenfeld, *Tikvat Zekhariah*, vol. 2, 6.

40 Ibid., 6–9. See b. Shab. 96b and Rashi, s.v. *maḥaneh* for the relationship between the Levite camp and a public domain; and *Ḥiddushei Ha-Ran al Massekhet Eruvin*, 6a, s.v. *kan*.

meet the six hundred thousand-person threshold for being a public domain according to the majority of rabbinic authorities. Furthermore, he noted that most people traveled the streets in electric or steam trolleys and argued that each trolley car had the status of a private domain (*reshut ha-yaḥid*), so their passengers did not count toward the six hundred thousand total. Even the ground underneath these trolleys had the status of a private domain. Finally, he argued that since the trolleys made it dangerous for people to cross the streets, St. Louis could not be considered public domain, since the inability of people to walk on the streets disqualified them as a public area. He went on to consider the possibility that the sidewalks might be wide enough to create their own public domain. However, he concluded that the width of the sidewalks could not be combined with the width of the streets to create a public domain.[41]

These two qualifications concerning the presence of trolleys on the streets of St. Louis requires further consideration, because they lie at the foundation of Rabbi Rosenfeld's determination that St. Louis did not have the status of a public domain. There is some precedent for Rabbi Rosenfeld's claim that the passengers in the trolleys should not be included in the tally of six hundred thousand. Rabbi Ephraim Margolioth, a Ukrainian rabbi (1762–1828), for example, wrote that people traveling on horses or in wagons are not included in the tally of six hundred thousand.[42] Rabbi Israel Trunk, a Polish rabbinic authority (1821–1893), wrote, in a similar vein, that the road over which train tracks run does not have the status of a public domain.[43] Rabbi Rosenfeld did not quote either of these authorities, but he seems to have combined their arguments in determining that passengers in trolleys are not included in the tally of six hundred thousand and that the roadway under the trolleys does not constitute a public domain. In defense of his claim that people's fear of traveling in the streets due to the risk of injury by the trolleys had legal implications for the classification of an area as a public domain, Rabbi Rosenfeld quoted the opinion of the early fourteenth-century Spanish scholar Rabbeinu Yeroḥam, who argued that a public domain needs to be accessible to the public without any interference.[44] Although Rabbi Rosenfeld made use of precedent regarding

---

41 Rosenfeld, *Tikvat Zekhariah*, vol. 2, 40–41.

42 Ephraim Zalman Margolioth, *She'elot u-teshuvot beit Efraim* (Warsaw, 1984), Oraḥ ḥayyim, no. 29, 98.

43 Israel Trunk, *She'elot u-teshuvot yeshu'ot malko* (Petrokow, 1927), no. 27. See also Sholom Mordechai Schwadron, *She'elot u-teshuvot Maharsham* (Jerusalem, 1958), Oraḥ ḥayyim, no. 161, who agrees with Rabbi Trunk.

44 Yeruham ben Meshullam, *Sefer toldot Adam ve-Ḥavvah* (Jerusalem, 1974), *netiv* 12, nos. 4 and 17. See also Abraham Yudelovitz, *She'elot u-teshuvot beit av*, 2nd ed. (New York, 1929), no. 9, section 2, who quotes Rabbi Rosenfeld's opinion regarding the nullification of the streets due

both of these issues, the way in which he applied past rulings to the reality of St. Louis required innovative thinking.

Rabbi Rosenfeld concluded his volume by reiterating that the population of St. Louis was under six hundred thousand people. However, he added that even if the population did reach six hundred thousand, the eruv in St. Louis would still be valid because the streets did not open into a market that itself had the status of a public domain. Therefore, these streets were not *mefulash,* open from one public domain to another, which is a necessary criterion for the existence of a public domain even if the population exceeds six hundred thousand.[45]

Rabbi Jaffe began his polemic in *Sho'el ka-inyan* by claiming that St. Louis had a population greater than six hundred thousand and therefore constituted a public domain, for which walls and gates that could be closed at night would be needed to allow carrying on the Sabbath. He explained that it would be impossible to erect these gates, since trains traveled in and out of the city all day and night. He asserted, however, that, even if there were not six hundred thousand people who traversed the city every day, the city would still be considered a public domain. This was based on the rabbinic position that a public domain is determined by the width of the streets and not the size of the population. Therefore, Rabbi Jaffe argued that carrying on the Sabbath could only be allowed in St. Louis if the city were to be enclosed by walls and gates.

Rabbi Jaffe continued his argument by analyzing the view of Rabbi Margolioth in his collection of responsa, *Beit Efraim.* He argued that Rabbi Margolioth only allowed carrying in the absence of walls and gates because it was impossible to build gates in the cities and towns of Eastern Europe. However, Rabbi Jaffe concluded, "Even if we are lenient and follow the opinion of the *Beit Efraim* and his followers [that a public domain is determined by the size of the population] and permit the surrounding of the city with a symbolic doorway (*ẓurat ha-petaḥ*), this symbolic doorway has to be constructed according to all the legal stringencies, since the idea that erecting a symbolic doorway is sufficient for creating an eruv boundary [in a public domain] is itself a leniency."[46]

Rabbi Jaffe claimed that even according to the opinion of the *Beit Efraim,* every street in St. Louis and in other American cities had the status of a *mavoi ha-mefulash,* an open alleyway, since they all led into public areas. Since each

---

to the trolleys and disagrees with him, claiming that the streets would still have the status of a *karmelit.*

45 Rosenfeld, *Tikvat Zekhariah,* vol. 2, 57.

46 Jaffe, *Sho'el ka-inyan,* 2–8, quote on p. 7.

street had the status of a *mavoi ha-mefulash*, it would require a symbolic doorway on the end that leads into the public space.

In *Teshuvah ka-halakhah*, Rabbi Jaffe continued to address Rabbi Rosenfeld's claims regarding the streets of St. Louis. First, he wrote that the claim that the road under the trolleys and cars had the status of a private domain was wrong, and "it is an embarrassment to mention it in front of Torah scholars." He went on to say that such an argument is "silly," because no one had ever suggested that people riding in trolleys or cars should not be included in the tally of six hundred thousand. He brought a proof from the *Magen Avraham* (Abraham Gombiner, 1635–1682), which states that people traveling on boats are still included in the tally of those people who negate the eruv boundary of the river even though the individual boats have the status of a private domain.[47] Furthermore, Rabbi Jaffe argued that Rabbeinu Yeroḥam's requirement that the streets be accessible to pedestrians did not mean that people regularly walked on the streets. If the streets were accessible to cars and trolleys, that would be sufficient according to Rabbeinu Yeroḥam, even if people did not regularly walk these streets. Finally, he noted that many people walked in the streets despite the fact that there were trolleys and cars on the street.[48]

Rabbi Jaffe claimed that Rabbi Rosenfeld also said that the manhole covers for the underground waterworks could be considered doorways that open and close and would constitute doors according to those rabbinic authorities who require that the city be enclosed by gates that can be opened and closed. Rabbi Jaffe disagreed that the manholes could be considered doors and argued that even if they were, the city would still be considered a public domain because the manhole covers did not sufficiently enclose the city. As previously discussed, Rabbi Jaffe's initial argument against the eruv was published prior to Rabbi Rosenfeld's defense of the eruv. Although most of the arguments that Rabbi Jaffe claimed that Rabbi Rosenfeld used in the creation of the St. Louis eruv were addressed by Rabbi Rosenfeld in *Tikvat Zekhariah*, Rabbi Rosenfeld did not mention the utilization of manhole covers as gates to enclose the city. Since this argument for the use of manholes has no basis in earlier rabbinic sources, it is possible that Rabbi Rosenfeld changed his mind or that Rabbi Jaffe attributed the argument to Rabbi Rosenfeld even though Rabbi Rosenfeld never actually used it in support of his eruv.[49]

---

47 Avraham Gombiner, *Magen Avraham*, Oraḥ ḥayyim, 363:30.

48 Jaffe, *Teshuvah ka-halakhah*, 21 and 26. The printed edition of *Teshuvah ka-halakhah* skips pages 22–25.

49 Ibid., 17–20.

In *Teshuvah ka-halakhah,* Rabbi Jaffe questioned Rabbi Rosenfeld's conclusion regarding the population of St. Louis. Rabbi Rosenfeld estimated that at the time of the creation of the eruv, there were about five hundred thousand people in St. Louis. In an attempt to bolster his credentials as someone knowledgeable about the realities of America, Rabbi Jaffe claimed that Rabbi Rosenfeld took this population figure from a Yiddish paper and that Rabbi Rosenfeld was no expert on numbers in St. Louis. Rabbi Jaffe claimed that he heard from several knowledgeable people and read in English-language books that the total population in St. Louis exceeded seven hundred thousand people. Furthermore, he said, since the main railroad station of the region was in St. Louis and passenger trains were constantly arriving and departing, there were bound to be even more people in the city at any one time. He concluded that during the World's Fair there were close to one million people in the city.[50] Rabbi Jaffe's view on who counts toward the necessary six hundred thousand reflects a departure from the traditional definition of "public domain" as expressed by the rabbinic authorities in Eastern Europe. For instance, Rabbi Margolioth, who was the accepted authority on eruvin, required that six hundred thousand individuals pass through one place or one street for the city to be considered a public domain.[51]

Luckily for us, we have access to information that allows us to determine the exact population of St. Louis in those years. The population of St. Louis in 1893, according to *Gould's St. Louis Directory,* was 574,569.[52] Rabbi Jaffe claimed that Rabbi Rosenfeld took his population estimate of five hundred thousand from a Yiddish paper. However, Rabbi Jaffe's claim that the population of St. Louis exceeded seven hundred thousand was also inaccurate. In 1896, the year in which *Teshuvah ka-halakhah* was published, according to *Gould's St. Louis Directory,* the population of St. Louis was 611,268.[53]

Eruv Boundaries

Rabbis Rosenfeld and Jaffe debated both the description of the eruv boundaries and the ability to utilize these boundaries as eruv walls. Rabbi Rosenfeld delineated the boundaries of the eruv that he claimed enclosed

---

50 Ibid., 21. The St. Louis World's Fair was first held in 1904. Rabbi Jaffe may have been referring to the annual St. Louis Fair.
51 Margolioth, *Beit Efraim,* Oraḥ ḥayyim, no. 26, 87.
52 *Gould's St. Louis Directory, 1893–1894,* 25.
53 *Gould's St. Louis Directory, 1896–1897,* 24.

the Jewish neighborhood of St. Louis. On the east side and north side, the boundary was the Mississippi River (numbers 1–2 and 5–6 on the map below) and on the south side, the River des Peres (numbers 3–4).[54] Closer to the city on the north side, the railroad ran along artificial embankments. One embankment was longer and steeper than the others and covered the pipelines that brought water into St. Louis (numbers 7–9). The west side created the greatest problem for the eruv. There was a deep artificial trench that ran south from the Mississippi River. There were also walls in the vicinity that consisted of fences surrounding Jewish and non-Jewish cemeteries (numbers 10–11). However, there were many breaks in these walls that exceeded ten cubits, the maximum size allowed for an eruv to be considered continuous. Therefore, Rabbi Rosenfeld suggested another alternative for the eruv boundary on the west side. Telegraph lines that began at the northern artificial embankment continued right to the banks of the River des Peres, so if these lines were relied on, there was no breach between the northern and southern boundaries of the eruv. (The telegraph lines ran from numbers 7–8 all the way to numbers 3–4).[55]

In *Sho'el ka-inyan,* Rabbi Jaffe rejected the eruv boundaries proposed by Rabbi Rosenfeld on several grounds. Based on the *Magen Avraham,* he argued that the Mississippi River could not be used as an eruv boundary, since there was a risk of sediment buildup. The *Magen Avraham* also maintained that if people cross a natural boundary, they disqualify that boundary as an eruv wall. Rabbi Jaffe therefore argued that the passengers embarking on and disembarking from ships negated the use of the river as an eruv boundary. Again citing the *Magen Avraham,* Rabbi Jaffe argued that that the river was not acceptable, since there was a break of more than ten cubits between the river and the walls of the houses.[56] In addition, he claimed that many of the roadways in St. Louis were not enclosed by the eruv boundaries at all.

Rabbi Jaffe also quoted the *Peri megadim,* which argued that a natural eruv boundary is not acceptable if the city is larger than five thousand square cubits, since these natural boundaries were not built specifically to enclose the city but preceded the building of the city.[57] Rabbi Shneur Zalman of Lyady applied this ruling to the case of a river that encloses a large city, which he disqualified as an eruv boundary, since it predated the building of the city.[58]

---

54 Rabbi Rosenfeld refers to this boundary as the Mississippi River even though it is really the Missouri River.

55 Rosenfeld, *Tikvat Zekhariah,* vol. 2, 42.

56 *Magen Avraham,* Oraḥ ḥayyim, 363:31.

57 Joseph ben Meir Teomim, *Peri megadim* (New York, 2006), Oraḥ ḥayyim, 363:31.

58 Shneur Zalman of Lyady, *Shulḥan arukh,* 363:44. See Jaffe, *Sho'el ka-inyan,* 12–14.

FIGURE 1. Map of St. Louis with possible *eruv* boundaries. Julius Pitzman, *Pitzman's New Atlas of the City and County of Saint Louis, Missouri* (1878).

Rabbi Jaffe rejected Rabbi Rosenfeld's use of the hills on the outskirts of town as an eruv boundary for the same reasons that he rejected the use of the Mississippi River. He claimed that the hills were not acceptable, since they were more than ten cubits from the continuation of the eruv wall created by the houses in the city and because they predated the creation of the city.[59]

Rabbi Jaffe claimed that Rabbi Rosenfeld had argued that eruvin could be built in all cities in America, since the streets in American cities were built on an incline that created an eruv boundary. Rabbi Jaffe contended that these streets did not have the necessary incline of four handbreadths over a ten-cubit area, since the trolleys or cars would not have been able to drive up such steep streets.[60] However, Rabbi Rosenfeld's published work does not make this claim.

Rabbi Rosenfeld addressed some of Rabbi Jaffe's concerns in *Tikvat Zekhariah*. First, he noted the view of the *Magen Avraham* that a river creates an eruv boundary only if the riverbank creates an acceptable eruv wall.[61] Rabbi Rosenfeld explained that the banks of the Mississippi River and the River des Peres rose ten handbreadths above the water line and therefore constituted a valid boundary even according to this opinion. He also noted that there was a bridge on which the railroad that crossed the River des Peres ran. However, he argued that this bridge did not create a breach in the eruv, since it had a structure at its entrance that could serve as a symbolic doorway. There were several additional bridges that crossed the artificial embankments. Rabbi Rosenfeld cited the opinion of Rabbi Shlomo Kluger that bridges do not negate the use of riverbanks as acceptable eruv boundaries.[62] However, so as not to rely on this leniency, he wrote that he preferred to rely on the telegraph wires that ran uninterrupted from the northern to the southern eruv boundaries.[63]

Rabbi Rosenfeld went on to address the concern that the risk of sediment buildup invalidated the rivers as a boundary. He argued that this was not an issue in St. Louis, since the eruv boundary was created by riverbanks that rose above the water line in both the Mississippi and Des Peres rivers. The opinion of the *Magen Avraham* that disqualified a river as an eruv boundary if its distance from the houses exceeds ten cubits was also not a problem in St. Louis, even though the Mississippi River was further than ten handbreadths from the houses,[64] since the *Magen Avraham* only referred to a situation in which the river

---

59 Jaffe, *Sho'el ka-inyan*, 14.
60 Ibid..
61 *Magen Avraham*, Oraḥ ḥayyim, 363:30.
62 Rabbi Shlomo Kluger, *Sefer u-vaḥarta ba-ḥayyim* (Vienna, 1934), no. 117.
63 Rosenfeld, *Tikvat Zekhariah*, vol. 2, 43–44.
64 *Magen Avraham*, Oraḥ ḥayyim, 363:31.

and the houses combine to form one of the eruv boundaries. In St. Louis, since the river formed an entire eruv boundary, its distance from the houses was of no consequence.

Finally, Rabbi Rosenfeld addressed the opinion of the *Magen Avraham* that if people cross a natural boundary, they disqualify that boundary as an eruv wall. In the case of St. Louis, passengers embarked on and disembarked from ships on the Mississippi River, which could potentially negate the eruv wall. However, Rabbi Rosenfeld argued that these passengers did not negate the eruv for three reasons. First, he cited the opinion of Rabbi Ezekiel Katzenellenbogen (1670–1749) that passengers only negate a natural eruv boundary if the city is not surrounded by man-made boundaries.[65] In St. Louis, two of the sides of the city were enclosed by telegraph poles as well as natural embankments, and since the telegraph poles were man-made, Rabbi Rosenfeld argued, these people did not negate the boundaries. Second, he quoted Rabbi Shneur Zalman of Lyady, who explained in his *Shulḥan arukh* that, if there were three sides of the eruv in which people did not cross over the boundary, the fact that they crossed over on the fourth side did not negate the eruv.[66] Lastly, he cited the *Magen Avraham*'s claim that the only time that people crossing the boundaries negated the boundary was a situation in which six hundred thousand people crossed the boundary in one day.[67] Since this was clearly not the case in St. Louis, passage across the rivers did not create a problem.[68]

In *Teshuvah ka-halakhah*, Rabbi Jaffe once again attacked the boundaries that Rabbi Rosenfeld delineated for the eruv. First, Rabbi Jaffe claimed that there was no exclusively Jewish neighborhood in St. Louis and that Jews lived together with non-Jews. Therefore, it was impossible to talk about enclosing the Jewish neighborhood. He argued that the Mississippi River did not adequately enclose the entire eastern side of the city, since the river did not run in a straight line, and even the streets that ran near the river were more than ten cubits from the river.[69]

Regarding the southern border of the eruv, Rabbi Jaffe claimed that the River des Peres was nothing more than a crevice that was dry most of the year. He also claimed that there were no riverbanks in St. Louis that rose ten handbreadths above the water line. Therefore, the riverbanks did not create acceptable eruv boundaries. Since the riverbanks did not rise above the water line, Rabbi Jaffe

---

65 Ezekiel Katzenellenbogen, *She'elot u-teshuvot kenesset Yeḥezkel* (Warsaw, 1883), no. 3.

66 Shneur Zalman of Lyady, *Shulḥan arukh*, no. 363.

67 *Magen Avraham*, Oraḥ ḥayyim, 363:40.

68 Rosenfeld, *Tikvat Zekhariah*, vol. 2, 44–54.

69 Jaffe, *Teshuvah ka-halakhah*, 27 and no. 10 (the page numbers are out of order at the beginning of *Teshuvah ka-halakhah*).

argued that the risk of the rivers freezing in the winter negated the rivers as acceptable eruv boundaries. In addition, he claimed that the banks of the Mississippi River tended to be eroded by the strong flow of the river.[70]

Rabbi Jaffe raised several questions concerning the eruv boundaries on the northern side of the city. First, he asked what role the Mississippi River played as a boundary on the north, since Rabbi Rosenfeld claimed that it was separated from the city by artificial embankments. Furthermore, Rabbi Jaffe questioned the existence of these artificial embankments. He claimed that in America all such embankments were leveled out. Finally, he explained that even if there were some small embankments closer to the city, they were still too far from the houses to be considered valid eruv boundaries.[71]

As far as the eruv boundaries on the western side of the city were concerned, Rabbi Jaffe rejected Rabbi Rosenfeld's use of telegraph lines as symbolic doorways, as discussed in the following section. Therefore, he focused on Rabbi Rosenfeld's arguments that there were other acceptable boundaries on the west side. First, Rabbi Jaffe claimed that the artificial trench that Rabbi Rosenfeld claimed could serve as a boundary did not actually exist. There were some small furrows, but they were far from the city. In addition, Rabbi Jaffe argued that the cemeteries were only one block long, so the fences surrounding the cemeteries did not provide an adequate enclosure.[72]

Rabbi Jaffe's disagreements with Rabbi Rosenfeld were based on both halakhic arguments and arguments over whether Rabbi Rosenfeld's boundaries actually existed. Although it is possible to identify several of these boundaries based on the contemporaneous map, it is difficult to ascertain whether the trenches and embankments actually existed or whether the River des Peres actually had river walls that could serve as eruv boundaries. Rabbi Rosenfeld seems to be intentionally vague in identifying some of these boundaries.

The fact that Rabbi Rosenfeld wrote that the northern border was created by the Mississippi River when in truth the Missouri River runs to the north of St. Louis highlights Rabbi Rosenfeld's lack of knowledge—or, perhaps, his intentional blurring of the details of the eruv boundaries. Given the importance of identifying these boundaries, one may surmise that Rabbi Rosenfeld and Rabbi Jaffe both approached these questions with foregone conclusions about the acceptability of the eruv.

---

70 Ibid., 27.
71 Ibid., 28.
72 Ibid., 28–29.

Telegraph Poles and Wires

Because Rabbi Rosenfeld did not have the money, political clout, or know-how to erect poles and wires in St. Louis, the use of preexisting telegraph poles played a vital role in his creation of the eruv. Rabbi Jaffe wrote that eruvin could not be built in any American city without erecting symbolic doorways, since the natural boundaries were insufficient. He argued that "it is impossible to construct them [symbolic doorways] due to the monetary issue and the fact that it would not be allowed by the governmental authorities."[73] Therefore, the use of telegraph wires was the only viable solution to complete this eruv, and the permissibility of telegraph poles and wires as eruv boundaries played a critical role in the debate between Rabbis Jaffe and Rosenfeld.

In *Tikvat Zekhariah,* Rabbi Rosenfeld made several different arguments in defense of his use of telegraph poles based on the opinion of Rabbi Joseph Nathanson of Lemberg, who was the major proponent of the use of telegraph wires as eruv boundaries in the nineteenth century.[74] Rabbi Rosenfeld explained that the objections of Rabbi Fradkin, the major opponent of the use of telegraph wires in the nineteenth century, did not apply in St. Louis.[75] First, Rabbi Rosenfeld claimed that since the telegraph wires in St. Louis were affixed on top of the crossarms, they were acceptable eruv boundaries and could not be disqualified by saying that they were not connected to the tops of the telegraph poles and therefore constituted a "symbolic doorway from the side" (*ẓurat ha-petaḥ min ha-ẓad*).[76] Second, he argued that the telegraph poles could be considered symbolic doorways even though they were not built explicitly for the purpose of creating doorways, since in St. Louis, the wires on top of the telegraph poles created the semblance of an entrance on different streets and roads. Rabbi Rosenfeld explained that since the telegraph poles were erected at the street corners and not in the middle of the street, their purpose was to provide entranceways to and from the street.[77] Finally, he addressed the fact that the telegraph poles were often located at a distance of greater than three handbreadths (*tefaḥim*) from the houses, thereby creating an unacceptable break in the eruv. He explained that the Gemara and the *Shulḥan arukh* considered a break of three handbreadths in the eruv walls a disqualification of the eruv.[78]

---

73 Jaffe, *Sho'el ka-inyan*, 8.

74 Joseph Nathanson, *Sho'el u-meshiv*, 1st ed. (New York, 1980), vol. 2, no. 88.

75 Shnayer Zalman Fradkin, *Torat ḥesed* (Warsaw, 1883), Oraḥ ḥayyim, no. 9, section 4.

76 Rosenfeld, *Tikvat Zekhariah*, vol. 2, 26–28.

77 Ibid., 28–31.

78 See b. Eruv. 5a and *Shulḥan arukh*, Oraḥ ḥayyim, 365:1.

However, Rabbi Rosenfeld claimed that this rule applied to a situation in which the symbolic doorway combined with the walls of the houses to create an eruv boundary, in which case there could not be a gap exceeding three handbreadths between the symbolic doorway and the other eruv walls. In the case of St. Louis, the symbolic doorway created by the telegraph poles extended along the entire street and created its own eruv boundary. Therefore, there was no concern about the fact that the symbolic doorway was more than three handbreadths from the walls of the houses. Rabbi Rosenfeld concluded this section of *Tikvat Zekhariah* explaining that, in St. Louis, this discussion was merely theoretical, since the telegraph poles and wires actually reached the other eruv boundaries, thereby enclosing the city within these boundaries.

Rabbi Jaffe argued that telegraph poles were not acceptable eruv boundaries for two reasons. First, he argued that the telegraph wire was connected to the side of the telegraph pole and did not run across the top of the pole (apparently disagreeing with Rabbi Rosenfeld's description), and that therefore the poles and wires had the status of a symbolic doorway from the side. He did not mention the disagreement between Rabbis Nathanson and Fradkin concerning utilizing telegraph poles and wires but simply stated categorically that telegraph poles and wires were not acceptable eruv boundaries.[79] Second, Rabbi Jaffe quoted Rabbi Jacob Sasportas, a member of the Rabbinical Court of Amsterdam at the end of the seventeenth century who allowed for the creation of an eruv in The Hague. Rabbi Sasportas argued that a symbolic doorway could not be used as an eruv boundary to enclose an open space that exceeded thirty cubits.[80] On this basis, Rabbi Jaffe argued that even if the telegraph poles and wires in St. Louis did constitute symbolic doorways, they would not be acceptable eruv boundaries, since the telegraph poles and wires extended for longer than thirty cubits. Therefore, "it is clear that there is no way to rely on the telegraph poles and wires in American cities."[81] By extending his claim about St. Louis to all of America, Rabbi Jaffe raised the stakes of the debate, showing that both rabbis thought of the local issue as having far-reaching consequences.

In *Teshuvah ka-halakhah*, Rabbi Jaffe reiterated his opposition to the use of telegraph wires as eruv boundaries because they were connected to the side of the poles. He added that the gaps between the telegraph lines and the houses disqualified them from serving as eruv boundaries. Rabbi Jaffe quoted

---

79 Jaffe, *Sho'el ka-inyan*, 9.

80 Jacob Sasportas, *Ohel Yaakov* (Amsterdam, 1737), no. 46; see also his *Sha'arei teshuvah*, Oraḥ ḥayyim, 363:12.

81 Jaffe, *Sho'el ka-inyan*, 9–12.

Rabbi Eliezer Grayewsky, who commented in his glosses on *Sho'el ka-inyan* that even though Rabbi Nathanson allowed for telegraph lines to be used as eruv boundaries in Lemberg, he required that small poles be erected under the symbolic doorways in Lemberg so that people would be reminded not to pass through the eruv boundary, thereby invalidating it. Again, Rabbi Jaffe highlighted the American Jewish community's lack of clout, asking sarcastically whether Rabbi Rosenfeld also intended to erect such small poles on every street in St. Louis.[82] At the conclusion of *Teshuvah ka-halakhah*, Rabbi Jaffe wrote, "I have drawn a picture of the telegraph wires and they are all connected from the side, and they are at a great distance from the houses. . . . I ask whether it is correct to place a stumbling block before the people for generations to come due to the corrupt assumptions of one rabbi who wishes to argue with the great rabbinic scholars of the generation."[83]

Leasing the City

Rabbis Jaffe and Rosenfeld also disagreed about the permissibility of leasing the city from the local authorities. Rabbi Rosenfeld addressed two issues relating to this in *Tikvat Zekhariah*. First, he discussed whether the right to lease the property of a non-Jew from his *sekhiro u-lekito*, his tenant or agent, extends to leasing the property of a Jewish Sabbath violator living in the city. Rabbi Rosenfeld quoted the opinion of Tosafot that leasing from a tenant or agent only applies to leasing from a non-Jew and not from a Jew.[84] Rabbi Akiva Eiger argued that this was indeed the halakhah and that the process of leasing from a tenant or agent does not work for leasing from a Jew.[85] Rabbi Rosenfeld, however, claimed that Rabbi Eiger was only addressing utilizing this process on behalf of an observant Jew, which he did not permit. According to Rabbi Rosenfeld, even Rabbi Eiger would allow leasing from the tenant or agent of a Sabbath violator. Rabbi Rosenfeld based his opinion on the view of Rabbi Meir of Rothenberg, who claimed that, since we treat the Sabbath violator as a non-Jew, all the laws of eruvin that apply to non-Jews apply to Sabbath violators.[86]

---

82 Jaffe, *Teshuvah ka-halakhah*, 19–20. See Rabbi Grayewsky's comments in *Sho'el ka-inyan*, 12 and 23; and Rabbi Nathanson's discussion about the use of telegraph lines in Lemberg in *Sho'el u-meshiv*, 1st ed., vol. 2, no. 88, section 2.

83 Jaffe, *Teshuvah ka-halakhah*, 29–30.

84 Tosafot on b. Eruv. 70a–b, s.v. *yoresh*.

85 Rabbi Akiva Eigder, *Gilyon ha-shas*, Eruv. 80a, s.v. *de-ishto*.

86 Asher ben Jehiel, *She'elot u-teshuvot le-Rabbeinu Asher* (Jerusalem, 1994), Eruvin, chapter 6, no. 13. For Rabbi Rosenfeld's discussion of this topic, see his *Tikvat Zekhariah*, vol. 2, 36–38.

Second, he addressed the question of whether the categories introduced by Rabbi Isaac ben Sheshet regarding the ability to lease the property of non-Jews from government officials applied in the United States. Rabbi Isaac ben Sheshet wrote that if a government official had the right to place objects in the homes in the city or the right to alter the public roads, the city could be leased from him for the purpose of creating an eruv.[87] Rabbi Rosenfeld believed that this level of authority was satisfied in the United States. Blending the laws of the Torah and the Constitution, he claimed that since the city government has the right of eminent domain—to acquire land and to demolish homes on it if the government determines that it needs the area for new roads—city officials are considered authorities from whom the area can be leased. Furthermore, he argued that since the government authorities also had the right to issue warrants to enter homes and that if they were not admitted they could break down the door, they had the status of the city official required by Jewish law. Finally, the fact that municipal health department representatives could examine the hygienic conditions of each home gave them a right of entry. He concluded that since these local officials, including police officers and all city authorities involved in municipal matters, were elected by the people and received their salaries from the people of the city, they had the status of tenants or agents, and lease of the city could be done through any of them.[88] On this basis, Rabbi Rosenthal apparently leased the property of the non-Jewish residents of St. Louis from a local police officer.

Rabbi Jaffe was not convinced by Rabbi Rosenthal's application of halakhic categories to American democracy and described Rabbi Rosenfeld's lease of the area as follows:

> The scholar who permitted the eruv was very proud of his discovery, and he asked some of his people to give something to a policeman. They gave the policeman something to satisfy him, and he sold him the authority for the entire city. And he added in a joking manner that he was also selling them Chicago. (This is true, for he had just as much right to sell Chicago as he did to sell St. Louis).... In all the cities in America, they are just waiting for

87 Isaac ben Sheshet, *She'elot u-teshuvot Rivash* (New York, 1974), no. 427.

88 Rosenfeld, *Tikvat Zekhariah*, vol. 2, 39–40. This view of Rabbi Rosenfeld regarding rental of the city is discussed by Yosef Gavriel Bechhofer, *The Contemporary Eruv: Eruvin in Metropolitan Areas* (Jerusalem, 1998), 111–117.

> rabbis to adopt this discovery. . . . For with this idea, he wanted to allow an eruv in Baltimore.[89]

Rabbi Jaffe asked by what authority Rabbi Rosenfeld considered the policeman the tenant or agent of the city mayor, beginning a debate between the two rabbis over the nature of democracy and its limits. Rabbi Jaffe claimed that, in a democracy, the mayor does not have the right to perform any action without the consent of the electorate and fulfillment of the laws of the land. Therefore, in America, one would not be allowed to lease the city from the city mayor for the sake of eruvin, and the only way to create an eruv would be to lease the property of each non-Jew in the city individually. He quoted the opinion of Rabbi Ezekiel Landau that, even in a city where the local authority can categorically lease property to the Jewish community, if there are certain houses that are excluded from the official's authority, they must be leased separately.[90] Rabbi Jaffe argued that every house in the United States would fall into the category of those houses excluded from the authority of the local governmental officials. Finally, he mocked Rabbi Rosenfeld's suggestion to lease the city from the local policeman. He wrote that this was merely "words of laughter and the cause of a desecration of God's name," for the policeman did not have any special rights in the private houses in the United States.[91]

In *Teshuvah ka-halakhah*, Rabbi Jaffe elaborated on his view on the status of the local authorities with respect to leasing the city. He wrote:

> In addition, no official has the authority to remove someone from his home, even if it is in the public's good, without paying the inhabitant of the home. This is not what the permitting rabbi wrote, as he does not know the truth. Yet, this is known to every child in America. Furthermore, all the rest of his arguments are useless words, for even the officer who is called a detective can only enter homes against the will of the owner in a case of suspected robbery but not for other reasons. In addition, there is a problem because the policemen are replaced every year.[92]

---

89 Jaffe, *Sho'el ka-inyan*, 20. Rabbi Jaffe probably chose the example of Baltimore since Rabbi Rosenfeld had lived in Baltimore before moving to St. Louis. There is no reference in Rabbi Rosenfeld's writings to an attempt to create an eruv in Baltimore.

90 Ezekiel Landau, *Nodah bi-Yehudah*, 2nd ed. (Jerusalem, 1990), no. 32.

91 Landau, *Nodah bi-Yehudah*, 2nd ed., 21–22.

92 Jaffe, *Teshuvah ka-halakhah*, 20.

Rabbi Jaffe elaborated on this issue in a reply to Rabbi Naphtali Hertz Vaidenboim of Jaffa, who wrote an approbation to *Sho'el ka-inyan* but questioned Rabbi Jaffe's claim regarding the inability to lease the area from a local government official. Rabbi Vaidenboim argued that the mayor had the status of the tenant or agent of the residents of the city. Rabbi Jaffe responded by quoting the opinion of Noah Zevi Hayyim Berlin, an eighteenth-century German rabbi who authored a volume entitled *Aẓei almogim* on the laws of eruvin, who claimed that the ability to lease the properties of non-Jews from a government official was dependent on whether the official had the right to evict the residents from their homes for not paying their taxes.[93] Rabbi Jaffe wrote that since in the United States people could not be evicted from their homes for not paying taxes, property could not be leased by these government officials.[94]

In addition, Rabbi Jaffe argued with Rabbi Rosenfeld about the ability to lease the property of a non-observant Jew from the tenant or agent. Rabbi Jaffe argued that the property of a Jew could not be leased from the tenant or agent. He quoted the opinion of Noah Zevi Hayyim Berlin, who wrote that the property of a Sadducee or a *mumar*, a Jew who has rejected Judaism, may not be leased from a tenant or agent.[95] Rabbi Jaffe added that "most of the Jews here, both the wealthy and the poor Jews, are public Sabbath violators and reject the basic principles of the Sabbath."[96]

Rabbi Jaffe concluded this section by noting that this discussion about leasing the space was theoretical, because leasing was not sufficient in a public domain such as St. Louis, where walls and doors must be erected.

Approbations

The volumes in which Rabbi Rosenfeld and Rabbi Jaffe presented their arguments over the eruv included approbations from rabbis in Europe, Israel, and the United States. These approbations and the way Rabbis Rosenfeld and Jaffe presented them reflect the ways they viewed their authority in the St. Louis community and the United States.

Rabbi Rosenfeld wrote in the introduction to the second volume of *Tikvat Zekhariah*, "As I am a wanderer and few know me in this country, and people

93 Noah Zevi Hayyim Berlin, *Sefer aẓei almogim* (Brooklyn, 1977), no. 391.
94 Jaffe, *Teshuvah ka-halakhah*, 31, 34.
95 Berlin, *Sefer aẓei almogim*, no. 391.
96 Jaffe, *Teshuvah ka-halakhah*, 20.

will definitely say, 'Who is this man who has come to make innovations that have never been practiced until now?' . . ."[97] For this reason, he decided to send his treatise to Rabbi Isaac Elchanan Spektor in Kovno, the great Lithuanian rabbinic authority, for approbation. Rabbi Spektor replied that it was difficult for him to enter a discussion concerning the streets of America, with which he was not familiar. Instead, he suggested that Rabbi Rosenfeld approach Rabbi Jacob Joseph, the chief rabbi of New York, for approbation.[98] Rabbi Joseph's approbation appears on the first page of the volume.

While Rabbi Rosenfeld wrote that he was sending his responsum to Rabbi Spektor for approval, Rabbi Jaffe took a different approach. Rabbi Jaffe concluded his introduction to *Sho'el ka-inyan* explaining that, although he sent his responsum against the eruv to many rabbis in America, the supporters of Rabbi Rosenfeld claimed that the rabbis with whom Rabbi Jaffe consulted were not capable of challenging the arguments of Rabbi Rosenfeld, who was accepted as a great rabbinic scholar. Therefore, Rabbi Jaffe wrote, he had decided to publish his own volume against the eruv and send it for approbation to the rabbis in Jerusalem, whose "words are holy." If these rabbis agreed with him, then his argument would be accepted as definitive.[99]

In order to receive the approbation of the Jerusalem rabbis, Rabbi Jaffe sent a long letter to Rabbi Shmuel Salant, the chief rabbi of the Ashkenazic community in Jerusalem at the time,[100] asking for his approbation for Rabbi Jaffe's views on the mikveh and eruv in St. Louis. Regarding the eruv, Rabbi Jaffe wrote to Rabbi Salant, "[I am sending you] my responsum concerning the eruv and carrying on the Sabbath that has been permitted by a new rabbi in the city. Already, the other rabbis in America have joined in opposing this eruv."[101] In his approbation, Rabbi Salant wrote:

> I am happy to know and to see that also in America there are rabbis who are Torah scholars. It would be fortunate if their numbers increased in all cities in America and if the generation listened to the voices of the rabbis to follow the path of Torah and commandments.[102]

---

97 Rosenfeld, *Tikvat Zekhariah*, vol. 2, 5.
98 Ibid., 5–6.
99 Ibid.
100 For a short yet interesting biography of Rabbi Salant, see his obituary in *The New York Times*, August 17, 1909, 7.
101 Jaffe, *Sho'el ka-inyan*, 37–44.
102 Ibid., n.p. (first page following the title page).

Although Rabbi Salant's approbation did not directly address the issues of mikveh or eruv, it provided support and credibility for Rabbi Jaffe. In addition, Rabbi Jaffe sent a request for approbation to Rabbi Grayewsky of Jerusalem. Rabbi Jaffe claimed that Rabbi Grayewsky had visited St. Louis and understood the layout of the city. Rabbi Grayewsky agreed with Rabbi Jaffe's assessment that an eruv could not be established in St. Louis.[103] Rabbi Jaffe believed that including these approbations from the Jerusalem rabbinate gave credibility to his view.[104]

In *Teshuvah ka-halakhah,* Rabbi Jaffe sought to strengthen his ties to the Jerusalem rabbinate while at the same time undermining Rabbi Rosenfeld's reliance on Rabbi Spektor. On the introductory page of *Teshuvah ka-halakhah,* Rabbi Jaffe explains that he showed both *Sho'el ka-inyan* and *Tikvat Zekhariah* to four rabbis in Israel, who agreed with his arguments prohibiting carrying in St. Louis on the Sabbath. In addition to the letters written by Rabbi Salant and Rabbi Grayewsky, Rabbi Jaffe included letters by Rabbi Naphtali Hertz Ha-Levi Vaidenboim of Jaffa and Rabbi Shaul Chaim Hurowitz of Jerusalem. Both of these letters addressed the issue of telegraph poles and wires as eruv boundaries and concluded that they could not be utilized, since they fell into the category of "symbolic doorways from the side."[105]

In an attempt to undermine Rabbi Rosenfeld's reliance on Rabbi Spektor, Rabbi Jaffe added the following anecdote in his introductory remarks. He claimed that he was told by his friend Rabbi Grayewsky of Jerusalem that Rabbi Grayewsky had heard from the rabbinical judge of Jerusalem, Rabbi Chaim Yaakov Spira, that when Rabbi Spira was a rabbi in Kovno, he had assisted Rabbi Spektor, who had been asked by the Kovno community to erect an eruv using telegraph lines. After Rabbi Spektor was made aware of the fact that Rabbi Spira's

---

103 In *Teshuvah ka-halakhah,* 28, Rabbi Jaffe wrote that his friend Rabbi Grayewsky had been to St. Louis and knew the layout of the city. In *Sho'el ka-inyan,* 45, Rabbi Grayewsky wrote that he knew the layout of the city but did not mention that he had visited. In his letter of introduction to *Sho'el ka-inyan,* Rabbi Grayewsky felt the need to justify his publication and writing of notes on a contemporaneous volume even though notes were usually only written on old books. He explained that he took an interest in this book due to the request of Rabbi Jaffe and the difficult situation of American Jewry. He also explained that Rabbi Jaffe had the book published in Jerusalem because it was less expensive than publishing it elsewhere. See *Sho'el ka-inyan,* 5–10.

104 When Rabbi Jaffe published *Teshuvah ka-halakhah* in 1896, he included another approbation from Rabbi Salant, co-signed by Rabbi Shneur Zalman Fradkin of Jerusalem, stating that telegraph poles could not be used to establish eruv boundaries as they constituted "symbolic doorways from the side." Rabbi Fradkin was a well-known rabbinic authority and author in Jerusalem.

105 Jaffe, *Teshuvah ka-halakhah,* 2–8.

grandfather, Rabbi Aryeh Leib Spira, the former rabbi of Kovno, had opposed the utilization of telegraph wires as eruv boundaries, Rabbi Spektor had stopped building the eruv. Rabbi Jaffe concluded that if Rabbi Rosenfeld continued to argue for the validity of his eruv against the decision of the rabbis of Jerusalem and what seemed to be the view of Rabbi Spektor, he would be considered a *zaken mamre*, one who rejects the official authority, and his punishment would be harsh.[106]

Both Rabbi Jaffe and Rabbi Rosenfeld felt that their volumes needed approbations from rabbis whose authority would provide legitimacy to their respective positions. They believed that these approbations must be from rabbis who lived in the rabbinic centers of Jerusalem and Lithuania. This decision to approach rabbis outside the United States reflected their unease with their positions in the United States. Rabbi Jaffe claimed that he did not have the authority to argue with Rabbi Rosenfeld, who was respected among American rabbis, while at the same time, Rabbi Rosenfeld stated that he was unknown in America. Rabbi Rosenfeld's and Rabbi Jaffe's ability to approach and rely upon rabbinic authorities from Jerusalem and Kovno provided the necessary support for these two immigrant Orthodox American rabbis.[107]

Although Rabbis Rosenfeld and Jaffe seem to have given more weight to the approbations from the leading rabbinic authorities in Lithuania and Jerusalem, each of them also sought and received approbations from American rabbis. Rabbi Rosenfeld received approbations from Rabbi Shabsi Rosenberg of Brooklyn, Rabbi Joseph Komisarsky of Chicago, Rabbi Todros Yukel Tiktin of Chicago, Rabbi Abraham Levinson of Baltimore, Rabbi Bernard Levinthal of Philadelphia, and Rabbi Moshe Sivitz of Pittsburgh. He also received an approbation from Rabbi Meir Feimer of Slutsk.[108] Each of these approbations

---

106 Ibid, 1–2.

107 For a discussion of approbation in rabbinic volumes written in America, see Menahem Blondheim, "Ha-rabbanut ha-Ortodoksi megaleh et Amerikah: Ha-ge'ografia shel ha-ruaḥ be-mitavim shel tikshoret," in *Be-ikvot Kolumbus: Amerikah, 1492–1992*, ed. Miri Eliav-Feldon (Jerusalem, 1996), 483–510.

108 Rabbi Rosenberg's approbation appears on page 2 of Rosenfeld's *Tikvat Zekhariah*. The National Library of Israel's copy of *Tikvat Zekhariah* contains three unnumbered leaves following page 2. The first leaf contains the approbations of Rabbi Komisarsky, Rabbi Tiktin, and Rabbi Levinson. The second leaf contains an approbation from Rabbi Feimer of Slutsk, and the third leaf contains approbations from Rabbi Levinthal and Rabbi Sivitz. The copy in Jewish Telegraphic Agency's archives contains one additional leaf after page 2 with approbations from Rabbis Komisarsky, Tiktin, and Levinson. The copy in Agudas Chassidei Chabad Ohel Yosef Yitzchak Lubavitch does not contain any additional leaves after page 2. For a discussion of the different editions, see Yosef Goldman, *Hebrew Printing in America 1735–1926: A History and Annotated Bibliography* (New York, 2006), vol. 2, 974.

praised Rabbi Rosenfeld for his initiative in creating the eruv and his knowledge of the rabbinic sources. However, none of them addressed the substantive issues in *Tikvat Zekhariah*, and none of the rabbis claimed to have visited St. Louis to verify that it met Rabbi Rosenfeld's description.

Rabbi Jaffe included letters of approbation from American rabbis at the beginning of *Teshuvah ka-halakhah*. He included letters from Rabbi Joshua Seigel of New York, Rabbi Abraham Lesser of Chicago, Rabbi Chaim Widerwitz of New York, and Rabbi Dov Baer Abramowitz of New York.[109] These approbations praised Rabbi Jaffe for his willingness to oppose the eruv in St. Louis but did not address the substantive issues. Rabbi Abramowitz said that Rabbi Jacob Joseph was ill and could not properly evaluate the situation in St. Louis.

Conclusion

The debate between Rabbis Jaffe and Rosenfeld reflects several features of the Orthodox community in North America at the end of the nineteenth century. First, the argument over the desirability of creating an eruv in St. Louis was shaped by the fact that a large portion of the Orthodox community did not observe the laws of the Sabbath stringently. For Rabbi Rosenfeld, the fact that many Jews would be carrying on the Sabbath regardless of the presence or absence of an eruv made creating one more urgent. To use Jeffrey Gurock's terminology, Rabbi Rosenfeld was an "accommodator" who sought to adapt halakhah to the reality of American Jewish life. For Rabbi Jaffe, the lax observance that characterized the Orthodox community made Rabbi Rosenfeld's leniencies more dangerous, since, he believed, less committed Jews would seek out permission to violate the Sabbath. His position was that of a "resistor" who attempted to use his position to strengthen Orthodoxy.

Second, the creation of an eruv entirely from preexisting boundaries was necessitated by the lack of any relationship between the Jewish community and local authorities, which made it impossible to erect wires or other structures. This same lack of relationship made it impossible to lease the property of St. Louis's non-Jewish residents from the mayor or another high official, leading Rabbi Rosenfeld to authorize leasing it from a local police officer.

---

109 Rabbi Seigel was the author of *Eruv ve-hoẓa'a* (New York, 1907), describing the eruv on the East Side of Manhattan. See the following chapter for a discussion of this eruv and how Rabbi Seigel could oppose the St. Louis eruv while promoting the eruv on the East Side of Manhattan.

Finally, Rabbi Rosenfeld's and Rabbi Jaffe's reliance on halakhic precedent from European eruvin and their dependence on approbations from European and Israeli rabbis reflect the newness of the American Orthodox community and tenuousness of these rabbis' authority in the United States. As immigrant rabbis, they were still establishing a foothold in their nascent communities.

The importance of the St. Louis eruv cannot be overstated. As the first eruv in North America, it had the potential to provide a model for other American eruvin. Both Rabbi Jaffe and Rabbi Rosenfeld understood the possibility that other cities could follow the lead of the St. Louis eruv. At the beginning of *Sho'el ka-inyan,* Rabbi Jaffe wrote, "He [Rabbi Rosenfeld] said that it was permissible to carry in all cities in America."[110] Rabbi Jaffe was afraid that other communities would model their eruvin on Rabbi Rosenfeld's lenient position. In addition, Rabbi Jaffe wrote that "all cities in America are constructed like this [St. Louis]."[111] It is easy to understand Rabbi Jaffe's fear. Did Rabbi Rosenfeld intend that his initiative be copied in other American cities? Rabbi Rosenfeld wrote in the introduction to the second volume of *Tikvat Zekhariah,* "My soul would rejoice if other worthy people would attempt to find a way to remove this source of shame of sin from the people [and find a way to allow carrying on the Sabbath]."[112] The idea of following Rabbi Rosenfeld's initiative was reflected in one of the approbations given to *Tikvat Zekhariah* by Rabbi Todros Yukel Tiktin of Chicago, in which he wrote that he hoped that rabbis in other cities would follow Rabbi Rosenfeld's example.[113]

The St. Louis eruv was not only significant for being the first eruv in America. It was also the first time that the creators of a city eruv had to address the issue of whether an eruv could be created in a city that might have a population greater than six hundred thousand. The earliest mention of the issue of six hundred thousand people in Eastern Europe, in connection with the Odessa eruv, did not take place until 1899. In St. Louis, this issue raised a variety of questions, such as how to properly determine the exact population of the city and whether people traveling in trolley cars were to be counted as part of the population.

Ephraim Deinard, the author and polemicist, wrote in 1913 about the eruv debate in St. Louis. He claimed that "the uncompromising rabbis who opposed the eruv placed the Jewish community of St. Louis in turmoil."[114] Deinard

---

110 Jaffe, *Sho'el ka-inyan,* 1.

111 Ibid., 2.

112 Rosenfeld, *Tikvat Zekhariah,* vol. 2, 5.

113 Ibid., vol. 2, National Library of Israel's copy.

114 Ephraim Deinard, *Sifrut Yisrael be-Amerikah* (Jaffa, 1913), vol. 2, 109; see also his *Kohelet Amerikah* (St. Louis, 1926), vol. 2, 147. Deinard referred to rabbis in the plural form to include those rabbis who had given approbations to Rabbi Jaffe's works.

suggested that in addition to the halakhic battle that accompanied the creation of the St. Louis eruv, the Orthodox community was divided on the question of whether to rely on the eruv. A small Jewish community in which some people carried on the Sabbath and others did not would undoubtedly experience friction and tension among both laymen and rabbis.

While the St. Louis eruv controversy touched on the issues facing the Orthodox Jewish community in America at the end the nineteenth century and the practical challenges that the rabbis faced in addressing the needs of this community, a fundamental aspect of the controversy revolved around the relationship between the halakhic arguments that were made by Rabbis Rosenfeld and Jaffe and the realities of the city of St. Louis and its natural and man-made structures. In St. Louis, the rabbis argued not only about the halakhic status of the eruv but about whether the eruv boundaries really existed. In *Teshuvah ka-halakhah,* Rabbi Jaffe dismissed Rabbi Rosenfeld's eruv by arguing that that the boundaries were not as Rabbi Rosenfeld described. For example, Rabbi Jaffe claimed that the Mississippi River did not actually enclose the entire east side of St. Louis and therefore could not serve the function of an eruv boundary as Rabbi Rosenfeld claimed.

It is impossible to determine which description of the St. Louis area is correct. The rabbis who wrote letters of approbations did not visit St. Louis to examine the boundaries. Even Rabbi Grayewsky, who purportedly once visited the city, lived in Jerusalem at the time and could not be considered an authority on the details of the city's topography. In the absence of evidence, we can only try to reconstruct the thinking of each of these rabbis as they approached the issue of the St. Louis eruv. Rabbi Rosenfeld explained that he believed that it was necessary to create an eruv around St. Louis to prevent Jews from violating the Sabbath. He received encouragement from Rabbi Jacob Joseph, who had been referred by the premier rabbinic sage of the period, Rabbi Spektor of Kovno. Yet, as Rabbi Jaffe pointed out, it was not possible to build symbolic doorways in St. Louis at the time. Therefore, the eruv would have to be constructed from existing natural and man-made boundaries. Did Rabbi Rosenfeld actually survey the city and its outlying areas? Did he explore the rivers and walk along the telegraph poles? Did he know that the population of the city did not exceed six hundred thousand? Or did he decide that an eruv had to be built in St. Louis and then determine the boundaries of the city to justify that decision?

Rabbi Jaffe clearly believed that Rabbi Rosenfeld had decided that an eruv had to be created and fabricated the details concerning the structure of the boundaries to satisfy the requirements for the eruv. Rabbi Jaffe felt so strongly that Rabbi Rosenfeld was mistaken that he wrote two volumes opposing the eruv. How would Rabbi Rosenfeld respond to this criticism? We do not know, because Rabbi Jaffe got in the last word on this debate with his *Teshuvah ka-halakhah*. However, there is some evidence from a contemporaneous drawing of St. Louis that at least some of the telegraph wires ran on top of the crossarms as Rabbi Rosenfeld claimed and that there were raised embankments on the northern edge of the city.[115]

The Jewish community of St. Louis moved to the western part of the city in the 1920s and 1930s and was no longer enclosed by Rabbi Rosenfeld's eruv boundaries.[116] However, this first documented eruv in North America stood at a critical juncture in the development of city eruvin. Both Rabbi Rosenfeld and Rabbi Jaffe used precedent in supporting their views regarding the St. Louis eruv. From their debate regarding the advisability of creating community eruvin to their disputes concerning the use of telegraph lines and river walls, earlier halakhic discussions laid the groundwork for the debate in St. Louis. Finally, their disputes concerning the way the six hundred thousand was calculated and the status of streets with cars and trolleys traveling on them were based on halakhic precedent, which was applied to situations that had not been the reality in the cases of earlier eruvin.

The importance of the St. Louis eruv in the history of city eruvin in North America can be measured in part by the utilization of the material from the works of Rabbis Rosenfeld and Jaffe in the literature regarding other eruvin that would be created in North America. Rabbi Spektor wrote that he could not offer a halakhic opinion regarding the streets of America, with which he was not familiar. Yet, as the Jewish communities in America grew in the first part of the twentieth century, American rabbis became familiar with the topography of American cities and the relevance of this material to the creation of city eruvin. Did they use this knowledge to create eruvin in other cities and, if so, did they rely on the precedent of the St. Louis eruv? The answer to this question will be explored in the coming chapters.

---

115 St. Louis Graf Engraving Co., c. 1896; and Richard J. Compton and Camille N. Dry, *Pictorial St. Louis, the Great Metropolis of the Mississippi Valley: A Topographical Survey Drawn in Perspective A.D. 1875 (St. Louis, 1876)*, plate 80.

116 For a history of the St. Louis Jewish community in the 1920s and 1930s and its move westward, see Ehrlich, *Zion in the Valley*, vol. 2, 46–49.

3

The East Side of Manhattan Eruv

In 1905, an *eruv* was created on the East Side of Manhattan, home to the majority of New York's Jews. The creation of this eruv and the debates surrounding it reflected many of the same issues that arose in the case of the St. Louis eruv. The population confronted by Rabbi Joshua Seigel, who created the East Side eruv, was less observant than the Jewish community he knew from Europe. And, as in St. Louis, the lack of a strong relationship between the Jewish community and local government affected the way the eruv was created. While Rabbi Seigel mentioned the theoretical possibility of creating an eruv that would include new structures, in the end, the eruv was created entirely from preexisting natural and man-made boundaries, and, as in St. Louis, leasing of the area was done through a local police officer. The approbations to the various responsa from Eastern European rabbis reflect a continued reliance on European precedent, with the only reference to the St. Louis debate coming from an opponent to the East Side of Manhattan eruv, who cited an argument of Rabbi Jaffe's opposing the eruv in St. Louis.

Yet there were also significant differences between the situations in St. Louis and the East Side of Manhattan, which were reflected in the eruv debates. Some of these differences pertained directly to halakhah. While in St. Louis there seems to have been some debate over the actual physical contours of the city, in Manhattan the nature of the physical boundaries was clear. Moreover, the tracks of the Third Avenue Elevated Train (the "El"), which traversed the island from north to south, created a convenient eruv boundary and avoided some of the halakhic issues raised by Rabbi Rosenfeld's reliance on telegraph poles in St. Louis. These factors may explain why Rabbi Seigel, who had opposed the eruv in St. Louis, found it acceptable to create an eruv in Manhattan.

The sociology of New York's Jewish community also differed from that of St. Louis owing to its larger size and greater diversity, which included a sizeable number of observant Jews. Whereas in St. Louis the debate took place between two individual rabbis, the controversy over the East Side of Manhattan eruv reflected existing divisions in the city, with Jews of different national origins following different authorities.

Background to the Eruv Dispute

New York City, and especially the Lower East Side, played a critical role in the experience of immigrants to the United States. Of more than twenty-three million immigrants to the United States between 1880 and 1920, seventeen million came through the port of New York. The number of Jews immigrating was particularly high during this period, and many settled in New York. By 1892, seventy-five percent of New York's Jews lived on the Lower East Side, with a peak population of 542,000 in 1910.[1]

The Jewish neighborhood of the Lower East Side extended from just north of Houston Street, south to Monroe Street, west to the Bowery, and east to the East River. Even in this small area, the Jewish community was divided along geographic lines. The Hungarian Jews lived in the northern quarters of the Lower East Side, the Galician Jews lived to the south, and the Romanians lived on the western tip of the neighborhood. The remainder of the area, from Grand Street south to Monroe Street, was the home of the group referred to as the "Russian Jews." These Jews arrived from Russian Poland, Lithuania, Byelorussia, and Ukraine, and the area housed more Jews than any other area of the Lower East Side.[2]

---

1 For a discussion of Jewish immigration to the United States prior to 1881, see Hasia R. Diner, *A Time for Gathering: The Second Migration 1820–1880* (Baltimore, 1992), 49–56. On the period following 1880, see Gerald Sorin, *A Time for Building: The Third Migration 1880–1920* (Baltimore, 1992), 69–108.

2 Moses Rischin, *The Promised City: New York Jews, 1870–1914* (Cambridge, MA, 1962), 76. An academic history of the Jews of the Lower East Side is yet to be written. Rischin's volume contains the most important material and set the stage for all subsequent work on the topic. See Hasia Diner, *Lower East Side Memories: A Jewish Place in America* (Princeton, NJ, 2000), 186, n. 47 for a discussion of the attempts to write a history of the Lower East Side. Shaul Stampfer has examined the origins of these immigrants through a study of the *landsmanschaft*

Although the Orthodox community of the Lower East Side had grown in the years prior to 1881, this growth accelerated sharply in the 1880s. These increased numbers, rather than serving as a boon to the community, instead translated into increased communal strife, which was manifest in the discord surrounding the selection of a chief rabbi of New York. With the selection of Rabbi Jacob Joseph of Vilna as the city's chief rabbi, the Polish Jews felt neglected and slighted. In July 1888, this tension resulted in a split in the Orthodox community on the Lower East Side, when Rabbi Joshua Seigel, known as the Sherpser Rav, was declared chief rabbi of over twenty Galician and Polish congregations, named the "Congregations of Israel, Men of Poland, and Austria."

Rabbi Seigel, who assumed the title "Chief Rabbi of Congregations of Israel, Men of Poland, and Austria," was the first rabbi to create an eruv in New York. Rabbi Seigel had come to New York from Poland in 1882.[3] He was born in 1846 in Kitzburg, a small town near the Prussian border, which was under the control of the Russian government. As a young man, he studied under Rabbi Leibel Charif of Plotzk and Rabbi Yehoshua of Kutna, who granted him rabbinical ordination. He inherited his father's rabbinical position in the town of Sherps, Poland, but was not accepted by the Hasidic sector of that community. Due to these conflicts and difficult economic conditions, Rabbi Seigel immigrated to the United States in 1882. He was appointed rabbi of a small Polish synagogue on the Lower East Side, consisting of a divided community of Hasidic and non-Hasidic families. In 1888, he was appointed Rav ha-Kollel ("head of the academy") of twenty Polish congregations on the Lower East Side.[4]

The rabbis living in Poland supported his leadership of the Polish Jewish community in America.[5] But their support did not make his task easier. In a responsum that was published in his collection of responsa *Oznei Yehoshua*, he

---

organizations in New York. See Shaul Stampfer, "The Geographic Background of East European Jewish Migration to the United States before World War I," in *Migration across Time and Nations: Population Mobility in Historical Contexts*, ed. Ira A. Glazier and Luigi De Rosa (New York, 1986), 220–230.

3 Moshe D. Sherman, *Orthodox Judaism in America: A Biographical Dictionary and Sourcebook* (Westport, CT, 1996), 193, claimed that Rabbi Seigel immigrated in 1884. Yosef Goldman suggested that he immigrated in 1875. However, the Twelfth Census of the United States of 1900 lists the immigration date of Joshua Seigel as 1882. This is significant, for the longer that Rabbi Seigel served in New York prior to the arrival of Rabbi Joseph, the stronger his claim that he should not be subservient to the new chief rabbi. See Yosef Goldman, *Hebrew Printing in America 1735–1926: A History and Annotated Bibliography* (New York, 2006), vol. 2, 998, which mentions 1875 as the possible year of his immigration to America.

4 Sherman, *Orthodox Judaism in America*, 193–194.

5 Eli Lederhendler, *Jewish Responses to Modernity: New Voices in America and Eastern Europe* (New York, 1994), 97–99.

described the challenges that he and other European-trained rabbis encountered in the United States, echoing some of the concerns that Rabbis Rosenefeld and Seigel expressed in St. Louis. He wrote:

> It has been over twenty years since I have arrived here in the United States, a land which was desolate without Torah but filled with those who were concerned with their employment. A new picture emerged for me, in which new questions arose that would never have been brought to rabbis in the land of my birth. I realized that it was not for naught that I came to this country, and maybe God placed me here to resolve these new issues.[6]

Rabbi Seigel saw himself as strengthening New York's Jewish community. His work to create an eruv in Manhattan was born, it seems, of a desire to support Judaism in a land that seemed averse to it.[7]

The earliest reference to the creation of the eruv in Manhattan is found in this same book, *Oznei Yehoshua*.[8] In an undated responsum, Rabbi Seigel addressed the question of whether Manhattan was a public domain, thereby precluding

---

6 Joshua Seigel, *Oznei Yehoshua* (Jerusalem, 1914), Introduction.

7 For a discussion of the views of Eastern European rabbis on their roles as rabbis in the United States, see Menahem Blondheim, "Ha-rabbanut ha-Ortodoksi megaleh et Amerikah: Ha-ge'ografia shel ha-ruaḥ be-mitavim shel tikshoret," in *Be-ikvot Kolumbus: Amerikah, 1492–1992*, ed. Miri Eliav-Feldon (Jerusalem, 1996), 483–510.

8 The earliest reference to the prohibition against carrying in Manhattan is found in a notice in *The Jewish Gazette*, August, 19, 1881, entitled "An Important Announcement to Prevent Religious Violation." In that notice, Rabbi Abraham Ash of Beth Hamidrash Hagadol wrote that, several weeks earlier, a religious teacher in New York had written to Rabbi Spektor in Kovno and received permission from Rabbi Spektor for Jews in New York to travel on the elevated trains on the Sabbath. Rabbi Ash wrote that Rabbi Spektor had sent him a letter describing the request and Rabbi Spektor's response. In that letter, Rabbi Spektor explained that this religious teacher had told him that, if travel on the trains was not permitted on the Sabbath, Jews would cease to be observant. In addition, this teacher had informed Rabbi Spektor that Rabbi Saul Nathanson of Lvov had permitted carrying in New York on the Sabbath. Therefore, Rabbi Ash explained, Rabbi Spektor had advised the Jews of New York to purchase their subway tokens prior to the Sabbath and not to travel outside the confines of the city. In addition, Rabbi Spektor wrote that such travel was only permitted for the sake of fulfilling a commandment. Rabbi Ash concluded the notice informing the readership of the newspaper that, now that Rabbi Spektor had been informed that Jews would not abandon observance due to this prohibition and that carrying was not permitted in New York on the Sabbath, Rabbi Spektor had withdrawn his permissive ruling. Rabbi Judah David Eisenstein recorded that, around the year 1878, there was a dispute in New York City over whether travel on the elevated trains was permitted on the Sabbath. Eisenstein wrote that Rabbi Ash prohibited such travel because of *mar'it ayin*, the possibility of appearing to sin, and because it had the appearance of a weekday activity. However, for the sake of a communal need or

the possibility of creating an eruv around Manhattan without enclosing the borough with walls and doors. Rabbi Seigel concluded that Manhattan was not a public domain, but he raised other questions about the eruv and the structural features that might be necessary to build. He concluded, "We look forward to the time when the wealthy Jews will create an eruv here like in all cities in Israel."[9]

In 1905,[10] Rabbi Seigel wrote a subsequent treatment of the eruv topic entitled *Eruv ve-hoẓa'ah*. The volume begins as follows:

> Concerning the city of New York where we live, I have written a lengthy responsum several years ago exploring whether it is a public domain concerning the laws of the Sabbath. Now, religious Jews have approached me and suggested that maybe we have the possibility to allow carrying on the Sabbath at least on the East Side of the city.[11]

His responsum explained the legal rationale for this eruv, and he appended several rabbinic approbations to it. In a different take from the one he expressed earlier, Rabbi Seigel concluded that an eruv existed naturally on the East Side of Manhattan because of the rivers and train tracks and that it was therefore permissible to carry on the Sabbath.

There were several rabbis who opposed Rabbi Seigel's eruv. The first rabbi to write in opposition was Rabbi Yehudah David Bernstein. Rabbi Bernstein was born into a rabbinic family in Kovno, Lithuania, and attended the Slobodka Yeshiva. He immigrated to the United States in 1894 and settled in New York. Not wanting to become a community rabbi, he was a businessman for a short time before he assumed the position of kashruth supervisor at a local winery. He helped found the Rabbi Isaac Elchanan Yeshiva and was one of its first Talmud instructors. He also served as an administrative assistant at the yeshiva. In 1910, Rabbi Bernstein published *Hilkhata rabbeta le-Shabbata*, a thirty-page responsum rejecting Rabbi Seigel's arguments and concluding that Jewish law did not permit the creation of an eruv on the Lower East Side.[12]

---

fulfilling a commandment, Rabbi Ash permitted such travel privately. (It is not clear how one would travel on trains privately.) See J. D. Eisenstein, *Oẓar zikhronotai* (New York, 1929), 352.

9 Seigel, *Oznei Yehoshua*, vol. 1, 180.

10 Joshua Seigel, *Eruv ve-hoẓa'ah* (New York, 1907), 1. While *Eruv ve-hoẓa'ah* was published in 1907, the responsum is dated September 5, 1905.

11 Seigel, *Eruv ve-hoẓa'ah*, 1.

12 Yehudah David Bernstein, *Hilkhata rabbeta le-Shabbata* (New York, 1910). The responsum is dated May 29, 1910.

The second responsum opposing the eruv was written by Rabbi Aharon Gordon. Rabbi Gordon was born in Miadziol, in the province of Vilnius, in 1845. Following his rabbinical ordination, he served as a rabbi in Vishnevo. He immigrated to the United States in 1890 and became a rabbi in Rochester, New York. He moved to New York City in 1900 and led a rabbinical court on the Lower East Side. The date of his responsum is not known, but Rabbi Gordon explained at the beginning of his work that he was responding to Rabbi Seigel's volume *Eruv ve-hoẓa'ah*, which was published in 1905. He stated that New York rabbis had published notices in the local Jewish newspapers that it was prohibited to carry in New York.[13] However, he said, the public had chosen to follow the more lenient position, even though it was based on lies.[14]

The last of the responsa opposing the eruv was written by Rabbi Azriel Herman. Rabbi Herman was born in Svirzh, Galicia, in 1859 and received his rabbinical ordination at the age of eighteen from, among other rabbis, Rabbi Shalom Mordekhai Schwadron of Brezhin. He arrived in America in 1891 and served as a rabbi on the Lower East Side and then in Brownsville, Brooklyn. According to his grandchildren, he was a colleague and friend of Rabbi Shalom Elchanan Jaffe, who was the fierce opponent of the St. Louis eruv.[15] In the introduction to his responsum, dated March 24, 1927, he wrote, "It has been over twenty years since this small volume filled with material was published by Rabbi Joshua Seigel permitting carrying in this neighborhood."[16] Rabbi Herman argued that Rabbi Seigel's leniency had no basis in Jewish law and that therefore it was forbidden to carry on the Sabbath in the area that Rabbi Seigel claimed was surrounded by the eruv.

There were many halakhic opinions in this debate. The pages that follow will explore the key issues and the various opinions that surrounded them.

---

13 The alleged notices cannot be found in the Jewish press of this period. Although there were a number of papers that were published during this time, the *Morgen zhurnal* is no longer extant from the year 1905, the year in which the eruv was created. It is noteworthy that the eruv controversies were not discussed in the Jewish press in America or in Eastern Europe, with few—if any—references in, for example, Cracow or Odessa to the disputes that divided the entire Orthodox community in those cities.

14 Rabbi Aharon Gordon, "Teshuvah be-niggud le-haẓa'ah le-tikkun eruvin be-ḥelek mi-mizraḥ Nu York," in *Kol ẓevi*, ed. Ari Zahtz and Michoel Zylberman, vol. 7 (New York, 2005), 37–48. This reprint is based on Ms. MS1300A in the Mendel Gottesman Library of Yeshiva University.

15 Azriel Herman, *Sefer mayyim ḥayyim*, in *Kovez̧ shut be-inyanei eruvin be-Arẓot ha-Berit* (n.p., n.d.), Introduction written by the grandchildren of Rabbi Herman, 1953. An abbreviated version of *Sefer mayyim ḥayyim* is found in *Kol ẓevi*, vol. 7, 49–66. (All page references will be to the complete version of the work.)

16 Herman, *Sefer mayyim ḥayyim*, Introduction, n.p.

Building an Eruv for Sabbath Violators

Unlike Rabbi Rosenfeld of St. Louis, Rabbi Seigel did not base his argument for creating an eruv on the low level of Sabbath observance among local Jews. His discussion of Manhattan's status as a public domain in *Oznei Yehoshua* was simply framed as a response to an unidentified questioner, and, at the end of the responsum, he expressed a hope that "there will be a time in the future when the wealthy Jews will establish an eruv in Manhattan just like there are *eruvin* in all cities where Jews live."[17] He did not elaborate on the role that the wealthy needed to play in the establishment of this city eruv, and it never came to fruition because Rabbi Seigel turned his attention instead to defending an eruv on the East Side that relied on preexisting boundaries. *Eruv ve-hoẓa'ah* similarly lacked any reference to the observance level of community. Rabbi Seigel simply wrote that "God-fearing people (*ḥaredim*) approached [him] and asked if an eruv could be established at least on the East Side of the city."[18] Evidently, there was at least a segment of the Jewish community that was punctilious enough in Sabbath observance to request an eruv. In his responsum opposing the eruv, *Hilkhata rabbeta le-Shabbata*, Rabbi Bernstein likewise referred to these God-fearing Jews: "Unfortunately, in New York there are God-fearing people who carry based on the eruv that was suggested by one of the rabbis here, who relied on arguments that had no basis. Therefore, I decided to publish this work to remove this stumbling block from the people."[19]

Rabbi Gordon's responsum, on the other hand, emphasized the lack of Sabbath observance among many of the Jewish residents of the Lower East Side, describing them in terms reminiscent of Rabbi Jaffe's description of the Jews of St. Louis:

> For whom did this rabbi work to permit this activity for which the punishment is stoning? If it is for the Sabbath violators who sit in their stores on the Sabbath selling and writing, smoking and extinguishing like on a weekday without any rabbinical dispensation, do they need an eruv, as they are violating biblical prohibitions . . . ? And if it is for the sake of those for whom the spark of Judaism has not been extinguished from their hearts and they observe the Sabbath, do we need to seek leniencies

---

17 Seigel, *Oznei Yehoshua*, vol. 1, 180.
18 Seigel, *Eruv ve-hoẓa'ah*, 1.
19 Bernstein, *Hilkhata rabbeta le-Shabbata*, 6. See also ibid., 8, where he makes a similar point.

> for them . . . for if so the laws and spirit of the Sabbath will be completely forgotten from the Jewish people?[20]

At the end of the responsum, he elaborated on his view of the two types of Jews in New York:

> Unfortunately, the epidemic has spread among the Jewish people, especially in New York, where Jews have removed the burden of the commandments . . . and they hate the observant Jews worse than the non-Jews hate them, and they barely consider them people.[21]

Rabbi Gordon did not deny that there were observant Jews on the Lower East Side, for whom "the spark of Judaism has not been extinguished from their hearts." But he did decry the prevalence of Jews who "removed the burden of the commandments" and argued that there was no need to build an eruv for their sake. His responsum also refers to animosity between observant and non-observant Jews, suggesting that these were two separate populations.

Defining the Public Domain

Rabbi Seigel begins his responsum in *Oznei Yehoshua* with a question that was asked of him:

> Our city, New York, does it have the status of a public domain? It has a population of close to two million, and a large river that is similar to an ocean surrounds it with ships that travel on the river. On three sides, the river is close to the city, but on the fourth side (the West Side), half of the river is close to the city, but half of the river is several miles from the city [houses]. . . . We would like to know whether the city has the status of a public domain or another type of domain.[22]

---

20 Gordon, "Teshuvah be-niggud," 42.

21 Ibid., 48.

22 Seigel, *Oznei Yehoshua*, vol. 1, 163. The actual population of Manhattan in 1900 was 1,850,093. See "New York (Manhattan) Wards: Population & Density: 1800–2910," Demogrpahia, http://www.demographia.com/db-nyc-ward1800.htm. Rabbi Seigel claimed that the population of Manhattan exceeded three million (*Oznei Yehoshua*, vol. 1, 180).

For the first time in the history of city eruvin, a rabbi addressed the possibility of creating an eruv around a city that definitely had a population that exceeded six hundred thousand. Because Manhattan had streets that were wider than sixteen cubits and had a population that exceeded six hundred thousand, Rabbi Seigel could not easily define Manhattan as anything other than a public domain. Therefore, he took several different approaches to explain how it would be possible to create an eruv in Manhattan despite its apparent status as a public domain. First, he argued that the river walls created eruv boundaries that were equivalent to walls and would adequately enclose even a public domain. The problem that remained was the question of whether traffic across the rivers negated the river walls as eruv boundaries. Although this was a dispute in the medieval sources, the Tosafot argued that even the Sages who believed that a boundary could not be negated by the passage of people only applied this to a man-made boundary and that a natural boundary, such as a river, could be negated by traffic.[23] Since people crossed the rivers around New York in boats and bridges, Rabbi Seigel suggested a novel interpretation to validate the New York eruv. He explained that, according to Tosafot, the natural eruv boundary would only cause a problem if crossing it were simple.[24] However, since it was impossible due to the steep incline of the rivers to even enter the water, Tosafot would agree that the people crossing the rivers around Manhattan did not negate the eruv. In addition, Rabbi Seigel argued that people entering the boats did not negate the eruv boundary, since the Gemara says that a ship on the water is considered stationary vis-à-vis the water.[25] Therefore, he explained that the people moving from the land to the ship were merely crossing from one stationary place to another and did not negate the eruv boundary. Finally, Rabbi Seigel cited the view of the *Magen Avraham,* also cited by Rabbi Rosenfeld in St. Louis, that the entire issue of an eruv boundary being nullified by traffic only applies if six hundred thousand people pass over the eruv boundaries each day.[26]

Rabbi Seigel also introduced another argument to justify the creation of an eruv around Manhattan. Rabbi Shmuel ben Meir (Rashbam), the grandson of Rashi and one of the Tosafists, defined a public domain as follows: "The camp of the Israelites was like a courtyard of partners because only the camp of the Levites had the status of a public domain."[27] Rabbi Seigel understood

23 Tosafot on b. Eruv. 22b, s.v. *dilma.*

24 Tosafot on b. Eruv. 22b, s.v. *Yehoshua.*

25 B. Metz. 9b.

26 Avraham Gombiner, *Magen Avraham,* Oraḥ ḥayyim, 363:40. Rabbi Seigel discusses this issue in *Oznei Yehoshua,* vol. 1, 172–175.

27 Rashbam on b. B. Bat. 60a, s.v. *vayar.*

this statement as establishing a different criterion for the creation for a public domain. According to Rashbam, a public domain is an area where six hundred thousand people congregate at one time, just as the Jews congregated in the Levite camp in the desert. The fact that six hundred thousand live in one area does not make it a public domain unless there is one place where they all gather at the same time.[28] Based on this explanation of the Rashbam, Rabbi Seigel concluded that no city could be considered a public domain even though there were cities whose population exceeded six hundred thousand, since none had a central place where six hundred thousand gathered. Rabbi Seigel acknowledged that common wisdom was that six hundred thousand people gathered on Broadway at one time, thereby classifying Manhattan as a public domain, even according to Rashbam. However, Rabbi Seigel argued that Broadway was only a large street in name, while in reality, many parts of it were no more than large alleyways. Therefore, he concluded that six hundred thousand never congregated in one place at one time. Thus, according to Rabbi Seigel's understanding of the Rashbam, Manhattan did not have the status of a public domain, even though its population far exceeded six hundred thousand.[29]

Although most of Rabbi Seigel's responsum went to great lengths to justify the creation of an eruv in Manhattan, the end of the responsum took a turn in the opposite direction. He explained that since the rivers were far away from the houses in the city, it was necessary to build symbolic doorways between the river and the houses,[30] but "this is something that is all but impossible." Therefore, he concluded, it was not permitted to carry in Manhattan. Finally, he wrote, "We eagerly await the moment when God will place it in the hearts of the wealthy people of New York to create an eruv like those in all other Jewish cities. . . . Who knows if we will ever have the ability to build such eruv walls here if God forbid the redemption is delayed?"[31]

In his later responsum *Eruv ve-hoẓa'ah*, Rabbi Seigel did not address the issue of whether Manhattan was a public domain. He explained,

---

28 The same essential argument was made by Rabbi Rosenfeld in St. Louis and attributed to Rabbeinu Nissim; see preceding chapter.

29 Seigel, *Oznei Yehoshua*, vol. 1, 179–180.

30 The need for a symbolic doorway in such a situation is a matter of dispute. See Rabbi Seigel's discussion in *Oznei Yehoshua*, vol. 1, 180 and Moses Sofer, *She'elot u-teshuvot Ḥatam Sofer* (Bratislava, 1841), vol. 1, no. 89, who argued that since these symbolic doorways are merely to create the impression that the inhabited area is enclosed, one can be lenient if they cannot be constructed.

31 Seigel, *Oznei Yehoshua*, vol. 1, 180.

> Concerning the city of New York where we live, several years ago I wrote a responsum defining whether it is a public domain or not. . . . Now, religious people have approached me and asked whether I could permit carrying on the Sabbath at least in the East Side of the city. Their argument was that the water surrounded the East Side on three sides . . . and on the fourth side there is an unequalled symbolic doorway created by the train track that runs from South Ferry in the south to the Harlem River in the north without any interruption.[32]

Rabbi Seigel wrote that there were fewer than six hundred thousand people within the East Side borders and that therefore, the issue of whether it was a public domain was not relevant. However, he did once again address the issue of whether public travel over the eruv boundaries nullified the eruv, quoting the *Magen Avraham*'s statement that an eruv boundary is only nullified if six hundred thousand people cross it in a single day. Rabbi Seigel concluded that since there were never six hundred thousand people in the area surrounded by the East Side eruv, this eruv was valid and could not be nullified.[33]

In the approbations at the end of *Eruv ve-hoẓa'ah,* Rabbi Sholom Mordekhai Schwadron of Brezhin and Rabbi Aryeh Leibush Horowitz pointed out that the author of the *Or zarua* disagreed with the *Magen Avraham* and maintained that even fewer than six hundred thousand crossing an eruv's boundaries each day invalidates the eruv.[34] Nevertheless, both Rabbi Schwadron and Rabbi Horowitz agreed that the view of the *Or zarua* did not render the East Side eruv unacceptable, because many rabbinic authorities agreed with the lenient position of the *Magen Avraham.*[35]

Rabbi Yehudah David Bernstein, one of the rabbis who wrote responsa in opposition to Rabbi Seigel, addressed the question of whether Manhattan was a public domain in his volume *Hilkhata rabbeta le-Shabbata.* He wrote that because Manhattan had streets that were sixteen cubits wide and a population exceeding six hundred thousand, it was a public domain according to all authorities. He discussed two considerations regarding the use of the rivers as eruv boundaries. First, he argued that Manhattan was faced with the problem of public travel over the eruv boundaries. He rejected Rabbi Seigel's suggestion

---

32 Seigel, *Eruv ve-hoẓa'ah*, 1.
33 Ibid., 12–13.
34 Isaac ben Moshe, *Or zarua* (Jerusalem, 2009), Hilkhot eruvin, no. 129.
35 Seigel, *Eruv ve-hoẓa'ah*, 28–30, 33–49.

(though without mentioning him by name) that crossing eruv boundaries made by rivers that are difficult to cross does not invalidate the eruv. Rabbi Bernstein argued that thousands of people crossed into Manhattan daily by boat and that more than six hundred thousand crossed into Manhattan through tunnels, thereby negating the eruv boundaries. Furthermore, he argued that the fact that the streets were elevated from the river wall did not create a sufficient eruv boundary. The purpose of eruv boundaries, according to Rabbi Bernstein, was to prevent passage in and out of the city; the elevation of the streets had nothing to do with it. Piers were not acceptable eruv boundaries because they facilitated docking of the ships and made embarking and disembarking from the boats more accessible, and so these piers could not be considered eruv walls. Finally, he argued that the bridges negated the eruv boundaries because they opened into the other boroughs, where there were more than six hundred thousand people at any given time.[36]

Rabbi Gordon, another of the opponents of Rabbi Seigel's eruv, also addressed the question of whether Manhattan was a public domain. He wrote simply, "You should know that New York City is the second largest city in the world after London, England, exceeding four million people."[37] The response of Rabbi Azriel Herman, another detractor, was lengthier. He explained that Rabbi Seigel's claim that the East Side of Manhattan did not constitute a public domain because its population did not exceed six hundred thousand was incorrect. Rabbi Herman quoted the opinion of Ritba, who said that as long as six hundred thousand congregate in an area on a single day, even if they do not live there, the area is considered a public domain.[38] Rabbi Herman wrote that the number of people on the East Side of Manhattan each day far exceeded six hundred thousand when counting the many people who traveled into Manhattan each day for work.[39]

Rivers as Eruv Boundaries

Rabbi Seigel's *Eruv ve-hoẓa'ah* included a lengthy discussion of whether the rivers surrounding the East Side of Manhattan could serve as eruv boundaries. According to Rabbi Seigel, the eruv consisted of the East River and the Harlem River on the east and north sides, New York Bay on the south side, and the Third

---

36 Bernstein, *Hilkhata rabbeta le-Shabbata*, 14–17.
37 Gordon, "Teshuvah be-niggud," 38.
38 *Ritba* on b. Eruv. 59a, s.v. *matnitin*.
39 Herman, *Sefer mayyim ḥayyim*, 48–49.

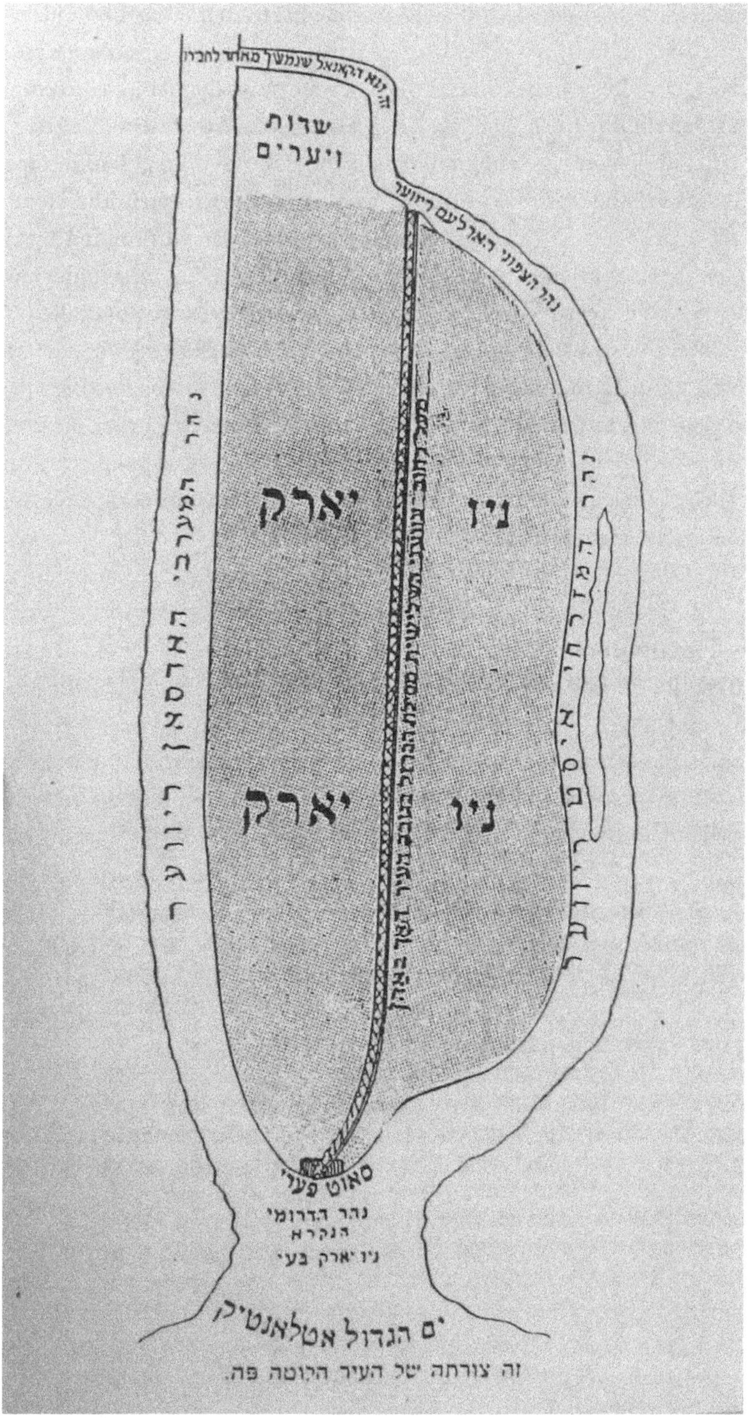

FIGURE 2. Seigel, *Eruv ve-hoẓa'ah*, 2.

Avenue Elevated (known as the Third Avenue El) train track as a boundary that connected South Ferry with the Harlem River at 155th Street on the west side. Rabbi Seigel addressed the concern that the waterways might build up sediment, which would nullify the eruv boundaries. He explained that, according to Rabbi Isaac ben Sheshet and the *Magen Avraham*, the risk of sediment buildup applied only to oceans and not rivers or other smaller bodies of water. Therefore, this was not a problem for the East Side eruv, which was surrounded by rivers and a bay.[40] Rabbi Seigel further explained that the issue of sediment was a problem only in a case where the water created only one eruv boundary, since the sediment would then create a breach in the eruv. However, in the case of Manhattan, the Third Avenue El tracks crossed the river on the northern border of the eruv and terminated at the water on the southern border. Even if the buildup of sediment invalidated the eruv boundaries created by the water lines, Rabbi Seigel explained, the East Side of Manhattan remained completely within the boundaries created by the Third Avenue El tracks.[41]

The fact that the East Side of Manhattan was completely enclosed by the Third Avenue El tracks also solved the problem of the rivers being farther than ten cubits from the houses. Rabbi Seigel explained, as Rabbi Rosenfeld had argued regarding the St. Louis eruv (although without mentioning Rabbi Rosenfeld), that the only time a breach of ten cubits invalidates an eruv is a situation in which the eruv wall is created through a combination of the river and the walls of the homes. In the case of the East Side of Manhattan, where the entire area was enclosed by the Third Avenue El tracks, the distance of the water from the houses was irrelevant.[42] Rabbi Seigel concluded his work decisively: "It is permissible to carry in the entire part of the city east of the elevated train tracks."[43]

Rabbi Bernstein, however, questioned whether the rivers could create eruv boundaries. In a short remark in the middle of his work *Hilkhata rabbeta le-Shabbata*, he wrote, "The permitting rabbi argued that since New York was surrounded by rivers, there was no fear of sediment buildup. However, this is an error because the sea surrounds these rivers." He noted that the rivers that enclosed New York were filled with salt water and were therefore extensions of the ocean. The status of New York City was as if it were surrounded by seas, so the risk of sediment buildup would invalidate the eruv even according to *Magen*

40 See Isaac ben Sheshet, *She'elot u-teshuvot Rivash* (New York, 1974), no. 405; and *Magen Avraham*, Oraḥ ḥayyim, 363:31, which is discussed by Seigel in *Eruv ve-hoẓa'ah*, 1.

41 Seigel, *Eruv ve-hoẓa'ah*, 6–7.

42 Ibid., 10–11.

43 Ibid., 13.

Avraham, who argued that sediment buildup was only a concern in oceans and not in rivers.[44]

Rabbi Herman similarly presented a lengthy analysis of whether the buildup of sediment invalidated the eruv. He concluded that Rabbi Seigel took for granted that all opinions agreed that this issue did not apply to rivers. However, Rabbi Herman quoted the opinion of the Vilna Gaon, who explained that the problem of sediment buildup lies in the fact that sediment can cause an eruv boundary to lose its necessary slope, thus invalidating the water as a boundary. This problem, according to the Vilna Gaon, applies both to oceans and to rivers.[45]

In the conclusion of his discussion of this topic, however, Rabbi Herman wrote that in the case of the East Side eruv, the fear of sediment buildup was not an issue, since the only time that sediment buildup is a problem is in a situation where the pier does not rise at least ten handbreadths above the water. In Manhattan, where the piers were significantly higher than the water, the possibility of sediment buildup could be ignored, since the pier, and not the river itself, created the eruv boundary.[46]

Elevated Train Tracks as an Eruv Boundary

The Third Avenue El was the second line of the elevated railway system in New York City. The first line, which ran up Ninth Avenue, was built in 1876. In 1886, the Third Avenue El was extended across the East River into the Annexed District, which was later known as the Bronx.[47] These train tracks served as the western boundary of the eruv and enclosed the Jewish area of the Lower East Side, which was situated to the east of the tracks.[48] Rabbi Seigel addressed the El as a boundary only in response to the specific question that was asked of him concerning the creation of the eruv. He wrote that religious people had asked him whether an eruv could be established on the East Side of Manhattan. He continued, "On the fourth side there is an unequalled symbolic doorway, which is the train tracks that run above the city from one end to the other. They extend

---

44 *Magen Avraham,* 363:31; and Bernstein, *Hilkhata rabbeta le-Shabbata,* 26–27.

45 *Biur Ha-Gra,* Oraḥ ḥayyim, 363; and Herman, *Sefer mayyim ḥayyim,* 7, 26.

46 Herman, *Sefer mayyim ḥayyim,* 26.

47 For the history of the Third Avenue El, see Lawrence Stetler, *By the El: Third Avenue and Its El at Mid-Century* (New York, 1995), 9.

48 See the map of Jewish residences on the Lower East Side in Rischin, *The Promised City,* 77.

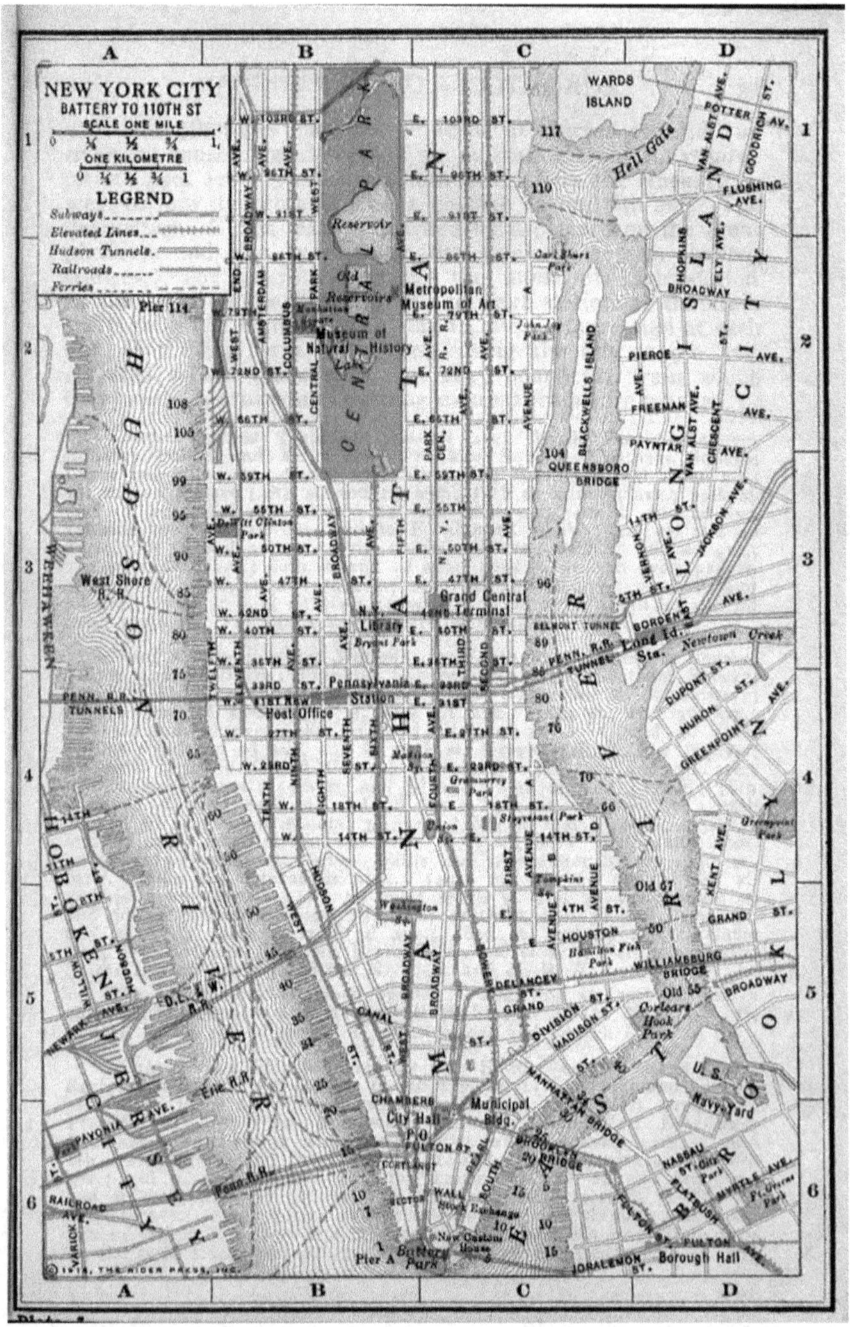

FIGURE 3. Rider's New York City, Henry Holt and Company, 1916.

from the water on the south side at South Ferry to the water on the north side without any interruption until Harlem.'"[49]

Rabbi Bernstein rejected the use of the Third Avenue El tracks as eruv boundaries for several reasons. First, he argued that iron beams were connected to the sides of the girders and that they constituted a "symbolic doorway from the side" (*ẓurat ha-petaḥ min ha-ẓad*), which rendered the eruv boundary invalid. He explained that the wooden frames of the tracks were also not acceptable as eruv boundaries, as there was significant distance between the girders and the wooden frame. Furthermore, he claimed that, even if the Third Avenue El tracks created an acceptable eruv boundary, the thousands of people who ascended and descended the steps of the stations each day and who passed underneath the Third Avenue train tracks created a breach in the eruv boundary.[50]

Rabbi Gordon also rejected the use of the Third Avenue El train tracks as eruv boundaries, though he did so for different reasons than Rabbi Bernstein. Rabbi Gordon argued that the underground subway that ran throughout the city crossed under the Third Avenue El train tracks in several locations and that therefore, passengers in the subway invalidated the Third Avenue El train tracks as a boundary. This was a novel use of the principle of traffic negating an eruv, since the rule had previously been used to invalidate eruv boundaries that people crossed over, not under. In this case, he said, the Third Avenue El train tracks were invalidated because people crossed under them.

Parks within the Eruv

The *Shulḥan arukh* addresses the question of a garden or park inside an eruv. It explains that if such a garden or park is not enclosed within its own walls, is more than five thousand square cubits, and is not suitable for human habitation, it invalidates the entire eruv. This is based on an assumption that the owners of the garden or park do not want people to traverse it and destroy the vegetation, so it is not considered part of the common space required for the creation of an eruv. According to the *Shulḥan arukh*, the only way to validate an eruv in which such an area exists is to totally enclose this smaller area.[51] Rabbi Seigel addressed the fact that there were gardens and parks on the East Side of Manhattan that would

---

49 Seigel, *Eruv ve-hoẓa'ah*, 1.

50 Bernstein, *Hilkhata rabbeta le-Shabbata*, 22–23.

51 *Shulḥan arukh*, Oraḥ ḥayyim, 358:9. See Yosef Gavriel Bechhofer, *The Contemporary Eruv: Eruvin in Metropolitan Areas* (Jerusalem, 1998), 96–98 for a discussion of whether the ability to walk in the field or park would render this area fit for human habitation.

seem to invalidate the entire eruv by the standards set by the *Shulḥan arukh*. He concluded that these areas did not create a problem for several reasons. First, many of these gardens or parks were, in fact, surrounded by walls or gates, thus fulfilling the requirement that they be enclosed and separate from the larger area. Second, since there were buildings designated in each of these parks or gardens as rest areas, the gardens and parks were considered fit for human habitation and would not invalidate the eruv.[52]

Rabbi Gordon agreed with Rabbi Seigel that the parks of the East Side were enclosed by gates. Yet, he wrote, the openings of the entranceways to the parks were wide (he claimed that he saw one gate with an opening fifteen feet wide), and since none of the gates had symbolic doorways, the parks were not properly sealed off from the larger area, thus invalidating the eruv.[53]

Leasing the Area

In *Eruv ve-hoẓa'ah*, Rabbi Seigel discussed the question of whether the Jewish community could lease the city through a city official. He began by quoting the responsum of Rabbi Isaac ben Sheshet, who maintained that a Jew could lease an area from the governmental head of the city or that person's representative. Since the head of the city had the right to prohibit people from traveling on certain streets, he also had the authority to lease the area to the Jewish community.[54] Rabbi Seigel applied this reasoning to the situation in New York City. He explained that the city could be leased from a city official, since the city official had the authority to close the street to traffic at will. He provided an example of this phenomenon from his own experience, where the mayor posted armed soldiers in the streets of Brooklyn during a strike. The presence of the soldiers altered the usual traffic through the streets. In addition, he suggested that the area could be leased from a police officer, who had similar authority to control the flow of traffic on the street. Even if the term of the city official ended in the middle of the term of the lease, the lease would not be cancelled according to the *Shulḥan arukh*.[55] Even without this dispensation, though, the area could be leased from the local police officers, since they were not elected for fixed terms.[56] Rabbi Seigel argued that even the Hakham Ashkenazi, who did

---

52 Seigel, *Eruv ve-hoẓa'ah*, 23–24.
53 Gordon, "Teshuvah be-niggud," 46.
54 Ben Sheshet, *She'elot u-teshuvot Rivash*, no. 427.
55 *Shulḥan arukh*, Oraḥ ḥayyim, 382:14.
56 Seigel, *Eruv ve-hoẓa'ah*, 25.

not permit the lease to extend beyond the term of the city official, would agree that it could be leased from a police officer.[57] The last words of Rabbi Seigel's responsum read: "So we did in practice lease the city from the representative of the governmental official for the duration of ten years. We make *eruvei ḥaẓerot* every Friday, and we carry on the Sabbath in the enclosed area."[58]

Rabbi Gordon, however, argued that Jews could not lease the city from the local police. He explained that the United States was unlike countries in which leadership was "passed from father to son." In a democracy, where the leaders are chosen by elections, the mayor and even the president of the United States do not have the right to enter private homes without permission. As a precedent for this opinion, he cited the view of Rabbi Shalom Elchanan Jaffe, who had opposed the eruv in St. Louis and had similarly distinguished between the democracy of the United States and the hereditary governments of other countries. Finally, he cited the opinion of Hakham Ashkenazi that the lease was only valid as long as the person from whom the area was leased remained in office. Since the national and city leadership changed every four years, the lease would not be valid upon the expiration of the official's term.[59] Rabbi Gordon did not address Rabbi Seigel's argument that this consideration did not apply to police officers, who have no fixed terms.

Approbations

Rabbi Seigel appended to his work approbations from four Polish rabbinic authorities: Rabbi Shalom Mordekhai Schwadron of Brezhin Rabbi Aryeh Leibush Horowitz of Stanislav, Rabbi Moshe Meizlish of Premishla, and Rabbi Moshe Nachum Yerushalimsky of Kiletz.[60]

The author of the first approbation, Rabbi Shalom Mordekhai Schwadron of Brezhin known by the acronym Maharsham, was one of the foremost rabbinic authorities in Galicia, as both Hasidic and Lithuanian rabbis accepted his decisions.[61] This approbation consisted of two separate letters. In the first letter, dated July 12, 1906, Rabbi Schwadron expressed reservations about the eruv, since he understood that the Third Avenue El train tracks reached from the southern tip of Manhattan to the northern tip. This would create a problem if

57 Tzvi Hirsch ben Yaakov Ashkenazi, *Sheelot u-teshuvot Ḥakham Ẓevi* (Jerusalem, 1995), no. 6.
58 *Sheelot u-teshuvot Ḥakham Ẓevi*, 26.
59 Gordon, "Teshuvah be-niggud," 46–48.
60 Seigel, *Eruv ve-hoẓa'ah*, 31–54.
61 For a biography of Rabbi Schwadron, see Meir Wunder, *Me'orei Galiẓyah: Enẓiklopedyah le-ḥakhmei Galiẓyah* (Jerusalem, 1997), vol. 5, 14–38.

the river developed sediment, creating a gap between the end of the train tracks and the point in the river that had the depth to create the eruv wall. However, he concluded, "In the end, there is room to allow carrying in the East Side of New York. However, a religiously stringent person who is able to avoid carrying is to be praised. However, in a case of emergency, there is reason to be lenient, and the rabbi has decided properly."[62]

In the introduction to the next letter from Rabbi Schwadron, dated January 14, 1907, Rabbi Seigel added a comment in parentheses in which he explained that Rabbi Schwadron had not properly understood the situation in Manhattan. In truth, the Third Avenue El train tracks crossed the Harlem River at 155th Street, and in the south, the tracks of the Third Avenue El reached the water line, at which point the river wall created the necessary eruv boundary. In this second letter, Rabbi Schwadron explained that he had received the letter of clarification from Rabbi Seigel and that therefore he believed that the eruv was acceptable even in a case that was not an emergency and that even religiously stringent people could rely on the eruv.

In his approbation, Rabbi Schwadron clarified certain matters regarding city eruvin that were utilized by later rabbinic authorities. First, he explained that since the issue of sediment buildup is only a rabbinic-level concern, the halakhah follows the lenient opinion of *Magen Avraham* that sediment buildup is not a concern in rivers and that the rivers that enclosed the East Side of Manhattan were therefore acceptable eruv boundaries. Rabbi Schwadron also cited the *Or zarua*,[63] which quotes the statement in *Halakhot gedolot* that a city surrounded by a river is considered enclosed with respect to the laws of eruvin.[64] Rabbi Schwadron concluded from the fact that the *Or zarua* quotes this opinion without any qualifications that an island such as Manhattan that is enclosed by rivers is considered enclosed and that there was no reason to worry about sediment buildup. He also addressed the issue of whether the rivers needed to be visible from the houses within the eruv, quoting the opinion of Ramban that natural eruv boundaries such as rivers must be visible to the people within the eruv.[65] This would create a problem for Manhattan and most cities surrounded by rivers, which are often far from the houses. However, Rabbi Schwadron explained that Ramban's criterion was limited to cases in which the water was not visible from anywhere in the city and could not be reached on the Sabbath.

---

62 Seigel, *Eruv ve-hoẓa'ah*, 28–30.
63 *Or zarua*, vol. 2, Hilkhot eruvin, no. 164.
64 Ezriel Hildesheimer, ed., *Halakhot gedolot* (Jerusalem, 1972), 260.
65 Moshe ben Nahman, *Ḥiddushei ha-Ramban* on b. Eruvin 59a, s.v. *u-mihu*.

Rabbi Schwadron argued that in a city in which the rivers are visible at least to the people living nearby and can be reached on the Sabbath, even Ramban would agree that the rivers are acceptable eruv boundaries.[66] His approbation to Rabbi Seigel's work established the credibility of *Eruv ve-hoẓa'ah* within the rabbinic community of Eastern Europe and the United States.

Rabbi Bernstein addressed Rabbi Schwadron's approbation in the introduction to his work. He wrote, "I wrote my work, yet, I was confused how to proceed, for the act of Satan has successfully misled the great Torah sage Rabbi Shalom Mordekhai, and he [Rabbi Seigel] received an approbation from him. However, after he [Rabbi Schwadron] explored the matter carefully, he changed his mind and decided to oppose the eruv. Now that he has changed his mind, I can publish my work."[67]

Rabbi Bernstein did not quote Rabbi Schwadron's purported retraction of his approbation. However, in the introduction to Rabbi Herman's work, his grandchildren explained that Rabbi Herman was so distraught over the fact that Rabbi Seigel had received such prominent approbations for an opinion that Rabbi Herman considered erroneous that he corresponded with Rabbi Schwadron, from whom he had received his rabbinical ordination, and then traveled to Poland for six months to prove to the rabbis who had given these approbations that Rabbi Seigel's eruv was based on faulty logic. According to his grandchildren, Rabbi Herman returned to New York only when these rabbis expressed agreement with him.[68] In his introduction to his work, Rabbi Herman wrote, "It was difficult for me because Rabbi Seigel received approbations from European rabbinic authorities who did not properly understand the situation, as Rabbi Schwadron explained to me. Rabbi Schwadron gave me a letter that stated that he retracted his approbation. This letter has been in my possession for fifteen years."[69] This letter from Rabbi Schwadron was discovered in 2000.[70] In the letter, dated July 22, 1908, Rabbi Schwadron wrote:

> Concerning my response regarding the eruv in New York, at the time I believed Rabbi Joshua Seigel, who signed his name as the

---

66 Seigel, *Eruv ve-hoẓa'ah*, 29–31.

67 Bernstein, *Hilkhata rabbeta le-Shabbata*, 8.

68 *Koveẓ shut be-inyanei eruvin be-Arẓot ha-Berit*, n.p.

69 *Koveẓ shut*; and Gordon, "Teshuvah be-niggud," 49.

70 The anonymous editors of the *Koveẓ shut be-inyanei eruvin be-Arẓot ha-Berit* printed a copy of the original letter. In the introduction to the letter, they wrote, "The letter was discovered in 2000 thanks to the will of God to fulfill the desire of this sainted rabbi [Rabbi Schwadron] who wanted to publicize the retraction of his approbation." *Koveẓ shut*, n.p.

> Rav Ha-Kollel, and all the diagrams of New York that he sent me. Later, I received letters from several rabbis that contradicted his diagrams and explained that he was not the Rav Ha-Kollel and that many rabbis oppose his eruv. . . . Therefore, I fear God, and I retract my approbation in which I allowed carrying in this one part of New York City.[71]

This attempt by the different rabbis to clarify the approbation of Rabbi Schwadron highlights the fact that Rabbi Schwadron was accepted as the premier rabbinic authority in Galicia and that his support or opposition was critical for much of the Jewish community. Even after Rabbi Schwadron's initial qualified approbation for the eruv, Rabbi Seigel felt the need to respond to him to seek stronger support. Rabbi Bernstein felt restricted in expressing opposition to the eruv until he heard that Rabbi Schwadron had in fact opposed it. Finally, Rabbi Herman went so far as to travel to Poland to clarify the issue for Rabbi Schwadron and receive a retraction from him. Although rabbinic approbations are always critical in rabbinic debate and played an important role in the debate regarding the St. Louis eruv, Rabbi Schwadron's approbation held an especially important place in the debate over the eruv on the East Side of Manhattan due to his stature in the Polish rabbinic world and among American rabbis at the beginning of the twentieth century, who continued to feel subservient to the rabbinic authorities of Eastern Europe.

Conclusion

The eruv on the East Side of Manhattan was the second documented city eruv in North America. Remarkably, Rabbi Seigel, the initiator of the New York eruv, wrote a letter of approbation for Rabbi Jaffe's anti-eruv treatise in St. Louis. At least in Rabbi Seigel's mind, there was no contradiction between supporting the eruv in New York and opposing the eruv in St. Louis. Although Rabbi Seigel did not elaborate on his reasons for opposing the St. Louis eruv, the halakhic issues that laid the foundation for his support of the East Side eruv in Manhattan evidently did not satisfy him regarding the eruv in St. Louis. This may have been in part because Rabbis Rosenfeld and Jaffe disagreed not only about halakhic principles but also about whether the eruv boundaries described by Rabbi Rosenfeld really existed and whether St. Louis had a population that exceeded

71 Gordon, "Teshuvah be-niggud," 50. This letter is also published in *Kovez̧ shut*, n.p.

six hundred thousand. In the case of the East Side of New York eruv, the physical boundaries were not open to dispute, as all the rabbis agreed that the East Side of Manhattan was bounded by rivers and the elevated train tracks. The issue was whether these boundaries constituted acceptable halakhic eruv boundaries, leading to a traditional legal debate based on the precedent of earlier city eruvin in Europe and St. Louis and centuries of halakhic material about eruvin.

Furthermore, the halakhic issues that were addressed in St. Louis differed from the ones that were raised regarding the New York eruv. In St. Louis, Rabbis Rosenfeld and Jaffe disagreed about the status of telegraph poles and wires as eruv boundaries. Although the rabbis who opposed the New York eruv mentioned the problem of "a symbolic doorway from the side" vis-à-vis the Third Avenue El train tracks, Rabbi Seigel did not address this issue and took it for granted that the Third Avenue El train tracks were acceptable eruv boundaries. In addition, even though the acceptability of rivers as eruv boundaries was an issue in both St. Louis and Manhattan, Rabbi Seigel's permissive ruling regarding the rivers in New York was based on the fact that three sides of the area were surrounded by rivers and that the elevated train tracks enclosed the entire area, a situation that did not pertain to St. Louis.

As previously mentioned, the impetus for the creation of the eruv differed in these two cities. In St. Louis, Rabbi Rosenfeld described how he initiated the idea of the eruv to save people from violating the Sabbath laws. In the case of the New York eruv, Rabbi Seigel did not identify the questioner in his first responsum, and it is even possible that he made up the question. In his subsequent treatment of the issue in 1905, he identified the questioners who requested an eruv on the east side of Manhattan as "the God-fearing people" (*ḥaredim*). Rabbi Seigel did not explain the reasons of these religious people for requesting the creation of an eruv. Yet it is notable that the rabbi initiated the eruv in St. Louis, whereas members of the community purportedly initiated the eruv in New York.

The dispute in New York reflected a deepening rift among the Eastern European Orthodox communities of the Lower East Side in the early decades of the twentieth century. Rabbi Herman wrote that the "God-fearing Jews" did not rely on the eruv, whereas the "common Jews" did rely on the eruv. Rabbi Judah David Eisenstein, the early historian of Lower East Side Orthodox Jewry, painted a different picture of those who relied on the eruv and those who did not. In his volume *Oẓar zikhronotai*, published in 1930, he wrote in the entry for the obituary for Rabbi Seigel:

> The Hasidim who follow his word are about two thousand people, and they do not hesitate to carry their *talleisim*, *siddurim*,

> and *ḥumashim* to the synagogue. This is in spite of the fact that the misnagdim complained and called out against them.[72]

In 1936, Rabbi Yosef Eliyahu Henkin, the rabbinic authority on the Lower East Side at the time, wrote, "There are many observant Jews and especially those Hasidim from Poland who carry here on the street on the Sabbath relying on the permission of Rabbi Joshua Seigel of Sherps."[73] Although Rabbi Seigel was not himself a Hasid, Hasidim tended to follow him, since he represented the Polish and Galician community.[74] The eruv controversy therefore reflected not only different interpretations of the law but also a contentious split between two groups of Orthodox Jews on the Lower East Side.

The eruv on the East Side of Manhattan played an important role in the history of the development of city eruvin. However, it is noteworthy that the precedent of the St. Louis eruv played very little role in the discussion surrounding the East Side of Manhattan eruv. The debate over the St. Louis eruv was cited only once in the entire discussion regarding the eruv on the East Side of Manhattan, when Rabbi Gordon referred to Rabbi Jaffe's discussion of whether the government authorities in American democracy have the status of "tenant or agent." Rabbi Seigel was obviously familiar with the dispute regarding the St. Louis eruv, since he gave his approbation to Rabbi Jaffe, and Rabbi Gordon was also clearly familiar with Rabbi Jaffe's work. Their failure to engage extensively with this material and their strong reliance on the views of the Polish rabbinic authority Rabbi Schwadron suggest that they were still thinking of this eruv as a continuation of the tradition of European eruvin rather than part of a new American tradition.

---

72 Judah David Eisenstein, *Oẓar zikhronotai* (New York, 1930), 118.

73 Yosef Eliyahu Henkin, *Luaḥ ha-yovel shel Ezrat Torah* (New York, 1936), 62, reprinted in his *Edut le-Yisra'el* (New York, 1949), 151. (In fact, *Edut le-Yisra'el* does not contain a date of publication. The date of 1949 seems to be the correct date of publication, as the calendar in the back of the book begins in 1950, and the copy of the book in the New York Public Library has a stamped date of acquisition of 1949.)

74 The exact number of Hasidim in New York at the beginning of the twentieth century is unknown. Eisenstein claimed that there were two thousand Hasidim. In *The Jewish Communal Register of New York City, 1917–1918*, Isaac Even claimed that the Hasidim were a small minority even at the end of World War I. However, he placed their number at thirty thousand in New York. See Isaac Even, "Chassidism in the New World," in *The Jewish Communal Register of New York City, 1917–1918* (New York, 1918), 341–346. For the history of Hasidism in North America prior to World War II, see Ira Robinson, "The First Hasidic Rabbis in North America," *American Jewish Archives* 44, no. 2 (1992): 501–517; and Ira Robinson, "Anshe Sfard: The Creation of the First Hasidic Congregations in North America," *American Jewish Archives* 62, no. 1–2 (2005): 53–66.

4

The Toronto Eruv

Created in 1921 by the Polish immigrant Rabbi Yehudah Leib Graubart, the Toronto eruv was the first in North America to face no opposition from other rabbinic authorities. This was the case even though Rabbi Graubart was confronted with many of the same sociological and halakhic issues as the creators of the more controversial eruvin in St. Louis and New York. Rabbi Graubart was aware of Rabbi Seigel's responsum justifying the creation of the eruv on the Lower East Side of Manhattan, however, he did not draw on Rabbi Seigel's own arguments but on the opinions written in the approbation by Rabbi Mordekhai Schwadron, the great Polish halakhic authority. When looking for halakhic precedent, Rabbi Graubart turned to the eruv in Warsaw and not those in North America. In this respect, the story of the Toronto eruv illustrates the continued reliance of immigrant rabbis on European precedent and the lack of an independent American halakhic tradition.

This chapter will explore the history of the Toronto eruv, beginning with Rabbi Graubart's efforts to strengthen Sabbath observance in Toronto and his eventual creation of the eruv. Next, it will look at the extension of the eruv in 1950 by Rabbi Abraham Price in response to northern migration of the Jewish community. Rabbi Price not only expanded the eruv's boundaries but also brought it into alignment with a stricter interpretation of the laws of eruvin by erecting small poles next to all the telephone poles along its boundary, which was made possible by the Jewish community's increasing ability to work with local governmental authorities. The end of the chapter will look at a controversey surrounding the eruv that arose in the 1980s and how Rabbi Price was again able to raise the standard of his eruv as a result of the growing clout of the Toronto Jewish community.

Background to the Eruv's Creation

Although there were already several thousand Jews in Canada by the 1870s, the mass migration from Eastern Europe in the last two decades of the nineteenth century transformed Canadian Jewish communities.[1] Between 1881 and 1901, Canada's Jewish population grew from 2,443 to 16,401, of whom 9,300 were immigrants. The increase in the Jewish population during this period was particularly acute in Toronto, where large numbers of Eastern European Jewish immigrants settled. In 1881, there were 534 Jews in Toronto. By 1891, that number had almost tripled, and by 1911, there were over 18,000 Jews in Toronto.[2]

Almost without exception, the Eastern European Jewish immigrants to Toronto gravitated to St. John's Ward. "The Ward," as it was called, was considered a slum from the beginning of its existence in the mid-nineteenth century. Most of these immigrants came with limited funds, and many arrived without their families and had little choice but to find inexpensive housing near the commercial center of the city. Initially, most of these Jewish immigrants worked in clothing factories. However, over time, some of them were able to open shops and factories that served the Jews of the Ward.[3]

Small synagogues and *landsmanschaften* congregations played an important role in the Toronto Jewish community, but there was no ordained rabbi in Toronto until 1899, when the Galician synagogue Shomrai Shabboth hired a young Romanian rabbi, Joseph Weinreb, to serve as its spiritual leader. Rabbi Weinreb was respected in the community, but the Russian and Lithuanian communities wanted a rabbi who had studied in one of the Lithuanian yeshivot, and they did not accept him as their rabbi. When Rabbi Jacob Gordon, a recently ordained rabbi from the yeshiva of Volozhin in Lithuania, arrived in Toronto in 1904 to collect funds for his school, he was immediately hired by the Russian and Lithuanian communities to serve as their rabbi. B. G. Sack, a historian of early Jewish life in Canada, writes that Rabbi Gordon "found a warm and friendly atmosphere and a community devoted to traditional Jewish values" in Toronto.[4] By World War I, Rabbi Gordon was the rabbi of at least six Lithuanian and Russian congregations.[5]

---

1 For a review of the early history of the Jews in Canada, see Gerald Tulchinsky, *Taking Root: The Origins of the Canadian Jewish Community* (Hanover, NH, 1993), 8–60. For an excellent study of the Jewish community in Toronto from its inception until 1937, see Stephen A. Speisman, *The Jews of Toronto: A History to 1937* (Toronto, 1979). For the early history of the Jews in Toronto, see Speisman, *The Jews of Toronto*, 11–20.

2 Speisman, *The Jews of Toronto*, 69–78; and Stephen A. Speisman, "St. John's Shtetl: The Ward in 1911," in *Gathering Place: Peoples and Neighbourhoods of Toronto, 1834–1945*, ed. R. F. Harney (Toronto, 1985), 108.

3 Speisman, "St. John's Shtetl," 107–113.

4 B. G. Sack, *Canadian Jews Early in This Century* (Montreal, 1975), 38.

5 A biography of Rabbi Gordon can be found in Kimmy Caplan, "There is No Interest in Precious Stones in a Vegetable Market: The Life and Sermons of Rabbi Jacob Gordon of Toronto," *Jewish History* 23 (2009): 149–155. Rabbi Gordon's experiences in Toronto can be found in Rabbi

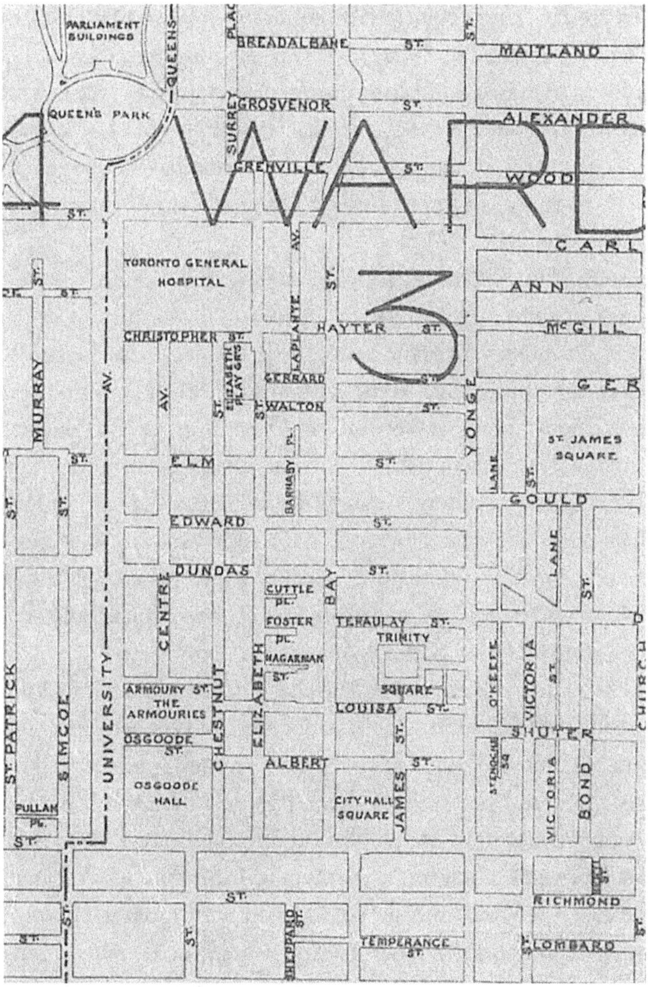

Figure 4. Plan of the City of Toronto, July 19, 1923. City of Toronto Archives, Series 725, File 17.

As the Toronto Orthodox community grew, its members became increasingly religiously lax. Rabbi Gordon wrote that, when he arrived in Toronto in 1905, the Sabbath was strictly observed in the Ward, and Jewish factories closed every Saturday. Most Jewish workers did not work on the Sabbath for the non-Jewish factory owners, even though they risked losing their jobs. However, as early as 1904, one religious Jew moved his family outside of the Ward in order to prevent

Jacob Gordon, "Zikhronos fun a Torontoer Rav," *Centennial Jubilee Edition Commemorating the Centenary of Jewish Emancipation in Canada and the Twenty-fifth Anniversary of the Jewish Daily Eagle* (Montreal, 1932), 67, 78.

his children from seeing other Jewish children violating the Sabbath.[6] When the Lyric Theatre opened in 1909, the *Yiddisher zhurnal* included a complaint that some Jewish women went to synagogue on Saturday morning and to the matinee in the afternoon.[7] By 1915, a few Jewish shops and kosher bakeries and groceries in the Ward remained open on the Sabbath.[8] Synagogue attendance also began to dwindle, and even large synagogues had difficulty assembling a minyan for weekday services.[9]

Additionally, the Polish Jews, who constituted the largest segment of the Orthodox community, were without a rabbinic leader. In an attempt to strengthen ritual observance and communal involvement, these Polish Jews sought someone to both serve as the rabbi of the Polish community and unify the Orthodox community of Toronto. In 1920, a group of Polish Jews from Toronto invited Rabbi Yehudah Leib Graubart to become the head of the Polish Jewish community there. Uncertain about the prospects for Jewish life in Toronto, he resisted the offer. However, in the summer of 1920, Rabbi Graubart traveled to London to participate in a conference. When fighting broke out between Russia and Poland, he was unable to return to Poland and accepted the position in Toronto as head of the Polish Jewish community.[10]

Rabbi Graubart was born in 1862 in the Slutsk Province of Lithuania. His father, a Hasid and follower of Rabbi Israel Meir of Gur, was Rabbi Graubart's first Talmud teacher and made sure that the young Graubart was acquainted with the teaching and practices of the Hasidim. In addition, Rabbi Yehudah Graubart took an interest in Jewish philosophy and modern Hebrew literature.

Graubart received his rabbinic ordination in 1882 from Rabbi Hayyim Elazar Wachs of Kalisch, Poland, and he received an additional letter of ordination from Rabbi Nathan Leipziger of Sarinsk two years later. He subsequently served as community rabbi in several towns in Lithuania and Poland. In 1901, Rabbi Graubart became the rabbi in Stashov, Poland, where he remained for the next twenty-five years. He gained a reputation as a great rabbinic scholar and a fiery preacher, often denouncing secularists and Bundists. He also established community boards throughout Poland to strengthen Jewish education and tradition. When World War I broke out, Rabbi Graubart was suspected of spying and was arrested with several other rabbis by the Russian authorities. Following

---

6 Gordon, "Zikhronos," 67.

7 *Yiddisher journal*, June 18, 1909.

8 Nachman Shemen, "Orthodoxy in Toronto," in *Sefer ha-yovel shel Talmud Torah Ez. Ḥayyim* (Toronto, 1943), 5.

9 Shemen, "Othodoxy in Toronto," 5, and Speisman, *The Jews of Toronto*, 278–279.

10 Shemen, "Orthodoxy in Toronto," 5.

his release from prison, he moved to Moscow, where he witnessed the Bolshevik Revolution. Rabbi Graubart was instrumental in raising money for needy families, establishing prayer services, and teaching children during this difficult period. Following World War I, Rabbi Graubart joined the Religious Zionism movement, Mizrachi, and became one of its most important spokespeople. He served as the editor of their journal, *Ha-Mizrachi,* and published several articles encouraging European Jewish youth to consider moving to Israel.[11]

Rabbi Graubart seemed to be the perfect rabbi for the Toronto Polish community. Many of the Polish Jews in Toronto came from Stashov, where Rabbi Graubart had established a stellar reputation. In addition, the Toronto community believed that his involvement in creating communal organizations would serve him well in Toronto. The Jewish community of Toronto also included a strong Zionist contingent, and Rabbi Graubart was respected for his leadership in Mizrachi. Rabbi Graubart seemed to understand the challenges that lay ahead in Toronto. In his autobiography, which mainly discusses his experiences during World War I, he wrote that the greatest problem facing the Jewish community in Toronto when he arrived was "that any city that does not have one chief rabbi for the city will lead to having nine different communities all involved in strife and conflict."[12]

Addressing the Issue of Sabbath Observance

Upon his arrival in Toronto, Rabbi Graubart committed himself to tackling the issue of Sabbath observance in the community. In April 1922, he published a short pamphlet in Yiddish and English entitled "A Sabbath Letter." He began the pamphlet speaking in the name of the Sabbath:

> I, Dame Sabbath, appeal to you. I am sufficiently known to you, and my lineage needs no introduction. I am as old as the Jew. I have ever played the greatest role and have occupied the greatest

11 A lengthy biography of Rabbi Graubart can be found in Nachman Shemen, "Rabbeinu Yehudah Leib Graubart" [Yiddish], in *Yovel-buch, Talmud Torah Ez Ḥayyim,* ed. N. Shemen and L. J. Zuker (Toronto, 1943), 13–45. A short biography can be found in Sherman, *Orthodox Judaism in America,* 81–83. See also Yitzchak Raphael, *Enziklopedyah shel ha-Ẓiyonut ha-datit* (Jerusalem, 1958), vol. 1, 561–565. Much of Rabbi Graubart's experience in Europe is contained in his autobiographical recollections, *Sefer zikaron* (Lodz, 1925).

12 Graubart, *Sefer zikaron,* 205.

> place in Jewish history. I am the crown of Judaism—God's cherished one—Israel's delight.[13]

He went on to criticize both Jewish employers for forcing Jews to work on the Sabbath and Jewish employees for working on the Sabbath. He ridiculed the employer who, he wrote, "goes to the synagogue on the Sabbath day, is called up to the scroll of the Law, the Reader recites in his honor 'Whoever doeth work therein shall be put to death.' . . . He leaves the synagogue with a parting 'Gut Shabbos' and immediately winds his way to the forbidden labor that had so recently been denounced."[14] He also compared the situation of the Jews in Poland to their situation in North America:

> You are indeed to be pitied, American Judaism. How lamentably deplorable is your status. You dwell in the happiest of lands, in an oasis surrounded by deserts of misery. You enjoy all rights; you suffer no restrictions, and no foes harm you or destroy your position, and yet you are ruining your own career. . . . Of what avail then is your stable economic condition when it is obtained at the expense of your spiritual life?[15]
>
> In the old country, in those dark and wretched regions where starvation rules, where one is lifelong engaged in the supreme struggle for a dry crust of bread, yet as in Warsaw, Lodz, Bialystock, Vilna—Shabbos is Shabbos as the Lord has ordained.[16]

Rabbi Graubart concluded his letter with several suggestions to rectify the problem, and he became involved in helping the Jews of Toronto to not have to work on the Sabbath. He wrote that he approached the officers of the Cloak Makers' Union and proposed a plan to divide the Saturday work hours among the other days of the week. Rabbi Graubart claimed that the union promised ratification of this policy as long as the employers agreed. Based on this promise, he appealed to the Jewish employers, "So you see, it is up to you, manufacturers. It is your move. Call a meeting and give this important question the full consideration to which it is entitled. Surely you will come to a decision—and

---

13 Yehudah Leib Graubart, *A Sabbath Letter* (Toronto, 1922), 2.
14 Graubart, *A Sabbath Letter*, 3.
15 Ibid., 5.
16 Ibid., 6.

to a favorable conclusion—that the Sabbath shall rest and your budget shall not suffer."[17]

Rabbi Graubart concluded his letter by placing additional pressure on those who insisted on working on the Sabbath:

> Furthermore, I appeal to all congregations to guard our honor and aid in eradicating this evil public violation of the Sabbath. Let not those who employ Jews on the Sabbath day and those who keep their stores open on this day hold any office. They must not be presidents or trustees, nor should they participate in any committees.[18]

Rabbi Graubart followed this letter by posting notices throughout the community urging Jewish workers and manufacturers not to work on the Sabbath, and he included lists of Sabbath-observing shops.

In 1924, Rabbi Graubart delivered a series of four lectures in Kensington Market. Known at the time as the Jewish Market, Kensington was founded at the beginning of the twentieth century by Jewish immigrants. Many Jews had small shops in the market that sold food and other goods, as well as services such as tailoring.[19] Rabbi Graubart's lectures took place on the Sabbath and criticized the people shopping in the stores and the shopkeepers whose stores were open. He began his first sermon in Kensington Market by pointing out the oddity of a rabbi delivering a sermon in the open market on the Sabbath.

> Who has ever heard of such a thing, a rabbi, head of a community, delivering a sermon outdoors? . . . This is my intention, that the assembled should ask such a question. . . . Is the custom that your children do not put on *tefilin* and you and your wives purchase on the Sabbath? Is this custom an ancient one derived from the practices of Poznan, Hordona, Lublin, and Cracow? . . . Had you maintained the traditions of your fathers and the practices of the past, the rabbi would also have maintained the tradition and not delivered a sermon in public.[20]

---

17 Ibid., 7.
18 Ibid., 7–8.
19 Speisman, *The Jews of Toronto*, 81–88.
20 Yehudah Leib Graubart, *Sefer devarim ki-khtavam* (Toronto, 1932), 197.

He continued, "What is the purpose of rebuking the Sabbath violators in the synagogue where only the Sabbath observers are found?"[21]

He went on to compare the situation of the Jews in Russia and Poland to the situation of the Jews in North America. In Poland during World War I, the government forced the Jews to keep their stores open on the Sabbath. In Russia, even following the war, the government forced the Jews to work on the Sabbath. In North America, there was freedom not to work on the Sabbath, yet Jews traveled on trolleys and purchased products from stores.[22]

In the second sermon in Kensington Market, Rabbi Graubart reiterated the importance of observing the Sabbath and concluded, "The one who closes his business on the Sabbath is worried about making a living. . . . However, God will provide a blessing in all his endeavors and allow him to become wealthy."[23] In the third and fourth sermons, he reiterated the value of the Sabbath for all those who observe its laws. At the conclusion of the fourth sermon, he provided some insight into the nature of the Orthodox Jews in Toronto at the time:

> If these women who violate the Sabbath were not religious, I would have remained silent. However, they are observers of the commandments, they do not eat non-kosher meat, they maintain a Jewish home, the stoves and ovens are kosher, they purchase meat and fish for the Sabbath, they are careful to light the Sabbath candles, and they observe the positive commandments of the Sabbath while violating its negative precepts.[24]

The Jews that Rabbi Graubart addressed were not assimilated Jews who had rejected the traditions of Judaism. They were, rather, observant Jews who had chosen to become lax in the observance of certain aspects of the Sabbath. For this reason, Rabbi Graubart concluded, it was worthwhile for him to publicly rebuke them.[25]

---

21 Graubart, *Sefer devarim ki-khtavam*, 198.

22 Ibid., 199.

23 Ibid., 203.

24 Ibid., 208.

25 Speisman wrote that Rabbi Graubart urged a boycott of Jewish stores that remained open on the Sabbath and encouraged picketing of these establishments. He also claimed that Rabbi Grabaurt risked being assaulted. See Stephen Speisman, "Orthodox Rabbinate Updates Toronto Eruv," *Canadian Jewish News*, January 11, 1996, 3.

This concern about Sabbath violation seems to have been the impetus for Rabbi Graubart's creation of the eruv in Toronto. In his collection of responsa, *Havalim ba-ne'imim*,[26] he describes the request that led him to establish this eruv. He began the responsum, dated 5681 (1920–1921), as follows:

> I have been requested here in Toronto by many people who are also righteous people to find a way to establish that all the members of this city will be allowed to carry on the Sabbath. They said that I must find a way to "remove the stumbling block."[27]

This introduction suggests that the eruv project was initiated in response to a request from members of the community, as in the case of the East Side of Manhattan eruv, rather than coming directly from the rabbi, as in the case of the St. Louis eruv. However, the idea of creating an eruv to "remove the stumbling block" suggests that the eruv was also created to prevent those who were already carrying on the Sabbath from being guilty of Sabbath violation. This is consistent with the concerns that Rabbi Graubart expressed about lax observance in the Toronto Jewish community.

The responsum goes on to underscore these concerns with several quotes from Eastern European rabbis on the importance of creating city eruvin. Among these is a quote from Rabbi Hayyim Elazar Wachs, one of the great Polish rabbinic authorities in the second half of the nineteenth century and the rabbi who ordained Rabbi Graubart, who wrote, "In a city where the Sabbath violators and those who carry on the Sabbath are rampant, we must gather all the possible leniencies to allow for the creation of an eruv in the city."[28] Rabbi Graubart concluded his introduction as follows: "It is obvious, as it is written in the Jewish books, that since the generation is sinful and carries even though it is forbidden, it is a mitzvah to save them from this prohibition."[29]

---

26 These responsa were published as follows: vol. 1 (Pietrokov, 1901), vol. 2 (Warsaw, 1910), vols. 3–4 (Lodz, 1929–1934), and vol. 5 (n.p., 1939). They were reprinted in two volumes (Jerusalem, 1975). All page references will be to the 1975 reprinting of *Havalim ba-ne'imim*.

27 Graubart, *Havalim ba-ne'imim*, vol. 3, 21.

28 Rabbi Hayyim Elazar Wachs, *Sefer nefesh ḥayyah* (Pietrokov, 1876), Oraḥ ḥayyim, no. 25. The discussion of the Pressburg eruv can be found in Moses Sofer, *She'elot u-teshuvot Ḥatam Sofer* (Bratislava, 1841), vol. 1, no. 89.

29 Graubart, *Havalim ba-ne'imim*, vol. 3, 21.

Borders of the Eruv and the Issue of Telephone Wires as Eruv Boundaries

Rabbi Graubart asserted that the Don River and the surrounding hills in the east, the Humber River and the hills of High Park in the west, Lake Ontario in the south, and the telephone poles and wires that ran the length of Bloor Street in the north created eruv boundaries around the Toronto Jewish community. The geography of Toronto meant that three sides of the eruv were natural boundaries and only one side was a man-made boundary. Rabbi Graubart began his responsum by discussing the acceptability of this constructed eruv boundary.[30]

By 1921, the telephone had replaced the telegraph in cities like Toronto, but telephone poles and wires were functionally the same as telegraph poles and wires when it came to forming eruv boundaries. Like Rabbi Rosenfeld in St. Louis, Rabbi Graubart was able to rely on the precedent of the Warsaw eruv, which used telegraph poles and wires as boundaries, but also wished to satisfy the requirements of even those who had opposed the Warsaw eruv. The concern in Warsaw was that the telegraph poles might constitute a "symbolic doorway from the side" and therefore be invalid. Rabbi Rosenfeld had argued that, since the telegraph wires in St. Louis were connected to the top of the crossbars rather than being bolted to the side of the pole like the ones in Europe, this was not a concern. Rabbi Graubart made the same argument in defense of the telephone wires in Toronto: since the cable was connected to the top of a crossbar that protruded from the main telephone pole, meaning that, at the point of the crossbar, the vertical beam did not extend above the cable, it formed a valid symbolic doorway and was acceptable as an eruv boundary.

In support of this argument, Rabbi Graubart cited a letter of approbation to his responsum written by Rabbi Shlomo Dov Kahane of Warsaw, in which Rabbi Kahane was able, based on drawings sent to him by Rabbi Graubart, to distinguish between the telegraph poles in Warsaw and the telephone poles in Toronto. Rabbi Kahane concluded that, although many halakhic authorities had disqualified the telegraph poles and wires in Eastern Europe as valid eruv boundaries, the telephone poles and wires in Toronto were valid symbolic doorways, because the wires were connected to the top of the crossbar that protruded from the vertical beam. Rabbi Kahane stated that he had shown Rabbi

30 Ibid., 21–22.

Graubart's letter to several rabbis in Poland, who agreed with the distinction between the situation in Eastern Europe and the one in Toronto.[31]

Rabbi Graubart made an additional argument to justify the use of the telephone poles and wires in Toronto as eruv boundaries. He quoted the thirteenth-century halakhic authority Mordekhai ben Hillel, who wrote that the only reason that a symbolic doorway from the side is not acceptable as an eruv boundary is that doors normally have crossbars attached to the top of the vertical beam and not the side.[32] Based on this argument, Rabbi Graubart wrote that, in the twentieth century, when most doorways had windows above the door (which could be considered part of the door), a crossbar or wire that was attached to the side rather than the top of the vertical bar should be permissible.[33] Rabbi Graubart concluded this section of the responsum writing, "Concerning the law, the tradition is to allow for telegraph poles to serve as eruv boundaries . . . and this is the custom in Warsaw and in several other holy communities."[34]

However, Rabbi Graubart added that, in order to satisfy the rabbinic authorities who did not permit telegraph poles to serve as eruv boundaries and would not accept the distinction between telegraph poles of Eastern Europe and the telephone poles and wires of Toronto, he had installed small poles next to the telephone poles at the two ends of the street. Because the poles were positioned directly under the crossbars, they eliminated the problem of "a symbolic doorway from the side." According to the *Shulḥan arukh,* such poles could serve as acceptable symbolic doorways even though they did not reach the wires.[35] Rabbi Graubart explained that these poles did not have to be inserted at every telephone pole, as the Gemara does not mention a maximum length for a symbolic doorway. Therefore, the symbolic doorway was created, according to the authorities who required the insertion of these small poles, by the telephone poles at the end of each street and the wires that ran between them. He wrote that this same advice was given to the Jewish community of Warsaw in order to allow them to rely on the telegraph poles as eruv boundaries.

While it might appear minor, the installation of these poles was a significant departure from the creation of previous North American eruvin, which relied

---

31 Ibid., 21–22. Rabbi Kahane's letter is included in the approbation contained at the conclusion of Rabbi Graubart's responsum. See Graubart, *Havalim ba-ne'imim,* vol. 3, 50. For a discussion of Rabbi Graubart's view on telephone poles and their use as symbolic doorways, see Bechhofer, *The Contemporary Eruv,* 68–69.

32 Mordekhai on Eruvin, no. 478.

33 Graubart, *Havalim ba-ne'imim,* vol. 3, 25.

34 Ibid., 26.

35 *Shulḥan arukh,* Oraḥ ḥayyim, 362:11.

exclusively on preexisting boundaries due to the lack of a relationship with local authorities allowing the Jewish community to do any construction. This had been an issue in Europe as well. In the nineteenth century, the government had prohibited the Jews of Cracow from erecting symbolic doorways. Rabbi Ben Zion of Bilsk, the rabbinic scholar who was quoted as the source of the suggestion to install small poles next to the telegraph poles in Warsaw, wrote that the Jews of Warsaw had to be careful that these poles remain inconspicuous. Rabbi Graubart did not mention any opposition from local authorities in Toronto regarding the insertion of these poles,[36] but there is also no evidence that he sought their permission.

Hills and Rivers as Eruv Boundaries

Rabbi Graubart addressed several distinct issues concerning the use of the hills and rivers that enclosed Toronto on the south, east, and west sides as eruv boundaries. First, he discussed whether the rivers and hills constituted eruv boundaries even though they were not *mukaf le-dirah*, created as eruv boundaries to enclose a preexisting city. Drawing on the *Peri megadim*,[37] he explained that the requirement that the boundaries be *mukaf le-dirah* was applicable only to one side of the eruv. As long as one of the four sides was built for the sake of the people and the houses, the entire eruv was valid. He added that the *Magen Avraham* states that a symbolic doorway is considered to be *mukaf le-dirah*.[38] Since the telephone poles in Toronto were built after the city was inhabited, the requirement was fulfilled, and the entire eruv was therefore valid. He also noted that the question of hills and rivers as eruv boundaries had been addressed throughout the past two hundred years, and the question of whether they were created for the purpose of surrounding the city was never mentioned, so this was clearly not a concern.[39]

Like the creators of the eruvin in St. Louis and Manhattan, Rabbi Graubart had to contend with the question of whether people moving in and out of the city through its natural boundaries—the rivers and hills—disqualified these

---

36 Graubart, *Havalim ba-ne'imim*, vol. 3, 26. See Ben Zion Sternfeld, *Sha'arei Zion* (Jerusalem, 2004), no. 3. Rabbi Ben Zion of Bilsk explains that these small poles were adequate to create symbolic doorways even in places where the telegraph wires did not run in a straight line, such as around a street corner.

37 See Joseph ben Meir Teomim, *Peri megadim* (New York, 2006), Mishbeẓot zahav, Oraḥ ḥayyim, 363:20.

38 Avraham Gombiner, *Magen Avraham*, Oraḥ ḥayyim, 358:5.

39 *Magen Avraham*, Oraḥ ḥayyim, 3:29–33.

features as eruv boundaries. Rabbi Graubart offered several explanations for why this was not a problem in Toronto. First, he explained that even according to Tosafot, who state that people passing through a natural eruv boundary invalidate it, this only applies if the eruv cannot be seen from the homes. In Toronto, since the river and the hills could be seen from the city, the eruv boundaries were valid even though people passed through them. Rabbi Graubart quoted Rabbi Abraham of Narbonne, who wrote that the distinction between constructed eruv boundaries and natural boundaries lay in the fact that constructed boundaries that could not be seen from the city are valid even if people passed through them, while natural boundaries that people passed through were only valid if the boundaries could be seen from the city.[40]

Regarding the risk of the rivers accumulating sediment, invalidating them as eruv boundaries, Rabbi Graubart made several arguments. First, he quoted the Rama, who stated that one must be concerned about the risk of sediment buildup.[41] Rabbi Graubart claimed, based on the opinion of *Magen Avraham,* that sediment buildup was only a concern in the ocean and not in rivers.[42] Furthermore, Rabbi Graubart claimed that the possibility of sediment buildup was only problematic if two sides of the city were bounded by water. If only one side was bounded by water, the three other eruv boundaries created a private domain, and then the risk of sediment buildup did not disqualify the eruv. He quoted the precedent of the Warsaw eruv, in which Rabbi Alter relied on the Vistula River as one of the eruv boundaries in the mid-nineteenth century. Rabbi Alter responded to his questioner regarding the possibility of disqualifying the eruv based on sediment buildup as follows: "Why are you looking for stringencies when the custom is to be lenient?"[43] Finally, Rabbi Graubart added that, in Toronto, the hills surrounded the city beyond the rivers, so even if the rivers were not acceptable eruv boundaries, the hills that surrounded the rivers on the east and south sides of the city would create acceptable eruv boundaries.[44]

Rabbi Graubart also quoted a disagreement between the *Magen Avraham* and the *Taz* about a city where the river froze for part of the year. The *Magen Avraham* prohibited carrying in such a city during the period when the river was frozen, since people might cross the river on foot and thus invalidate the boundary, and the *Taz* prohibited carrying during the summer months as well. Rabbi Graubart quoted Rabbi Moses Sofer, who argued that the Sephardic halakhic authorities

---

40 Abraham of Narbonne, *Sefer ha-eshkol* (Halberstadt, 1868), no. 65.

41 Rama, Oraḥ ḥayyim, 363:29.

42 *Magen Avraham*, Oraḥ ḥayyim, 363:31.

43 Isaac Meir Alter, *Teshuvot ha-Rim* (Warsaw, 1882), no. 4.

44 Graubart, *Havalim ba-ne'imim*, vol. 3, 33–34.

allowed carrying even during the winter months. Rabbi Sofer explained that he too agreed that the river freezing was not a concern because people would be afraid to cross the frozen river and so would not negate the eruv boundary.[45] Therefore, Rabbi Graubart concluded that the frozen rivers did not invalidate the eruv even during the winter season, when the rivers were actually frozen.[46]

Bridges and Gardens

Rabbi Graubart also discussed whether Toronto's bridges created breaches in the eruv wall, which would mean that each bridge would require a symbolic doorway to close these breaches.[47] Rabbi Graubart concluded that all the bridges on the Don River and the bridge that connected the Don River to Lake Ontario had structures at their entrances that served as symbolic doorways, thus creating unbroken eruv walls.[48]

On the question of whether the gardens and parks within the city negated the entire eruv, Rabbi Graubart made an important distinction. He argued that the only time that gardens and parks negated an eruv was when the garden or park was separated from the rest of the city or not used by the people in the city. In that case, the garden or park interfered with the creation of an eruv community. However, if, after the garden or park was planted, it was incorporated into the city and used by the people in the city, then it did not negate the eruv and could be included in the eruv, since it became part of the eruv community. Notably, while the issue of gardens and parks was also addressed in connection with the eruv on the Lower East Side of Manhattan, the halakhic justification for allowing the parks to be incorporated into the eruv was entirely different. Here as elsewhere, Rabbi Graubert does not display any engagement with the earlier North American responsa on eruvin or the controversies surrounding them.

Leasing of the City

Finally, Rabbi Graubart analyzed the laws of leasing the property of non-Jews and the Jews who did not accept the principle of the eruv from the

---

45 Sofer, *She'elot u-teshuvot Ḥatam Sofer*, vol. 1, no. 89.

46 Graubart, *Havalim ba-ne'imim*, vol. 3, 34–35.

47 Ezekiel Landau, *Nodah bi-Yehudah*, 2nd ed. (Jerusalem, 1990), Oraḥ ḥayyim, no. 42.

48 Graubart, *Havalim ba-ne'imim*, vol. 2, 35–37.

civil authorities. He raised an issue that had not been brought up in prior discussions, namely whether the leasing of space from these civil authorities would successfully exclude the Jews who did not accept the principle of eruv from the eruv community or whether leasing of space only excluded non-Jewish residents. Rabbi Graubart began his analysis by explaining that the leasing of property was instituted to exclude non-Jews from the eruv community, as a way to prevent Jews from interacting with non-Jews. As Rashi explained, the difficulty of leasing the property of the non-Jew each week would cause the Jews to move into an exclusively Jewish neighborhood.[49] This rationale does not apply to Jews and, therefore, Rabbi Graubart argued that leasing of property did not exclude a Jew from the eruv community. However, Rabbi Graubart added that, since public Sabbath violators have the status of non-Jews, leasing their property would exclude them from the eruv community. Rabbi Graubart expressed uncertainty as to whether Jews whose only Sabbath violation was the fact that they rejected the principle of eruv had the status of non-Jews, allowing for their property to be leased, but he suggested that the incentive of preventing Jews from living with non-Jews should be extended to preventing Jews from living with non-observant Jews. It was only because non-observant Jews were not common in the talmudic period that the rabbis did not explicitly address the right to lease their property.

Rabbi Graubart concluded this discussion by quoting the opinion of Rabbi Jacob Reischer, who lived at the beginning of the eighteenth century and stated that leasing property from the local government authorities would suffice for both non-Jews and Jews who were Sabbath violators.[50] Rabbi Graubart applied this reasoning to Toronto, allowing the leasing of the property of non-Jews and non-observant Jews from the local authorities.[51] Unfortunately, Rabbi Graubart did not identify the authority from whom he ultimately leased the city.

Rabbinic Precedent

Rabbi Graubart concluded his responsum as follows:

---

49 Rashi on b. Eruv. 62a, s.v. *ela*.

50 Jacob Reischer, *Sefer shevut Yaakov*, vol. 3 (Brooklyn, 1961), Oraḥ ḥayyim, no. 29.

51 Graubart, *Havalim ba-ne'imim*, vol. 3, 39–40. See Malkiel Tzvi Tenenbaum, *Divrei Malkiel* (Jerusalem, 1976), 4:3 for the responsum by Rabbi Malkiel of Lomza. The responsum of Rabbi Hayim Berlin that Rabbi Graubart quoted in both of these responsa has been reprinted and can be found in Hayim Berlin, *Sefer nishmat ḥayyim* (Jerusalem, 2008), Oraḥ ḥayyim, nos. 29–31.

> After all this discussion, one can see clearly that concerning the eruv here one does not need to turn to paths that are far away and difficult or to rely on leniencies and get involved in differing opinions. This eruv has been made according to the tradition of the rabbinic authorities from whose waters we drink. All of the rules and the disagreements have been addressed in other cases, and in the city of Warsaw, the great city to God, people carry on the Sabbath with the permission of the great rabbinic authorities of Israel.[52]

From these concluding comments, several things can be understood about Rabbi Graubart's approach to the creation of the eruv in Toronto. First, he once again makes reference to the eruv in Warsaw, which was based on the "permission of the great rabbinic authorities of Israel." Rabbi Graubart relied on the precedent of eruvin in large cities in Eastern Europe and utilized the eruv in Warsaw as his model for a permissible eruv in a large city. Furthermore, Rabbi Graubart stated explicitly that he did not rely on leniencies that would make his eruv controversial or open to dispute. He believed that his arguments for the eruv were irrefutable.

Analysis of Rabbi Graubart's Responsum

As noted above, the case of the Toronto eruv differed from that of other early eruvin in North America in that it faced no rabbinic opposition. We can only speculate as to why this was the case. There had been rabbinic disputes over other matters in Toronto, including over kashrut supervision. The eruv may have been less controversial than kashrut supervision in part because it did not involve the same level of economic interest. However, this factor did not prevent the controversies in St. Louis and Manhattan.

It is notable that one of the major topics of controversy with respect to the earlier eruvin, namely the question of whether the city qualified as a public domain, was not addressed by Rabbi Graubart at all. The population of Toronto in 1921 was 521,893,[53] making it less of an issue than Manhattan, where the population was definitely over six hundred thousand, and St. Louis,

---

52 Graubart, *Havalim ba-ne'imim*, vol. 2, 40.

53 *The Canada Year Book, 1921*, issued by Canada Dominion Bureau of Statistics (Ottawa, 1922), 108.

where the size of the population was in dispute. However, it is interesting that Rabbi Graubart did not feel it necessary to state explicitly that Toronto had a population less than six hundred thousand even though its population did approach that number.

Another subject of dispute with respect to the earlier eruvin was the desirability of creating an eruv for a community in which Jews regularly violated the Sabbath. As discussed earlier, the laxity of Sabbath observance in Toronto was a major concern of Rabbi Graubert's and seems to have been one of the reasons for his creation of the eruv. However, unlike in St. Louis and New York, there does not seem to have been disagreement over this issue and Rabbi Graubart's approach to it in Toronto. The establishment of the eruv helped strengthen Sabbath observance in Toronto without impacting the economic stability or authority of the other rabbis.

Interestingly, Rabbi Graubart's eruv received little publicity, either at the time that it was created or in subsequent years. During the years 1921 through 1922, in which Rabbi Graubart created the eruv, there was no mention of it in the *Yiddisher zhurnal*, the local Yiddish daily. This omission is even more surprising given that the *Yiddisher zhurnal* covered many aspects of Rabbi Graubart's tenure in Toronto, including his arrival[54] and a speech that he delivered on behalf of Yeshivat Etz Chaim in October 1921.[55] Rabbi Graubart's obituary in the *Yiddisher zhurnal* in 1937 called him "the head of the Vaad ha-Rabbanim of Toronto for many years and one of the most important rabbis on the American continent."[56] The obituary went on to praise Rabbi Graubart for his rabbinic writings and his expertise as a talmudic scholar. Over the course of the days following his death and on the occasion of the observance of the thirty-day mourning period, there were several articles about Rabbi Graubart and his contribution to Toronto Jewry.[57] Among the topics covered in these articles were the eulogies delivered at his funeral, his biography and background in Poland, and his involvement in the Toronto Jewish community. There was not one mention of the eruv that he built in any of these articles. The only mention of Rabbi Graubart's eruv in the *Yiddisher zhurnal* appeared in the history of Orthodoxy in Toronto written

---

54 *Yiddisher zhurnal*, August 20, 1920, 1; August 22, 1920, 1; August 23, 1920, 1; and August 25, 1920, 4.

55 Ibid., October 5, 1921, 1.

56 Ibid., October 7, 1937.

57 See *Yiddisher zhurnal*, October 8, 1937, 4; October 10, 1937, 1, 4; October 11, 1937, 5; October 14, 1937, 4; and November 8, 1937, 1, 5. There is also no mention of the Toronto eruv in the obituary in *Ha-Pardes*.

by Nachman Shemen, which was serialized in the *Yiddisher zhurnal* in 1950.[58] When describing Rabbi Graubart, Shemen wrote, "Graubart used his energy for the sake of Sabbath observance and Jewish education. He created an eruv in the town, an innovation in America."[59] It would seem that although Rabbi Graubart considered his eruv important for curbing Sabbath violation, he did not think it necessary to publicize it beyond the community of observant Jews that had requested it. Any Jew who worked on the Sabbath would not have thought twice about carrying without an eruv, so publicizing it would not have prevented the Sabbath desecration that Rabbi Graubart believed had to be addressed through his public sermons on Saturday morning in Kensington Market.

The Extension of the Toronto Eruv

In December 1950, Rabbi Abraham Price wrote an article in the rabbinical journal *Ha-Pardes* outlining his extension of the Toronto eruv, which was necessitated by the movement of the Toronto Jewish community to northern Toronto.[60] Rabbi Price was born in 1900 in Kielce, Poland, and was a disciple of Rabbi Abraham Borenstein, founder of the Sochatchover Hasidic dynasty and author of the well-known volume of responsa *Avnei Nezer*. Rabbi Price spent some time in Berlin and Paris before arriving in Toronto in 1937, where he became the dean of the newly founded Torat Chaim yeshiva and the rabbi of a number of congregations consisting mainly of Polish Jews called Chevra Shas. In 1941, he ordained three students, who were the first rabbis to be ordained in Canada. He served this rabbinic role in Toronto until his death in 1994.[61]

Between 1921, when Rabbi Graubart's eruv was created, and 1951, the Jewish population in Toronto grew from 34,000 to 66,000. This growth, caused by immigration and natural population increase, created an "almost impassable mass of human beings" in the Kensington area, and the Jewish community began

---

58 Ben Kayfetz records in his recollections of the *Yiddisher zhurnal* that Shmuel Meyer Shapiro, editor of the paper, commissioned Nachman Shemen to write a history of Orthodoxy in Toronto. A fundraising dinner was held, but it did not raise enough money, so the project was cancelled even though the special supplement had already been printed. It is not clear whether the serialized version that appeared in the paper predated or postdated this fuller version. See Ben Kayfetz, "The Toronto Jewish Press," *Canadian Jewish Historical Society Journal* 7, no. 1 (Spring 1983): 40–42.

59 *Yiddisher zhurnal*, April 19, 1950, 5.

60 Avraham Aharon Price, "Tikkun eruvin," *Ha-Pardes* 25, no. 4 (Tevet 5711/1951): 11–38.

61 His obituary appeared in *Ha-Pardes* 68, no. 8 (Iyyar 1994): 30–31.

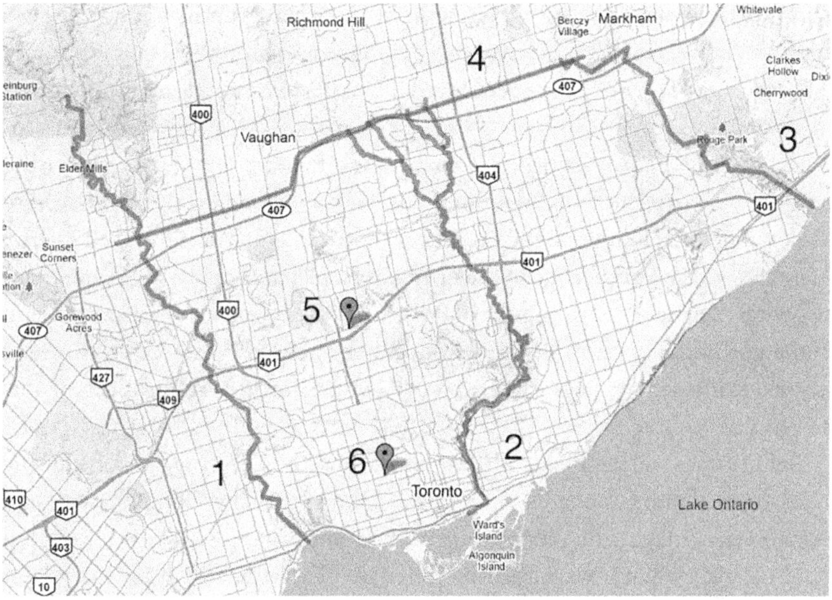

FIGURE 5. Boundaries of the extended Toronto Eruv. Image from Google Maps, accessed April 30, 2011.

to move northward.[62] However, this relocation occurred with minimal Orthodox participation. In 1954, only seven of the city's forty-eight synagogues lay north of Bloor Street, the northern border of Rabbi Graubart's eruv. The majority of synagogues and the social service agencies remained in the downtown area still enclosed by the eruv. However, even the first trickle of northern movement of the Jewish community, which included a small portion of the Orthodox community, required an expansion of the boundaries of the eruv.[63]

Rabbi Price began his article by explaining that he had been asked by many Jews in Toronto to expand the eruv to allow for Jews in the new neighborhoods to carry on the Sabbath. He added that the expanded eruv would also save many people from Sabbath violation, since even religious people were carrying on the Sabbath. Although he clearly accepted the legitimacy of Rabbi Graubart's eruv, he wrote that he had the opportunity to create an eruv without the leniencies that Rabbi Graubart had relied upon. He explained that he had received letters of approbation from rabbis in Israel regarding the extension of the eruv in

---

62 See *Jewish Standard*, June 1949.

63 For a description of the suburbanization of the Toronto Jewish community and its significance, see Etan Diamond, *And I Will Dwell in Their Midst: Orthodox Judaism in Suburbia* (Chapel Hill, NC, 2000), esp. 26–54.

Toronto. However, he chose not to publicize these letters until he had shared his explanation with the American rabbinic community through the publication of this article in *Ha-Pardes*. He encouraged all rabbis to respond to his article and to correct any errors.[64]

Rabbi Price began his halakhic analysis by defining the boundaries of the new eruv. He explained that the three sides of Rabbi Graubart's eruv that were enclosed by the Humber and Don Rivers and Lake Ontario still served as eruv boundaries. The only change in the eruv was his reliance on the telegraph poles and wires that ran the entire length of Wilson Ave (see #5 on map). The expansion of the northern border of the eruv from Bloor Street to Wilson Avenue served to include most of the Jews who had moved to the northern suburbs during this period.[65]

Rabbi Price went on to explain the ways in which this new eruv was halakhically superior to Rabbi Graubart's eruv. First, in the 1920s, the Humber River had been on the outskirts of Toronto and far from any houses. Rabbi Price quoted Rabbi Yisrael Walfish, who described the eruv that he had built in his town of Zakroczym, Poland, at the end of the nineteenth century. Rabbi Walfish stated that if the eruv boundary were too far from the city, the eruv would be invalid.[66] Rabbi Price pointed out that, by 1950, there were houses built all the way to the Humber River, so this would not create a problem regarding the Toronto eruv. Furthermore, he explained that Rabbi Graubart had had no choice but to rely on telephone poles and wires that ran in the middle of Bloor Street, thereby excluding the northern sidewalk from the eruv. This created potential confusion for people. However, on Wilson Avenue, the telegraph poles and wires were located on the northern side of the northern sidewalk, so both sidewalks were included in the new eruv.[67]

At this point in the article, he discussed the most significant difference between his eruv and the earlier one. In 1921, the population of Toronto had been less than six hundred thousand, so Rabbi Graubart was able to avoid the issue of whether Toronto constituted a public domain. Writing in 1950, Rabbi Price explained, "In Toronto, the city where I reside, the population is approximately 1.2 million, and the streets are very wide, with many of them exceeding the width of sixteen cubits. Is it therefore possible that Toronto has

---

64 Price, "Tikkun eruvin," 11–12.
65 Ibid., 11.
66 Yisrael Yaakov Walfish, *Maḥshevot Yisra'el* (Warsaw, 1900), no. 105.
67 Walfish, *Maḥshevot Yisra'el*, 11–12.

the status of a public domain?"[68] Rabbi Price went on to argue that modern cities do not have the status of a public domain.

First, Rabbi Price explained that local law limited the access that people had to the main streets: people were not allowed to walk on the streets and were only allowed to cross the streets at certain designated places and walk on the sidewalks. He explained that a public domain must have streets of sixteen cubits that are accessible to people and that this requirement was not met by the streets of Toronto. Furthermore, Rabbi Price explained that the large streets in each city were reserved for cars and trolleys and that these cars and trolleys had the status of their own private domains. Therefore, the people riding in cars and trolleys would not count toward the six hundred thousand needed to constitute a public domain. Rabbi Price cited Rabbi Israel Trunk, who claimed in the late nineteenth century in Poland that people who rode the trains were not included in the tally of six hundred thousand.[69]

Rabbi Price wrote that his student Rabbi Gedalia Felder had shown him that this argument for city streets not having the status of public domain was mentioned in the responsa of Rabbi Abraham Yudelovitz in the name of a volume abbreviated TK"Z.[70] Rabbi Price wrote that he was not familiar with this volume and did not know what the abbreviation stood for. In his own volume on eruvin, Rabbi Felder wrote that the TK"Z was the *Tikvat Zekhariah*, written by Rabbi Rosenfeld, who used this same argument to claim that the streets of St. Louis did not constitute a public domain. Rabbi Yudelovitz disagreed with Rabbi Rosenfeld for the following reasons: First, he argued that the even though people did not walk in the streets, the street was included in the public domain, thus creating a combination of street and sidewalk that was wider than sixteen cubits. Furthermore, he argued that the reason people didn't walk on the street was fear of being injured and not a law prohibiting it. Therefore, Rabbi Yudelovitz argued that the street was accessible to people and that if the population of a city exceeded six hundred thousand, the city would have the status of a public domain. Rabbi Price disagreed, arguing that there was no real distinction between the inability to walk on the street due to fear or due to a law

---

68 Ibid., 15. While it is difficult to determine the exact boundaries of Toronto that Rabbi Price considered in his population estimate, the population of the area that is occupied by the City of Toronto in 2010 was 1,117,470 in 1951. See "Population," City of Toronto Archives, http://www.toronto.ca/archives/toronto_history_faqs.htm#population.

69 Israel Trunk, *She'elot u-teshuvot yeshu'ot malko* (Petrokow, 1927), no. 27; and Price, "Tikkun eruvin," 15–16.

70 Abraham Aaron Yudelowitz, *Sefer she'elot u-teshuvot beit av*, 2nd ed. (New York, 1919), no. 5, paragraph 10, and no. 9, section 2. See Zecharia Rosenfeld, *Tikvat Zekhariah* (Chicago, 1896), vol. 2, 40–41.

prohibiting such activity. Therefore, Rabbi Price agreed with Rabbi Rosenfeld that even though Toronto had a population that exceeded six hundred thousand, it was not a public domain.[71]

Regarding the use of telephone poles and wires to create the eruv boundary, Rabbi Price agreed with Rabbi Graubart's explanation that because in North American cities, the wires ran on top of the crossbar that protruded from the main telephone pole, the telephone wires constituted an acceptable symbolic doorway that even the rabbinic authorities who disqualified the use of telegraph poles and wires in Eastern Europe would allow. Rabbi Graubart, however, had argued that it was sufficient to place small poles at the foot of the telephone poles at each end of the street, while Rabbi Price argued that small poles should be placed at the foot of each and every telephone pole that would be used as part of the eruv boundary. He cited Rabbi Walfish, who inserted these poles of ten handbreadths under each telegraph pole in Zakroczym.[72] Rabbi Price explained that these small poles should be inserted because the government permitted the Jewish community to insert these poles, and so there would be nothing lost by adding them to the eruv. He also addressed the concern that the rivers were not adequate eruv boundaries because they were not *mukaf le-dirah*, created to enclose the city, and that it was necessary for at least one side of the eruv to be *mukaf le-dirah*. Rabbi Price explained that the symbolic doorway created by the telephone poles and wires on Wilson Avenue was *mukaf le-dirah*, since it was constructed after the city was inhabited. However, he added that since the entire eruv relied on the fact that this symbolic doorway was *mukaf le-dirah*, it was preferable to include as many stringencies as possible, such as the insertion of small poles at regular intervals.[73]

Finally, regarding the use of bridges as eruv boundaries, Rabbi Price explained that there were many bridges that crossed the Don and Humber Rivers. Each one of them had a structure at each end to prevent workers from falling into the water. However, none of these bridges was covered, and it would be impossible to install symbolic doorways on them. Did these bridges create breaches in the eruv? Rabbi Price made several arguments for the inclusion of the bridges as eruv boundaries. First, he suggested that the reason that bridges create a breach in an eruv is that people pass over the bridges and thereby nullify the separation between domains that the bridge creates. However, since the bridges were

---

71 See Gedaliah Felder, *Yesodei Yeshurun* (Jerusalem, n.d.), 2:277. Rabbi Price's discussion of this topic can be found in Price, "Tikkun eruvin," 17–23.

72 Walfish, *Maḥshevot Yisrael*, no. 68.

73 Price, "Tikkun eruvin," 28–29.

utilized mainly by cars and trolleys and not pedestrians, and the walking traffic on the bridges did not come close to six hundred thousand, the bridges did not create a break in the eruv wall. Nonetheless, Rabbi Price stated that the bridges that were wider than ten cubits still created a potential break in the eruv wall. To solve this, he explained that Rabbi Ezekiel Landau only considered bridges to create a break in an eruv wall when a bridge was within ten cubits (about fifteen feet) of the water.[74] The bridges in Toronto were much higher than fifteen feet above the water and therefore did not create a break in the eruv wall.

Although Rabbi Price combined these different explanations to defend the use of bridges as eruv boundaries in Toronto, he concluded his article with the following comment:

> However, it is preferable when possible to fix the bridges and to fulfill the various opinions regarding the eruv. Therefore, I have searched for a way in which we can create symbolic doorways on the bridges.[75]

He wrote that he had decided to close off each of the streets that reached the bridges with their own symbolic doorways, thereby eliminating the need to rely on the bridges as eruv boundaries.[76]

Later Controversy

Initially, Rabbi Price's eruv was accepted without rabbinic opposition in Toronto. In the 1980s, however, Rabbi Price's eruv became a point of conflict within the Orthodox community in Toronto. While the opposition was initially muted, in 1987, Rabbi Jacob Sofer, a rabbi brought to the community by the Reichmann family, publicly denounced Rabbi Price's eruv and claimed that anyone who relied on this eruv would be in violation of the laws of the Sabbath. Immediately, Rabbi Price's supporters issued statements in support of his eruv, and Rabbi Price wrote an unpublished defense of his eruv.[77] In this twenty-seven page typewritten draft, Rabbi Price presented further support from rabbinic sources

---

74 Landau, *Nodah bi-Yehudah,* 2nd ed., Oraḥ ḥayyim, no. 42.
75 Price, "Tikkun eruvin," 37.
76 Ibid., 37.
77 The anti-eruv declaration was signed by five Toronto rabbis, including Rabbi Sofer. For a description of the dispute concerning the eruv, see *The Canadian Jewish News,* March 26, 1987, 5; August 27, 1987, 3; and December 17, 1987, 20.

for his eruv, and he described the extensions of the eruv that he had undertaken since 1950 and certain minor improvements that he had made to the eruv.[78]

In the last section of his essay, Rabbi Price addressed the *maḥmirim*, "stringent ones," who had tried to bring together all the possible stringencies in order to declare the Toronto eruv invalid. He asserted that the tradition throughout the ages, from the talmudic period to the present day, was to be lenient in the laws of eruvin. He cited a proof from the Gemara stating that if the rabbis were strict and did not allow the creation of *eruvei ḥaẓerot* ("courtyard eruvin") on festivals, there would be great harm, since people would forget and carry on the Sabbath. Rabbi Price understood this gemara as stating that being strict regarding eruvin leads people to sin.[79] In support of the idea that the tradition had always been to be lenient regarding eruvin, he pointed to the example of eruvin in large European cities.

Although Rabbi Price emphasized the tradition of being lenient regarding eruvin, he described his Toronto eruv without any reference to leniencies. He wrote: "Anyone with a brain in his head will realize that the eruv that I have built in Toronto is ideal, with its three sides surrounded by water and the fourth side having a symbolic doorway that is better than any symbolic doorway that I have seen in the world."[80]

He concluded by warning those who announced that it was forbidden to carry in Toronto on the Sabbath that they would "pay the religious price" and that their remorse after the fact would not suffice. He cited as proof the letter Rabbeinu Asher sent to the rabbi in Fredes threatening to excommunicate him if he did not build an eruv in that city.[81]

In spite of Rabbi Price's defense of his eruv, there was a group of Jews in Toronto who believed that Rabbi Price had relied on certain leniencies in the expansion of the eruv. At the suggestion of Rabbi Shlomo Miller, head of the Kollel Avreichim of Toronto, several members of the Toronto community travelled to Israel to meet with Rabbi Sholom Yosef Eliashiv, one of the leading rabbinic authorities of the ultra-Orthodox community in Jerusalem. Rabbi Eliashiv permitted the eruv in Toronto because there had been a tradition of having an eruv in Toronto since 1921. However, he only consented on the condition that a majority of the eruv boundaries consist of fences and not symbolic doorways. By this time, the Jewish community was in a position to

---

78 Abraham Price, *Tikkun eruvin he-ḥadash be-ir Toronto Canada* (Toronto, 1987).

79 B. Beiẓ. 16b; and Rashi on Beiẓ. 16b, s.v. *keivan*.

80 Price, *Tikkun eruvin he-ḥadash*, 21.

81 Ibid., 25–26.

work with the two railway companies, Canadian Pacific and Canadian National, to construct the necessary fences to serve as eruv boundaries. This eruv was completed in 1995, shortly after Rabbi Price's death.[82]

Conclusion

The Toronto eruv was the first of the North American eruvin that did not engender initial opposition. Halakhically, the Toronto eruv posed few problems for Rabbi Graubart. The population did not exceed six hundred thousand, and three of the eruv boundaries were created by the rivers and hills. The fourth eruv wall was created by the telegraph poles on Bloor Street, which ran uninterrupted from east to west, resulting in an uncomplicated eruv configuration. Rabbi Graubart relied heavily on the precedent of the Warsaw eruv, which had been supported by Rabbi Yitzchak Meir Alter in the mid-eighteenth century. He was clearly familiar with the eruv on the Lower East Side of Manhattan, as he cited a letter written to him by Rabbi Levinstein and also referred to Rabbi Seigel's volume. However, he did not engage with Rabbi Seigel's responsum itself (or that of Rabbi Rosenfeld before him), referring only to the approbation to Rabbi Seigel's volume by Rabbi Mordekhai Schwadron, the great Polish halakhic authority. Rabbi Graubart's reliance on the Polish rabbinic authorities and the precedent that he drew from the Warsaw eruv are not surprising, since Rabbi Graubart had only recently arrived in Toronto when he began his eruv project. He was both more familiar and more comfortable with the Polish rabbinic world than with the world of the American Orthodox rabbinate.

When Rabbi Price began to address the Toronto eruv in 1950, there had been significant changes in the Toronto Jewish community. Population growth required Rabbi Price to address the issue of whether Toronto was a public domain, which Rabbi Graubart had been able to ignore. In addition, although Rabbi Price praised Rabbi Graubart's eruv, he attempted to improve upon it. The biggest improvement involved the insertion of small poles underneath each telephone pole on the new northern boundary of the eruv. Rabbi Price explained that even though this addition to the eruv was not necessary, since the Jewish community was able to receive permission to insert these poles, it should be done. This is the first mention of a Jewish community in either Europe or

82 See "History of Eruvim in Toronto," Toronto Eruv, https://www.torontoeruv.org/history-of-eruvim-in-toronto/; and the pamphlet "The Toronto Community Eruv," published by the Toronto Community Eruv Committee in 1998.

North America receiving explicit permission to erect any kind of constructed eruv boundary.

The ability of the Jewish community to receive permission from the government to assist in the construction of city eruvin changed the mindset of community rabbis. No longer did they need to rely only on leniencies. In his 1950 article, Rabbi Price emphasized many times that even though Rabbi Graubart's eruv was acceptable, his own eruv was acceptable according to a greater number of rabbinic sources. It is unfortunate that neither Rabbi Graubart nor Rabbi Price described the manner in which they leased the city, as that may have also reflected this change in relationship with local officials.

In response to the criticism of Rabbi Sofer and his supporters, Rabbi Price defended the principle of leniency regarding the creation of eruvin throughout Toronto's history. Nevertheless, Rabbi Price wrote in his 1987 defense of his eruv that the symbolic doorway that he utilized was the best in the world. In that unpublished responsum, he tried to strike a balance between defending the principle of leniency regarding eruvin and arguing that his eruv was based on the strictest interpretation of the laws of city eruvin.

Rabbi Price wrote that he was not familiar with Rabbi Rosenfeld's work and was unable to decipher its abbreviation. It is interesting that Rabbi Price, a rabbinic scholar who was writing an article about eruvin in North America in 1951, was not familiar with *Eruv ve-hoẓa'ah*. It is not clear whether this was because *Eruv ve-hoẓa'ah* was not available or because Rabbi Price, like Rabbi Graubart, was more interested in the Polish precedent and rabbinic authorities than the American Orthodox rabbis who had addressed this issue. In any case, there was yet to be a tradition of North American eruvin in which later eruvin were based on the precedent of earlier eruvin.

5

The Manhattan Eruv, 1949–1962

The creation of the Manhattan *eruv* in the decade following the Holocaust represented the start of a new period in the history of American *eruvin*. The debate surrounding this eruv involved a large number of rabbinic authorities, many of whom had come to the United States following World War II. They had come from cities and towns in Eastern Europe that had been enclosed by eruvin, and they wanted to recreate at least this part of their previous lives. Yet for the first time, their halakhic argumentation looked not only toward European precedent but to the halakhic literature on earlier North American eruvin.

As an island, Manhattan would seem to be easier to enclose with an eruv than the other North American cities in which eruvin had been built. Yet its large population and the particulars of its bridges and sea walls made the creation of this eruv the most complex yet. In the debate surrounding the eruv, several rabbis seriously considered the possibility of adding new construction rather than relying entirely on existing boundaries, and new symbolic doorways were ultimately added. This, along with the leasing of the city from Mayor Wagner rather than a local police officer, reflected an increasingly strong relationship between the Jewish community and local authorities.

Background to the Eruv Debate

In 1936, Rabbi Yosef Eliyahu Henkin, the leading rabbinic authority on the Lower East Side, wrote, "There are many observant Jews, and especially those Hasidim from Poland, who carry here on the street [Lower East Side] on the Sabbath relying on the permission of Rabbi Joshua Seigel of Sherps."[1] However, by the time Rabbi Henkin made this observation, many of New York's Orthodox Jews had migrated from the Lower East Side. In the early twentieth century, almost seventy-five percent of all New York Jews lived on the Lower East Side within Rabbi Seigel's eruv. However, by the 1920s, many Jews had begun to move to other neighborhoods in Manhattan and the outer boroughs. During the 1920s, 160,000 Jews left the Lower East Side, leaving 100,000 Jews in a neighborhood where there had once been over a quarter of a million.[2]

Large numbers of Russian Jews from the Lower East Side had already moved to the northern parts of the city shortly after the turn of the century. In 1904, the superintendent of the YMHA on Ninety-Second Street and Lexington Avenue observed, "Numbers of people are moving uptown from the lower sections of the city and we are feeling the effects of the invasion."[3] The first decade of the twentieth century saw a mass movement of Russian Jews to Harlem. By 1910, over 100,000 Jews lived in Harlem. The Jewish presence in Harlem began to decline in the 1920s. Slowly, the synagogues of Harlem began to relocate, with Congregation Anshe Emeth leading the way in 1917 by merging with a new congregation in Washington Heights, in northern Manhattan. By 1926, Shaarei Zedek, Ohab Zedek, and Anshe Chesed had all relocated to the Upper West Side.[4]

This relocation of Jews to the northern and then western parts of Manhattan meant that a majority of Manhattan's Jews no longer lived in the area enclosed by Rabbi Seigel's eruv. In addition, Rabbi Henkin argued that Rabbi Seigel's eruv was no longer halakhically acceptable because of new bridges that had been built since Rabbi Seigel wrote his defense of the eruv, such as the Triborough Bridge, which was built in 1936 and connected Manhattan to Queens. Rabbi

---

1 Yosef Eliyahu Henkin, *Luaḥ ha-yovel shel Ezrat Torah* (New York, 1936), 62, reprinted in his *Edut le-Yisra'el* (New York, 1949), 151.

2 Deborah Dash Moore, *At Home in America: Second-Generation New York Jews* (New York, 1981), 19.

3 *Thirteenth Annual Report and Yearbook of the YMHA, 1904*, 68, quoted in Jenna Weissman Joselit, *New York's Jewish Jews: The Orthodox Community in the Interwar Years* (Bloomington, IN, 1990), 9.

4 For the history of Jewish Harlem, see Jeffrey S. Gurock, *When Harlem Was Jewish, 1870–1930* (New York, 1979).

Henkin also claimed that Rabbi Seigel had leased the city for ten years and that this lease had never been renewed.[5]

As a result of these demographic and halakhic issues, the New York rabbinic community began to reexamine the possibility of creating an eruv that would surround the entire borough of Manhattan. In 1949, according to one report, Rabbi Shimon Kalish, the Amshinover Rebbe, would telephone other rabbis every Friday afternoon to encourage them to create an eruv around Manhattan.[6] Rabbi Tzvi Eisenstadt, a respected rabbinic scholar who had been head of a yeshiva in Cracow and immigrated to Brooklyn in 1948, surveyed the entire borough and wrote a piece in 1948 outlining the issues in creating an eruv around Manhattan, deciding that the creation of an eruv was halakhically permissible. Manhattan was an island surrounded by sea walls and met the requirements of eruv enclosures that had been built throughout the centuries. He concluded his work by explaining that he had "written all of this as a suggestion that should be addressed by the rabbinic authorities of the city. And, even if they find a problem with these conclusions according to one opposing view, they should consider whether it is preferable to permit carrying on the Sabbath according to most rabbinic authorities or to leave the situation as it is without any eruv at all."[7]

In April 1949, Rabbi Michael Weissmandel, the head of the Nitra Yeshiva in Mt. Kisco, New York, wrote to Rabbi Eisenstadt, urging him to have Rabbi Yonatan Steif, "a rabbi in Brooklyn whose authority is respected by the masses," lead the initiative.[8] Rabbi Weissmandel also encouraged Rabbi Eisenstadt to begin by creating an eruv around Brooklyn before moving on to the rest of Manhattan. A Brooklyn eruv, he explained, would involve erecting symbolic doorways. Consequently, uninformed people would see that care and precaution was being used in the eruv's creation. On the other hand, the proposed Manhattan eruv did not involve any physical changes because the river walls created acceptable eruv boundaries. Consequently, uninformed people might question what steps had been taken by the rabbis to alter the conditions that had precluded the establishment of an eruv earlier. However, Rabbi Weissmandel

5 Henkin, *Luaḥ ha-yovel ſhel Ezrat Torah*, 62, reprinted in hif *Edut le-Yiſra'el*, 151.

6 Menahem Mendel Kasher, "Tikkun eruvin be-Manhattan New York," in his *Divrei Menaḥem* (Jerusalem, 1980), vol. 2, 5 (special pagination at conclusion of volume).

7 Rabbi Menahem Tzvi Eisenstadt, "Kuntres haẓa'ah le-tikkun eruvin be-ir Manhattan Nu York," in Menahem Tzvi Eisenstadt, *Sefer minḥat Ẓevi* (New York, 2003), 28–38. An abridged version of the article can be found in Kasher, "Tikkun eruvin," 117. For a biography of Rabbi Eisenstadt, see the introduction to *Sefer minḥat Ẓevi.*

8 Michael Dov Weissmandel, *Torat ḥemed* (Mt. Kisco, NY, 1958), no. 1, especially 156–157.

did agree that an eruv could be created in Manhattan and was posthumously included in a list of rabbis who supported it.[9]

Rabbi Eisenstadt sent a copy of his article to Rabbi Steif. In a responsum dated May 25, 1950, Rabbi Steif agreed that an eruv could be created around Manhattan. However, he wrote that the purpose of eruvin is to create peace among Jews, and there were some rabbis who opposed the idea. Therefore, he argued that it would be preferable for each neighborhood to build its own eruv, which would be supervised by the local rabbi. This would avoid the controversy that was brewing in Manhattan.[10]

Rabbi Eisenstadt also sent a copy of his article to Rabbi Menahem Pollak, a great Hungarian rabbinic authority who immigrated to America in 1940 and became a rabbi on the Lower East Side. Rabbi Pollak wrote a lengthy article explaining the permissibility of creating an eruv around Manhattan. He began by explaining that there was a specific need for an eruv in Manhattan "because many people, including Sabbath observers, fail in their observance due to the prohibition of carrying on the Sabbath, and no words of rebuke will prevent this transgression."[11] Regarding Rabbi Eisenstadt's article, Rabbi Pollak wrote, "There has come to my possession an article by my close friend Rabbi Tzvi Eisenstadt, who also wrote about the creation of an eruv in our city, and I have found in it that which is beloved in my eyes."[12]

In 1949, a committee was created for the establishment of the Manhattan eruv under the leadership of Rabbi Yonatan Steif. Rabbi Steif sent a letter to New York Orthodox rabbis and included Rabbi Eisenstadt's and Rabbi Pollak's proposal for a Manhattan eruv.[13] The letter read as follows:

---

9 See Rabbi Weissmandel's letter, Yeshiva University MS 1300 1/9, reprinted in the anonymously edited *Sefer ḥai anokhi le-olam* (New York, 2003), 148; and Kasher, *Divrei Menaḥem*, vol. 2, 10, where Rabbi Weissmandel is included in a list of the rabbis who supported the eruv.

10 The undated responsum to Rabbi Eisenstadt can be found in Yonatan Steif, *Sefer she'elot u-teshuvot ve-ḥiddushei Mahari Steif* (New York, 1968), no. 68, and a more complete version of the letter can be found in Eisenstadt, *Minḥat Ẓevi*, 39–43. The original letter is found in the Yeshiva University Archives MS 1300 1/12. Rabbi Steif wrote additional material on the Manhattan eruv that was published in "Kuntres tikkun eruvin," *Ohr Yisro'el* 8, no. 4 (Sivan 5763 [2003]): 6–9; and "Kuntres tikkun eruvin," *Ohr Yisro'el* 9, no. 1 (Tishrei 5764 [2003]): 6–15.

11 Rabbi Menahem Seigel Pollak, "Kuntres be-inyan tikkun eruvin be-Manhattan," in *Kol ẓevi*, ed. Ari Zahtz and Michoel Zylberman, vol. 7 (New York, 2005), 67–82. The original article is located in Yeshiva University Archives MS 1300 1/8. An abridged version of this article can be found in Kasher, "Tikkun eruvin," 13–14.

12 Pollak, "Kuntres be-inyan tikkun eruvin."

13 Kasher, "Tikkun eruvin," 6.

December 27, 1949
Dear Rabbis,

We are presenting you with the following article written as a suggestion for the creation of an eruv around Manhattan by one of the members of the Vaad Harabonim of New York, who has worked on this article and seeks our reactions. [This refers to Rabbi Menahem Tzvi Eisenstadt together with another article on the topic by Rabbi Menahem Seigel Pollak.]

Therefore, it is our desire to receive the approbations of other Torah giants so that we may begin this work immediately to establish an eruv in Manhattan so that thousands and tens of thousands will not violate the laws of the Sabbath. . . .

If anyone has any suggestions, they should mail them to our most important colleague, Rabbi Yonatan Steif, at the above address. In order to facilitate this process, if we do not receive your reply within ten days, we will record you as agreeing with this proposal.

Vaad Le-Ma'an Ha-Eruv Be-Manhattan Nu York
[Committee for the Sake of the Manhattan Eruv, New York][14]

The next rabbi to address the issue of an eruv in Manhattan was Rabbi Menahem Kasher. A well-known rabbinic scholar and author, Rabbi Kasher wrote a lengthy article arguing for the permissibility of creating an eruv around Manhattan in an appendix to a volume called *Torah sheleimah*.[15] When the article was republished in his collection of responsa, he added the following note: "Three years ago I received from one of the illustrious rabbis in New York, the head of the Committee for the Sake of the Manhattan Eruv, two articles from important rabbis that explained the permissibility of creating an eruv around Manhattan. At that point, I was inclined to be strict and not allow the eruv. However, now I have returned to the topic and I realize that there is room to permit the Manhattan eruv, as I will describe."[16]

In 1954, Rabbi Joseph Moskowitz, the Shatzer Rebbe, who lived on the Lower East Side of Manhattan, wrote an article in the rabbinic journal *Ha-Ma'or* in which

---

14 Ibid., 6.
15 Menahem Kasher, *Torah sheleimah* (New York, 1953), vol. 15, appendix.
16 Kasher, "Tikkun eruvin," 43.

he outlined his reasoning for allowing an eruv to be created in Manhattan.[17] He concluded his article: "Here there is a mitzvah [to create an eruv] to save the tens of thousands who unintentionally violate the Sabbath. Furthermore, even for the religious Jews, it is impossible to avoid carrying on the Sabbath."[18] He included several comments from Rabbi Menachem Mendel Schneerson, the Lubavitcher Rebbe, in his article. Rabbi Schneerson stated, "When Rabbi Eisenstadt asked my opinion, I praised him and all those involved in this project for the sake of the community. However, this endeavor should be done without any publicity in order to avoid several concerns."[19] Rabbi Schneerson later wrote to Rabbi Moskowitz that, although he had earlier commented upon the importance of creating this eruv, his family tradition was not to rely on city eruvin.[20]

There was, however, more opposition to the creation of the Manhattan eruv. In the spring of 1952, Rabbi Moshe Feinstein, the renowned Lithuanian rabbinic authority who lived on the Lower East Side, wrote a letter to Rabbi Eisenstadt in which he explained that he believed that one should be strict and not create an eruv around Manhattan.[21] Additionally, in his article in *Ha-Ma'or,* Rabbi Moskowitz explained that he had shown his article to Rabbi Yoel Teitelbam (the Satmar Rebbe) and Rabbi Feinstein, who both opposed the creation of an eruv in Manhattan. In response to these rabbinic opponents of the eruv, Rabbi Moskowitz wrote, "If we follow each of these stringencies . . . how could we eat meat, marry, or divorce, and especially how could we sell our *ḥameẓ*?"[22]

In his 1959 volume, Rabbi Moskowitz included letters from both Rabbi Henkin and Rabbi Feinstein. Rabbi Henkin reiterated his doubts about whether an eruv could successfully be constructed around Manhattan, noting that there were breaks in the sea walls under the bridges and in other places and that there were points where high beaches replaced the sea walls. However, he concluded that if the sea walls were determined to be acceptable eruv boundaries, the eruv would be valid because no action would be required.[23] Rabbi Feinstein complimented the rabbinic scholarship of the volume, commenting that he agreed with certain aspects of the book and disagreed with other aspects. Despite these disagreements, he encouraged everyone to assist Rabbi Moskowitz in

---

17 Joseph David Moskowitz, "Tikkun eruvin be-Manhattan Nu York," *Ha-Ma'or* 5, no. 8 (October 1954): 11–14.

18 Moskowitz, "Tikkun eruvin," 14.

19 Ibid., 12.

20 Ibid., 10.

21 The three responsa that constitute Rabbi Feinstein's answer to Rabbi Eisenstadt are found in Moshe Feinstein, *Iggerot Mosheh* (New York, 1959), Oraḥ ḥayyim, vol. 1, nos. 138–140.

22 Moskowitz, "Tikkun eruvin be-Manhattan," 15–16.

23 Joseph David Moskowitz, *Sefer tikkun eruvin be-ir Manhattan* (New York, 1959), 5–8.

the publication of the volume and added, "The rabbis will address the issues included within it." Rabbi Feinstein neither supported nor opposed the eruv in this letter.[24] Both Rabbi Henkin and Rabbi Feinstein wrote about the Manhattan eruv in several different publications, in some cases expressing opposition to the creation of the eruv and in other places taking a more neutral stance.

In 1959, Rabbi Moskowitz, together with Rabbi Eisenstadt and Rabbi Raphael Zilber, toured the entire borough of Manhattan to determine the viability of constructing an eruv. They drove around the island and then rented a boat to allow them to investigate the piers more carefully. On March 26, 1959, the rabbis gathered in the home of Rabbi Henkin to hear a report from Rabbi Eisenstadt on their findings. At that meeting, Rabbi Eisenstadt reiterated his belief that an eruv could be created around Manhattan.[25]

The next episode in the debate regarding the Manhattan eruv took place in June 1959, when the Committee for the Sake of the Eruv joined a meeting of the Orthodox rabbinate of New York to discuss the Manhattan eruv and it was decided that each rabbi would have three months to submit his comments about the eruv.[26] During this three-month period, Rabbi Moshe Bunim Pirutinsky, the Secretary of the Committee for Sake of the Eruv, wrote a lengthy article in *Ha-Pardes* reviewing the major issues regarding the eruv and concluding that it was permissible to create an eruv around Manhattan. He included a note at the beginning of the article that his purpose was to assist other rabbis in responding to the issue in a timely fashion.[27]

At this first meeting in June 1959, several rabbis suggested that the matter be presented to rabbis in Israel to solicit their opinions. The matter was thus taken to Rabbi Tzvi Pesach Frank, the Chief Rabbi of Jerusalem. Rabbi Frank responded that although some rabbis opposed the creation of an eruv in Manhattan and that their reasons were valid, the need for an eruv in Manhattan was great, and the rabbis in New York should be lenient and allow for the creation of an eruv. He cited as precedent the creation of the Warsaw eruv in the mid-nineteenth century, where there was also legitimate opposition to the eruv and rabbis nonetheless supported the creation of an eruv in order to support

---

24 Moskowitz, *Sefer tikkun eruvin*, 8.

25 Moshe Bunim Pirutinsky, "Haẓa'ah le-tikkun eruv be-Manhattan," *Ha-Pardes* 33, no. 9 (June 1959): 10. A more complete version of this article with four additional pages can be found in Yeshiva University Archives MS 1300 2/6.

26 Moskowitz, *Sefer tikkun eruvin*, 169–170; and letter found in Kasher, "Tikkun eruvin," 10.

27 Pirutinsky, "Haẓa'ah le-tikkun eruv be-Manhattan," 8–19.

Sabbath observance.[28] After receiving Rabbi Frank's response, the Committee for the Sake of the Eruv sent a letter to the New York rabbis in March 1960 and stated that, with Rabbi Frank's approval now confirmed, they were prepared to begin the project.

However, the debate continued. In an article in *Ha-Pardes,* Rabbi Pirutinsky explained that he had approached Rabbi Feinstein to discuss Rabbi Feinstein's opposition to the eruv. Rabbi Feinstein responded that, although he followed the rabbinic views that did not allow for the creation of an eruv in Manhattan, other rabbis had the right to create an eruv in Manhattan, as the rabbis who permitted an eruv in Manhattan were more numerous than those who prohibited it.[29] Based on the opinions of Rabbi Henkin and Rabbi Feinstein, Rabbi Moskowitz and Rabbi Kasher wrote a letter, dated June 2, 1962, noting that Rabbis Henkin and Feinstein supported the creation of the eruv and informing the recipients that the eruv was functional, as Rabbi Eisenstadt had leased the borough from Mayor Robert Wagner on October 16, 1959, for one dollar for a period of forty-nine years.[30]

Rabbi Aharon Kotler, the head of Beth Medrash Govoha in Lakewood, New Jersey, wrote a responsum in 1962 in which he said that he believed that an eruv could not be created around any city with streets that were more than sixteen cubits wide, clearly prohibiting Manhattan.[31] In addition, Rabbi Simon Schwab of the Khal Adath Jeshurun in Washington Heights, New York, wrote two letters to the Vaad opposing the creation of the Manhattan eruv.[32] This opposition to the eruv continued even after the completion of the project. In June 1962, the Agudath Harabonim distributed a letter that reported on a meeting that took place on June 20, 1962. The letter read:

> In the meeting of the Agudath Harabonim that took place on Wednesday, *Parashat Beha'alotkha,* the 18th of Sivan 5762, it

---

28 Kasher, "Tikkun eruvin," 31–33. Rabbi Frank was first approached for his opinion on the Manhattan eruv in 1955 by the members of the Vaad. See the letter in Yeshiva University Archives MS 1300 2/3.

29 Pirutinsky, "Haẓa'ah le-tikkun eruv be-Manhattan," 14–15.

30 Kasher, "Tikkun eruvin," 16–17. A copy of the lease agreement can be found in the Jewish Center Archives. A handwritten note outlining the terms and length of the lease is located in Yeshiva University Archives 2/12.

31 See the responsum in Aharon Kotler, *Mishnat Rabbi Aharon* (Jerusalem, 1985), 1:6; and the note in Kasher, "Tikkun eruvin," 16.

32 The first letter is found in the Yeshiva University Archives MS 1300 2/10. The second letter was published in Simon Schwab, "Mikhtav be-inyan tikkun eruvin be-Manhattan," *Ha-Pardes* 36, no. 5 (February 1962): 26.

> was decided to publicly announce the decision already made by the Agudath Harabonim that it is absolutely forbidden to establish an eruv in Manhattan and that it is forbidden to carry in Manhattan even after the repairs that have been made or that will be made by some rabbis. Whoever relies on the Manhattan eruv is considered a Sabbath violator.
>
> Aharon Kotler
> Yaakov Kamenetsky
> Gedalia Halevi Schorr
> Chaim Bick
> Moshe Feinstein[33]

This letter was reprinted in *Ha-Pardes* in 1966, announcing that a meeting of the Agudath Harabonim had taken place in April under the leadership of Rabbi Feinstein, at which the decision was made to call upon rabbis to urge their communities not to rely on the Manhattan eruv.[34]

This opposition, however, did not deter the supporters of the eruv. In 1977, Rabbi Israel Silverstein, the chairman of the Committee, wrote to Rabbi Kasher, who was living in Jerusalem, to report that "regarding the Manhattan eruv, all is in order."[35] In 1986, Rabbi Gavriel Zinner, a rabbi in Brooklyn who specialized in the building of eruvin, wrote a responsum in which he supported the Manhattan eruv but suggested that additional symbolic doorways should be constructed to repair certain breaches in the eruv.[36] These symbolic doorways were built under the leadership of Rabbi Jacob J. Schacter of The Jewish Center.[37] The Manhattan eruv remained in operation until 2005, at which point Rabbi Haskel Lookstein, whose father, Rabbi Joseph H. Lookstein, had been one of the original rabbinic supporters of the Manhattan eruv, wrote:

> After months of discussion, it appears that the Manhattan eruv which was established almost fifty years ago can no longer be

---

33 The letter can be found in "The 1979 Flatbush Kol Korei Exposed," Eruv Online, December 01, 2005, http://eruvonline.blogspot.com/2005/12/1979-flatbush-kol-korei-exposed.html, accessed October 5, 2010.

34 *Ha-Pardes* 40, no. 7 (April 1966), inside of front cover.

35 Kasher, "Tikkun eruvin," 17.

36 This responsum is located in The Jewish Center Archives.

37 Documentation of the construction of these symbolic doorways and the correspondence with other rabbis is located in The Jewish Center Archives.

> maintained as a proper eruv. The problem is not halakhic but rather structural. Many changes have taken place over the last decade or two which make it extremely difficult to maintain the kashrut of the eruv. The necessary improvements to bring the eruv up to the standards that Rabbi Kasher, of blessed memory, established would be very expensive to make and, in any event, the nature of traffic and construction in Manhattan make it virtually impossible to assure the *kashrut* of the *eruv* on any given Shabbat.[38]

At that point, the Mechon L'Hoyroa, a rabbinical group from Monsey, New York, built an eruv around sections of Manhattan utilizing the constructed symbolic doorways that had become popular in most community eruvin at the end of the twentieth century.[39]

An Eruv for Observant Jews

In some respects, the debate over the creation of an eruv surrounding Manhattan in the 1950s and 1960s echoed the earlier debates around the creation of eruvin in St. Louis and on the Lower East Side. Rabbis questioned whether the eruv was intended to meet the needs of observant Jews or to prevent those who already violated the Sabbath from being guilty of carrying, and they debated whether having an eruv would prevent Sabbath desecration and lead to greater sin. Yet while Rabbi Rosenfeld in St. Louis, Rabbi Seigel in Manhattan, and Rabbi Graubart in Toronto addressed communities that were, in their view, overwhelmingly lax in their observance of the Sabbath, in 1950s Manhattan there was unquestionably a sizeable community of observant Orthodox Jews.

Rabbi Kasher wrote at the end of his work on the Manhattan eruv:

> It is important to emphasize that we are not establishing this eruv simply for the "sinners." Rather, there are religious people

38 Private communication between Rabbi Haskel Lookstein and the Manhattan Orthodox rabbis, July 1, 2005.

39 For a detailed map of the Manhattan eruv created by the Mechon L'Hoyroa, see "Manhattan Eruv Map," GoogleMaps, http://maps.google.com/maps/ms?hl=en&ie=UTF8&msa=0&msid=113076836900840950588.00044dbfc593b01e16fc3&ll=40.834593,-73.996353&spn=0.121826,0.219727&z=12, accessed November 8, 2010. Mechon L'Hoyroa was later invited to build a community eruv on the Upper West Side of Manhattan, which has been in operation since 1999.

> who are careful even about the prohibition of *mukẓeh* [touching objects that cannot be used on the Sabbath, such as money or electronics] but still carry glasses or handkerchiefs or papers and even *tallitot*. Any rabbi who does not want to fool himself and to recognize the truth will realize this.[40]

Rabbi Kasher went on to point out that this phenomenon was not a new one and that, for hundreds of years, otherwise religious Jews had carried personal items on the Sabbath. While the issue may not have been new, Rabbi Kasher seems to have been the first North American rabbi to promote an eruv specifically for the sake of Orthodox Jews who wanted to enjoy the Sabbath.

Rabbi Bloch, in his 1950 letter to the Vaad, also acknowledged that religious Jews were carrying on the Sabbath. However, he reached a different conclusion. He argued that if an eruv was established in Manhattan, even religious people would forget that carrying on the Sabbath was prohibited when there was no eruv, and this would lead them to carry when they spent the Sabbath outside of Manhattan. Furthermore, he explained that it was very possible for the eruv boundaries to be broken and that no one would be authorized to repair them, leading to mass violation of the Sabbath. Rabbi Bloch concluded that the Vaad must consider whether the benefits of the eruv outweighed the risks or vice versa.[41]

In a letter in February 1950, Rabbi Pollak responded to Rabbi Bloch, defending the establishment of the eruv by explaining that religious Jews in New York who observed the details of Jewish law nevertheless carried on the Sabbath. He argued that it was therefore the obligation of the rabbis to remove this stumbling block and to build an eruv in Manhattan, noting that the mission of the Agudath Harabonim—of which Rabbi Bloch was president—was to promote Sabbath observance.[42]

Rabbi Feinstein held a different view, which he expressed in response to a 1959 article by Rabbi Pirutinsky:

> I do not see a need to establish an eruv here, for it is not like cities in Europe where there was a need for an eruv in order to survive, as it was impossible to prepare water for the animals and other similar things that were crucial for people. However, here

---

40 Kasher, "Tikkun eruvin," 90.

41 Eliyahu Meir Bloch, "Mikhtav be-inyan eruvin be-Manhattan," in *Kol ẓevi*, vol. 7, 20–22.

42 Yeshiva University Archives MS 1300 1/8.

> everything is in the home, and there are even *siddurim* [prayer books] and *ḥumashim* [books containing the Torah readings] in the synagogues. It is only for the sake of the sinners who violate all the laws of the Torah in order to remove the prohibition of carrying on the Sabbath. This must be balanced with the dangerous state that will be created for the religious Jews who will rely on the lenient view without knowing the opinions of the more stringent ones. . . . However, if after proper consideration the supporters of the eruv consider it a necessity for the children or those who carry unintentionally, I do not object, but I cannot participate with them.[43]

Rabbi Feinstein reiterated this point in a letter to Rabbi Leo Jung of The Jewish Center in Manhattan in December 1960. Rabbi Feinstein wrote that although he had decided that it was not acceptable to build an eruv around Manhattan, there were many reputable rabbis who supported the eruv, and he did not criticize them. However, he warned Rabbi Jung that the eruv would cause religious Jews to carry based on lenient opinions that were not acceptable according to many rabbinic authorities.[44]

Rabbi Feinstein made one additional argument opposing the Manhattan eruv for social reasons. He wrote in his response to Rabbi Eisenstadt that perhaps Jerusalem did not have an eruv in the temple period because people came to Jerusalem from other cities, and, if they had been allowed to carry in Jerusalem, they would have assumed that it was permissible to carry in the cities in which they lived. Rabbi Feinstein wrote that, in this regard, Manhattan was similar to Jerusalem, since people came from all over the world, and if they were permitted to carry on the Sabbath in Manhattan, they would assume that it was permissible to carry when they returned to their homes.[45]

Rabbi Pirutinsky, who had quoted Rabbi Feinstein's objections in his article in *Ha-Pardes,* replied to Rabbi Feinstein that the eruv was for the sake of the

---

43 Although Rabbi Pirutinsky wrote in support of the eruv, he wrote that he had shown his article to Rabbi Feinstein, and he included included Rabbi Feinstein's response in his published article, "Haẓa'ah le-tikkun eruv be-Manhattan," *Ha-Pardes* 33, no. 9 (Sivan 5719): 13. Rabbi Moshe Bick said in an interview in 1975 that he had accepted the need for Rabbi Seigel's eruv since at that time the bathrooms were outdoors and people needed to carry keys in order to enter. However, he agreed with Rabbi Feinstein that there was no need for eruvin in the second half of the twentieth century in New York. See Lyle Kamlet, "Eruv Controversy in New York," *Ha-Mevaser* 14, no. 3 (December 30, 1975): 5.

44 Feinstein, *Iggerot Mosheh,* Oraḥ ḥayyim, vol. 4, no. 89.

45 Ibid., vol. 1, no. 139, section 5.

observant Jews who carried personal items on the Sabbath and especially for observant women who could not take their children outside the home without an eruv. Rabbi Pirutinsky was not concerned that people would erroneously conclude that the eruv extended beyond Manhattan, as the Vaad would post eruv maps and signs in all the synagogues outlining the borders of the eruv. Because the eruv was for observant Jews, Rabbi Pirutinsky was confident that these Jews would listen to the rabbis and not irresponsibly carry outside of the eruv.[46]

At the end of his *Tikkun eruvin*, Rabbi Moskowitz enumerated several responses to Rabbi Feinstein's opposition to the Manhattan eruv. He wrote that he disagreed with Rabbi Feinstein's claim that the eruv was only for the sake of the "sinners," arguing that there were thousands of "regular Jews" who observed the Sabbath and did not go to work but had a hard time avoiding carrying. For these people alone, Rabbi Moskowitz said, it was worthwhile to build the eruv. Rabbi Moskowitz also rejected Rabbi Feinstein's claim that an eruv was not needed in America as it was in Europe, arguing that, in America, where people worked hard all week and wanted to walk with their families on the Sabbath, they needed an eruv to allow them to push their children in baby carriages. Otherwise, they would have been stuck at home for the entire day. He wrote that one woman had heard that he was working on building an eruv in Manhattan and had told him that he would be doing her a big favor.

Finally, Rabbi Moskowitz took issue with Rabbi Feinstein's argument that, if carrying was allowed in Manhattan, travelers would return home and assume that carrying was permitted in their hometowns. Rabbi Moskowitz noted that many people claimed that they had no need for a mikveh because their bathtub was more sanitary than a public mikveh, and that did not prevent communities from building mikvaot. The same was true regarding eruvin. The fact that people might do something wrong was not grounds to prevent or even discourage the community from providing the necessary services for the community.[47]

In a subsequent letter dated May 22, 1960, Rabbi Moskowitz addressed a prominent Manhattan rabbi who wrote a letter to many other rabbis arguing that there was no need for an eruv in Manhattan and outlining the risks involved in building this eruv. Rabbi Moskowitz responded to "the rabbis of the synagogues in Manhattan" pointing out that the problem of observant Jews carrying on the Sabbath had not originated in New York. The prophet Jeremiah had warned the

---

46 Pirutinsky, "Haẓa'ah le-tikkun eruv be-Manhattan," 19. There is an elaboration on this issue in the copy of the article in Yeshiva University Archives MS 1300 2/6, 12–13.

47 Moskowitz, *Sefer tikkun eruvin*, 161–164.

people against carrying on the Sabbath, and the tradition of relying on leniencies in the laws of eruvin was based on the fact that observant Jews were nonetheless carrying. He also explained that the concern that people might think that the eruv extended to the other boroughs was not relevant because the Jews who were surrounded by the eruv attended synagogue, and signs would be posted identifying the borders of the eruv. Finally, Rabbi Moskowitz criticized this rabbi for distributing his letter to the broader community of rabbis. He wrote, "A man whose intentions are for the sake of heaven would first approach the members of the Vaad and speak to them face to face."[48]

Two additional letters were written on this issue by Rabbi Simon Schwab, the rabbi of Khal Adath Jeshurun in Washington Heights, New York. In the first letter, dated April 20, 1960, Rabbi Schwab, with the approbation of Rabbi Joseph Breuer, Senior Rabbi of Khal Adath Jeshurun, wrote to the Vaad opposing the establishment of the Manhattan eruv. He explained that most of the rabbis with whom he had spoken believed that Manhattan was a public domain. However, much of Rabbi Schwab's opposition was social. He argued that, if the eruv were created in Manhattan, Jews living in other boroughs would assume that they too could carry on the Sabbath in their neighborhoods. Furthermore, he argued, because the Manhattan eruv did not require any structural changes to the city, Jews would think that halakhah was a joke merely dependent on the rabbinical whim. [49] It is interesting that this argument does not seem to have been made regarding the previous North American eruvin even though they did not require structural changes. It is possible that this heightened sensitivity to how the eruv process would be perceived resulted from the growing sense in the 1970s that Orthodoxy faced a threat from the Conservative movement.[50]

In his second letter, printed in *Ha-Pardes*, Rabbi Schwab elaborated on his opposition to Rabbi Kasher's support for the Manhattan eruv. Rabbi Schwab wrote:

> Everyone agrees that it is a great mitzvah to establish eruvin to prevent Sabbath violation. . . . However, in this time and especially in this country, which is corrupted by arrogance and ignorance, at a time when the ignorant have taken control and young people stand in the place of elders and are not

48 This letter is located in Yeshiva University Archives MS 1300 2/11.

49 This letter is located in Yeshiva University Archives MS 1300 2/10.

50 For a similar fear of the Conservative movement during this period, see Jonathan D. Sarna, "The Debate over Mixed Seating in the American Synagogue," in *The American Synagogue: A Sanctuary Transformed*, ed. Jack Wertheimer (Cambridge, 1987), 363–394.

> embarrassed to misinterpret the Torah . . . we must consider the problems that could arise and the destruction that might come from this innovation . . . for if even one person carries four cubits in a public domain due to this eruv, what will you answer on the Day of Judgment?[51]

Rabbi Schwab was concerned that the eruv would lead this "arrogant" generation to become lax in the general observance of the laws of the Sabbath. Furthermore, he claimed that carrying on the Sabbath was the marker by which one could tell whether someone was part of the observant Jewish community. If they did not carry on the Sabbath, then one could assume that they were strict about the laws of kashrut and that they sent their children to yeshivot. If they carried on the Sabbath, he argued, it would be safe to assume that they were not observant in other areas of Jewish law. In this generation, in which the identification of a Jew as being either Orthodox or Conservative was an important cultural and religious demarcation, this consideration loomed large in the American Orthodox community.

Rabbi Schwab admitted that the eruv would help to prevent the inadvertent Sabbath violator from violating the laws of carrying on the Sabbath. Therefore, he suggested that the eruv be created around Manhattan and the city be leased from the governmental authorities. However, he suggested that the rabbis keep the eruv a secret so that those who carried by accident would not be liable but those who wanted to use the eruv as a vehicle to allow for further Sabbath desecration would not be aware of its existence.[52]

Is Manhattan a Public Domain?

In 1949, the population of Manhattan approached two million people,[53] and the streets were wider than sixteen cubits, which would seem to make it a public domain according to all authorities. In order to create an eruv around the borough, the rabbis had two options: either they could identify walls that surrounded Manhattan, or they could determine that, for some reason, Manhattan did not have the status of a public domain.

---

51 Schwab, "Mikhtav be-inyan tikkun eruvin," 26.

52 Schwab, "Mikhtav be-inyan tikkun eruvin," 26–28.

53 Rabbi Eisenstadt claimed that the population of Manhattan was approximately 1,906,000. See Eisenstadt, *Minḥat Ẓevi*, 28.

In his initial article about the Manhattan eruv, Rabbi Eisenstadt observed that the East Side of Manhattan eruv was the first time in the history of American eruvin where population size became an issue, although it had come up in the context of Eastern European eruvin at the beginning of the twentieth century. He explained that the source of the view that an area must have a population that exceeds six hundred thousand people to be considered a public domain is that the Israelite camp in the desert contained six hundred thousand Jewish men. That calculation, he argued, did not include women, children, or non-Jews. Since Manhattan did not contain six hundred thousand Jewish men, one could argue that it was not a public domain. As he noted, the Ritba states that the number six hundred thousand refers to the number of people who pass through the city and not the number of people who live in the city, and there were six hundred thousand Jewish men who passed through Manhattan each day. However, Rabbi Eisenstadt explained, these people did not travel to Manhattan on the weekends, and so it might not be a public domain. In the end, Rabbi Eisenstadt concluded that, although the arguments against considering Manhattan a public domain were reasonable, they were not conclusive, and so Manhattan must nevertheless be considered a public domain.[54]

Rabbi Steif argued that Manhattan did not have the status of a public domain because a public domain requires that the streets be *mefulash*, that is, run straight from one end of the city to the other. Since Manhattan did not have any streets that ran straight from one end to the other, it was not to be considered a public domain. In addition, Rabbi Steif claimed that if an area was filled with houses, then it did not have the status of a public domain. He supported this opinion by noting that while the Levite camp in the desert had the status of a public domain, the Israelite camp was not a public domain even though six hundred thousand passed through it daily, which he attributed to the fact that the Israelite camp was filled with tents.[55]

Rabbi Pollak observed that, according to Rashi, six hundred thousand must pass through the city each day for it to be considered a public domain,[56] and Manhattan would meet that criterion. However, according to the *Shulḥan arukh*, six hundred thousand must pass through at least one of the streets of the city

54 Eisenstadt, *Minḥat Ẓevi*, 28. See Ritba on b. Eruv. 59a, s.v. *matnitin*.

55 See Rabbi Steif's opinion in "Kuntres tikkun eruvin," *Ohr Yisro'el* 8, no. 4 (Sivan 5763 [2003]): 7; and "Kuntres tikkun eruvin," *Ohr Yisro'el* 9, no. 1 (Tishrei 5764 [2003]): 6 and 13.

56 Rashi on b. Eruv. 59a, s.v. *ir shel rabbim*. Rabbi Pollak infers Rashi's view that the six hundred thousand must pass through the city from the fact that Rashi offers his definition of a public domain in reference to a "city of many people."

each day.[57] Rabbi Pollak claimed that even on streets such as Broadway, where there were six hundred thousand people during the week, there were fewer on Sundays, and so Broadway would not be considered a public domain.[58]

Rabbi Moskowitz also believed that Manhattan did not have the status of a public domain. He argued that the number of people in Manhattan each day did not reach six hundred thousand because each person counted only once even if they entered and left Manhattan several times during the day.[59] Additionally, Rabbi Moskowitz quoted Rabbi Ephraim Margolioth, who was the first to claim that people who rode in carriages were not included in the tally of six hundred thousand.[60]

Rabbi Kasher discussed the issue of whether Manhattan was a public domain in great detail. He argued that the number six hundred thousand referred to the number of people who passed through the eruv boundaries on a regular basis. Therefore, he explained, the fact that there were fewer than six hundred thousand on the streets of Manhattan on the weekends did not preclude Manhattan from being considered a public domain. He also maintained that while the six hundred thousand people must live in the city, they did not need to travel the streets, and he included non-Jews in his calculation of six hundred thousand.[61] Nonetheless, he maintained that Manhattan was not a public domain because, according to Rashi, a public domain must have streets that are *mefulash* and *mekhuvanim mi-sha'ar le-sha'ar*.[62] According to Rabbi Kasher, *mefulash* means that the streets must open into a public domain, and *mekhuvanim mi-sha'ar le-sha'ar* means that the streets must run straight from one end of the city to the other. Rabbi Kasher said that, even though some streets opened onto bridges that had the status of a public domain, there was no street that ran straight from one end of Manhattan to the other end. Therefore, Manhattan did not have the status of public domain.[63]

The opponents of the Manhattan eruv cast the situation in a different light. Rabbi Bloch argued that Manhattan had the status of a public domain and rejected the claim that non-Jews were not included in the six hundred thousand, since that idea was not found in the writings of any of the Rishonim. He also rejected the claim that Manhattan was not a public domain because there were fewer than six hundred thousand people on the weekends, arguing that there were in fact six hundred thousand people in Manhattan even on the weekends.

---

57 *Shulḥan arukh,* Oraḥ ḥayyim, 345:6.
58 Pollak, "Kuntres be-inyan tikkun eruvin," 68.
59 Tosafot on b. Eruv. 6a, s.v. *keiẓad.*
60 Moskowitz, *Sefer tikkun eruvin,* 104–106.
61 Kasher, "Tikkun eruvin," 43–48.
62 Rashi on b. Eruv. 6b, s.v. *Yerushalayim.*
63 Kasher, "Tikkun eruvin," 23–27, 87–90.

Additionally, he argued that six hundred thousand were required to be in the city on a regular basis but not every minute of the day or night. He based this argument on Rashi's definition of a public domain. Rashi states that six hundred thousand must pass through the area "always."[64] Rabbi Bloch explained that the word "always" could not possibly be taken literally and must mean that there were six hundred thousand in the area on a regular basis.[65]

Rabbi Moshe Feinstein discussed the status of Manhattan in several different places in his *Iggerot Mosheh*. In a letter dated 5 Adar 5712, he stated, "Regarding a public domain, the custom has already been established to follow the opinion of Rashi and Tosafot, who are lenient [and require six hundred thousand to consider an area a public domain]." He went on to say that, based on this understanding, there might be places in New York and Brooklyn that would be considered public domains since more than six hundred thousand people traveled there.[66] He explained that this traffic could include Jews and non-Jews, including women and children, and he even included people driving in cars and riding buses.[67] However, in several responsa written in the late 1970s and early 1980s, Rabbi Feinstein argued that, in order to meet the definition of six hundred thousand, a city would need to have five times that many people living in or commuting to the city. He stated that this must be true since the rabbis established an eruv in Warsaw even though the population exceeded six hundred thousand. He never explicitly wrote whether he believed that Manhattan had the status of a public domain based on this definition.[68]

The Eruv Boundaries

In his 1949 article on the eruv, Rabbi Eisenstadt wrote that Manhattan was surrounded on all sides by rivers ten handbreadths deep that might serve as acceptable eruv boundaries. However, he explained that the boundaries created by the Atlantic Ocean, the East River, the West Channel, and the Hell Gate had the status of seas and not rivers and were therefore not acceptable eruv boundaries because of the risk of sediment buildup. He added that natural boundaries are unacceptable according to Tosafot based on the principle of *atu rabbim u-mevatlei meḥiẓah,* meaning that people nullify the eruv boundaries by

64 Rashi on b. Eruv. 59a, s.v. *ir shel rabbim*.
65 Bloch, "Mikhtav be-inyan eruvin be-Manhattan," 17–19.
66 Feinstein, *Iggerot Mosheh*, Oraḥ ḥayyim, 1:109.
67 Feinstein, *Iggerot Mosheh*, Oraḥ ḥayyim, 1:139.
68 See Feinstein, *Iggerot Mosheh*, Oraḥ ḥayyim, 4:87 and 5:28–29.

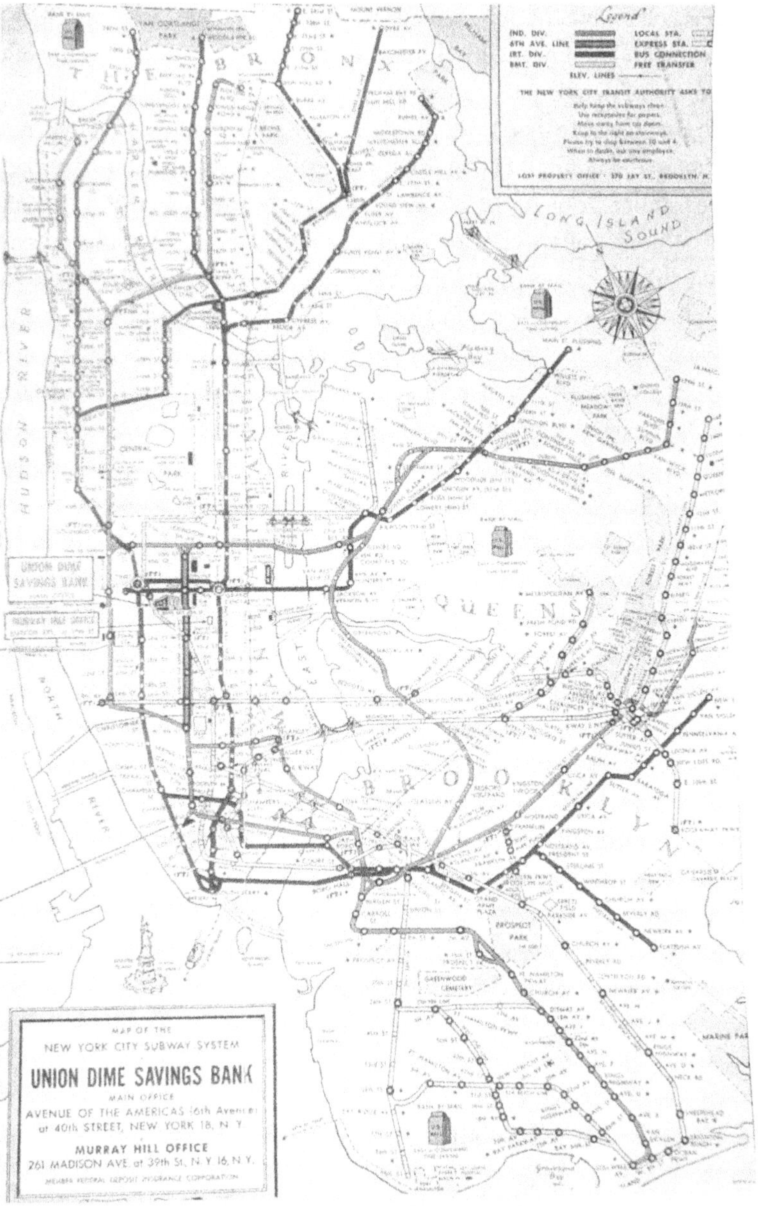

FIGURE 6. Map of the New York City Subway System, Union Dime Bank, 1954.

passing through them.[69] Therefore, he argued that the eruv boundaries around Manhattan were created by constructed piers and sea walls that rose at least ten handbreadths above the water line.[70]

---

69 Tosafot on b. Eruv. 22b, s.v. *dilma*.
70 Eisenstadt, *Minḥat Ẓevi*, 29–31.

Rabbi Pollak, on the other hand, accepted the rivers as satisfactory eruv boundaries. He did not mention the risk of sediment buildup but did address the problem of people passing through the eruv and potentially nullifying the boundaries. He wrote that, since the piers were constructed rather than natural, public traffic did not nullify these boundaries. He raised the issue that the river was in existence prior to the creation of the city, thereby creating a situation where the eruv walls were not *mukkaf le-dirah,* created for the purpose of enclosing the city. However, he quoted the *Shulḥan arukh,* which stated that as long as most of the eruv is *mukkaf le-dirah,* the eruv was acceptable.[71]

In his *Tikkun eruvin be-Manhattan,* Rabbi Moskowitz wrote that he had surveyed the boundaries of Manhattan several times and saw that constructed river walls surrounded the entire city and served as acceptable eruv boundaries. He addressed the fact that the rivers were not visible from the houses and cited Ramban who argued that, if natural boundaries were not visible from the houses, those natural boundaries were not acceptable.[72] However, Rabbi Moskowitz quoted the opinion of Rabbi Schwadron in his approbation to *Eruv ve-hoẓa'ah,* in which he explained that Ramban's comments applied only to the case of the ocean, which was not visible from anywhere in the city and could not be reached on the Sabbath. Rabbi Schwadron argued that, in a city where the rivers were visible at least to the people living nearby and could be reached on the Sabbath, even Ramban would agree that the rivers served as acceptable eruv boundaries.[73]

In the approbation letter that Rabbi Henkin wrote to Rabbi Moskowitz upon the publication of his *Tikkun eruvin be-Manhattan,* he stated that if the river walls were in existence as Rabbi Moskowitz had claimed, then he supported the eruv. However, if, as he suspected, the eruv boundaries still needed symbolic doorways, then he believed that these symbolic doorways would not endure in New York.[74]

Public Traffic Crossing the Eruv Boundaries

Although all of the rabbinic authorities agreed that the sea walls constituted acceptable eruv boundaries, the issue of people crossing over these boundaries

---

71 Pollak, "Kuntres be-inyan tikkun eruvin," 68–69; and *Shulḥan arukh,* Oraḥ ḥayyim, 365:2.

72 Moshe ben Nahman, *Ḥiddushei ha-Ramban,* b. Eruv. 59a, s.v. *u-mihu.*

73 Schwadron, *Eruv ve-hoẓa'ah,* 29–31.

74 Moskowitz, *Sefer tikkun eruvin,* 5.

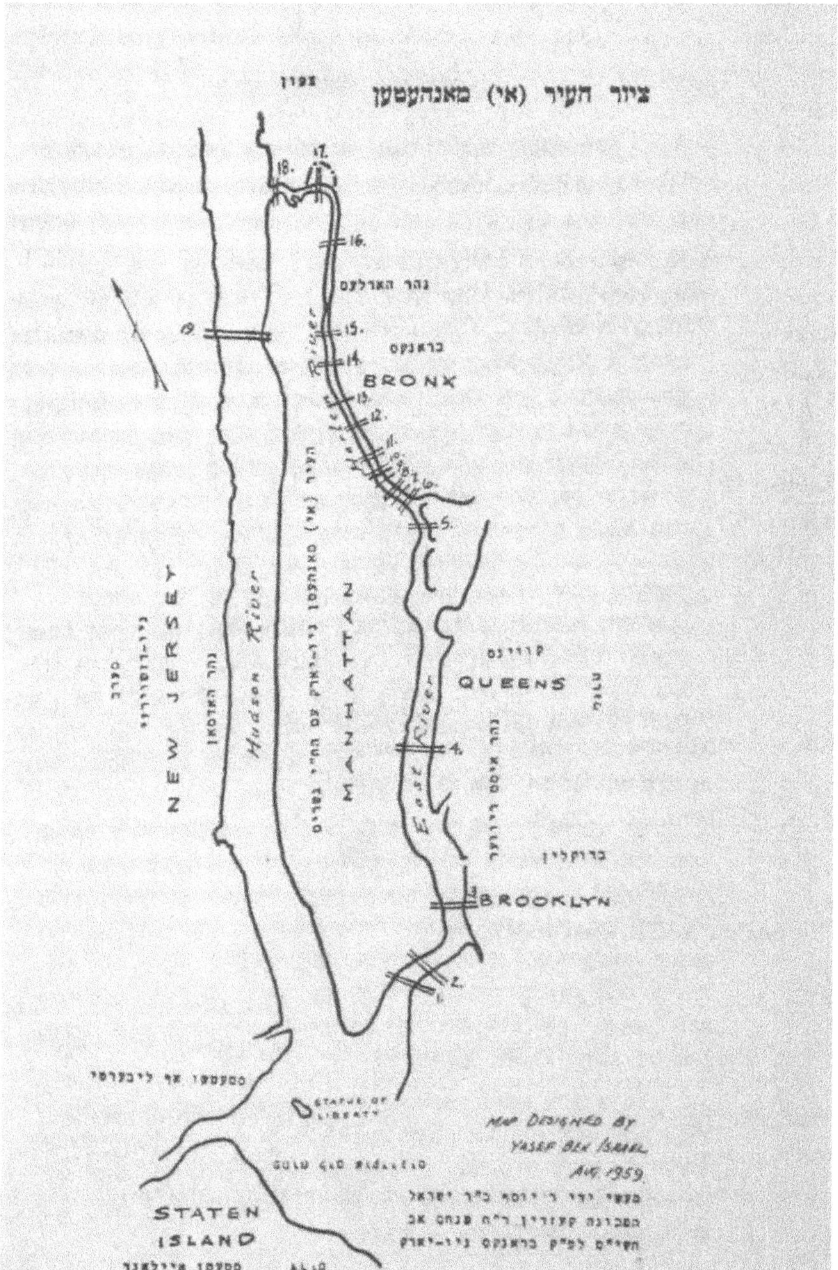

FIGURE 7. Moskowitz, "Tikkun eruvin," 175, reprinted in Kasher, "Tikkun eruvin," 12.

needed to be addressed. Rabbi Eisenstadt quoted the opinion of the *Magen Avraham* that people exiting ships would negate the eruv boundary.[75] Rabbi Eisenstadt explained that the view of the *Magen Avraham* did not pose a problem in Manhattan for several reasons. First, Rambam rejected the entire principle that boundaries are nullified by people crossing them. Second, each pier was enclosed by its own fenced-in area, so, even according to the *Magen Avraham,* the eruv boundary would be established by these enclosures and not by the river walls. Rabbi Eisenstadt wrote that, if symbolic doorways were created around the few piers that were not already enclosed, the Manhattan eruv would be acceptable even according to the *Magen Avraham.* He also explained that the sea walls were constructed by people and that traffic does not nullify constructed boundaries.[76]

In 1949, Rabbi Henkin raised the issue of whether public traffic nullified the eruv around Manhattan. He wrote that this issue had already been addressed by Rabbi Seigel in his *Oznei Yehoshua,* in which he explained that public traffic did not nullify the eruv in New York because Manhattan was enclosed by acceptable eruv walls and did not have the status of a public domain since there was no one street that had six hundred thousand people on it.[77]

Rabbi Kotler, however, argued that the halakha was to follow the *Mishkenot Ya'akov,* which stated that, even if there were four walls surrounding a city, there was still a potential problem of the boundaries being nullified by traffic.[78] Rabbi Kotler stated that, according to the *Magen Avraham,* people disembarking would nullify the eruv boundaries. Therefore, Rabbi Kotler required gates around Manhattan in order for Manhattan to be considered a private domain.[79]

Fear of Sediment Buildup

Rabbi Moskowitz included in his volume a lengthy discussion about the risk of sediment buildup in the rivers and the possibility that this risk would disqualify the eruv boundaries. First, he explained that all the waterways surrounding Manhattan had the status of a river and not a sea or ocean because they had banks on both sides. Second, he explained that all rabbinic authorities, with the exception of the *Taz,* believe that sediment buildup is only an issue for seas and

---

75 *Magen Avraham,* Oraḥ ḥayyim, 363:30.
76 Eisenstadt, *Minḥat Ẓevi,* 31.
77 Seigel, *Oznei Yehoshua,* 180; and Henkin, *Edut le-Yisra'el,* 151.
78 *Mishkenot Ya'akov,* Oraḥ ḥayyim, 1:120.
79 Kotler, *Mishnat Rabbi Aharon,* 1:6.

oceans and not for rivers.[80] Since the rule regarding eruvin is to follow the more lenient opinion, the opinion of the *Taz* was to be rejected, and sediment buildup was not a concern.[81]

Bridges

When Rabbi Eisenstadt first addressed the issue of bridges negating the eruv boundary in 1949, there were eighteen bridges connecting Manhattan with the outer boroughs and New Jersey. He explained that most of them had symbolic doorways, which were the entrances to the bridges and thus were not considered breaches in the eruv wall. Rabbi Eisenstadt included a lengthy footnote in his 1949 article that listed and described each bridge and the reason why it did not negate the eruv wall. He argued that the bridges were not lined up opposite one another, and so Manhattan was not to be considered an "open alleyway" (*mefulash*) and therefore did not have the status of a public domain. For this reason, the symbolic doorways would be adequate to create an eruv boundary around the city. Rabbi Eisenstadt added that if a bridge did not have a symbolic doorway, it would be simple to construct one.[82]

Rabbi Eisenstadt also raised a concern brought up by *Nodah bi-Yehudah* and *Ḥatam Sofer*[83] that bridges themselves create breaches in an eruv wall. Rabbi Eisenstadt suggested that a canister be built on each side of the bridge entrance with mesh wrapped around it. These mesh-covered canisters would serve as gates that could theoretically be closed at night and would satisfy rabbinic authorities who do not require that the gates actually be closed at night. However, in his footnote describing the details of the twenty bridges around Manhattan written in 1959, Rabbi Eisenstadt argued that each bridge could be considered closed off without relying on these canisters, which he recognized would be impractical.[84]

Rabbi Steif believed that Manhattan did not have the status of a public domain. Therefore, the symbolic doorways on the bridges would suffice to enclose the breach created by the bridges. However, since there was significant

---

80 David Ha-Levi Segal, *Taz*, Oraḥ ḥayyim, 363:20.

81 Moskowitz, *Sefer tikkun eruvin*, 78–93. Rabbi Steif also addresses this issue in a short paragraph in which he explains that the prevalent view follows the *Magen Avraham* that sediment buildup is not an issue in rivers. See Steif, "Kuntres tikkun eruvin," *Ohr Yisro'el* 9, no. 1 (Tishrei 5764 [2003]): 10.

82 Eisenstadt, *Minḥat Ẓevi*, 32.

83 Landau, *Nodah bi-Yehudah*, 2nd ed., Oraḥ ḥayyim, no. 42; and Moses Sofer, *She'elot u-teshuvot Ḥatam Sofer* (Bratislava, 1841), vol. 1, no. 89.

84 Eisenstadt, *Minḥat Ẓevi*, 32–33. See his description of the bridges in n. 2.

debate concerning bridges in an eruv, Rabbi Steif suggested building symbolic doorways around the area in front of the bridges, thereby relying on the symbolic doorways as eruv boundaries and not including the bridges in the eruv.[85]

Rabbi Henkin addressed the problem that the bridges posed in the creation of the Manhattan eruv in 1936. He wrote that the city landscape had changed since the days of Rabbi Seigel. Specifically, he explained that the bridges that were not part of Rabbi Seigel's original eruv nullified the eruv boundaries that were underneath them, as they broke the enclosure created by the sea wall.[86] In a second paragraph added to this description when Rabbi Henkin republished this discussion in 1949, he wrote that the entranceways to the bridges might create a symbolic doorway to alleviate the problem that the bridges created. However, he was not satisfied with this solution, because he did not think that these entranceways actually functioned as symbolic doorways.[87] In his approbation to Rabbi Moskowitz's volume, Rabbi Henkin explained that Rabbi Moskowitz had claimed to him that the bridges surrounding Manhattan had symbolic doorways, but Rabbi Henkin wrote that he was "not sure."[88]

Rabbi Feinstein, in his response to Rabbi Eisenstadt, took a different approach to the issues of the bridges surrounding Manhattan. Rabbi Feinstein explained that the eruv wall around Manhattan rose all the way up to the sky. Therefore, the bridge did not create a breach in the eruv wall. However, Rabbi Feinstein argued that the part of the bridge that extended beyond the eruv wall would be considered a public domain if six hundred thousand people passed over the bridge or a *karmelit* if fewer than six hundred thousand passed over the bridge. Rabbi Feinstein added an additional element that created a serious problem for the establishment of the Manhattan eruv. He argued that even a *karmelit* required gates and that the only difference between a public domain and a *karmelit* was that a public domain required gates that actually closed at night, while a *karmelit* only required gates that could theoretically be closed. This being the case, Rabbi Feinstein explained that an eruv could not be built around Manhattan because it would be impossible to close off the bridges with gates. But at the end of the responsum, he added that since there were clearly fewer than six hundred thousand people passing over any of the bridges and the prevalent view was that it was acceptable to enclose such an area with symbolic

---

85 Steif, "Kuntres tikkun eruvin," *Ohr Yisro'el* 9, no. 1 (Tishrei 5764 [2003]): 13–14.
86 Henkin, *Luaḥ ha-yovel shel Ezrat Torah*, 62, reprinted in his *Edut le-Yisra'el*, 151.
87 Henkin, *Edut le-Yisra'el*, 151.
88 Moskowitz, *Sefer tikkun eruvin*, 5.

doorways and not to consider it a *karmelit* that required gates, he would not nullify the eruv on account of the bridges alone.[89]

Tunnels

Rabbi Eisenstadt addressed the twenty tunnels that went in and out of Manhattan, fifteen of which were used for trains or subways and five of which were for cars. Rabbi Eisenstadt wrote that train and subway tunnels were not problematic since they were blocked off on the side of the tunnel outside of Manhattan by closed gates. Regarding the other five tunnels, he argued that the entrance to every tunnel constituted a symbolic doorway and that the toll booths served as gates that closed off the tunnels.[90]

Rabbi Moskowitz argued that tunnels did not constitute a breach in the eruv walls because the roofs of the tunnels extended downward and created eruv walls based on the principle of *pi tikrah yored ve-sotem*, "the edge of the beam descends." This means that eruv walls may be created not only upward toward the heavens but also downward into the ground. In addition, he explained that he had joined Rabbis Eisenstadt and Kasher in surveying the tunnels of Manhattan and that they had seen that the openings of the tunnels did not exceed ten cubits and therefore did not create breaches in the eruv.[91]

The Public Square (*Pelatya*)

The baraita in tractate Eruvin gives several examples of public domains. One of the examples is of a *pelatya*, a public square. Rabbi Shlomo Ibn Adret introduced a novel explanation of the status of a *pelatya*. He wrote that a *pelatya* is any open space of at least sixteen square cubits in which people come to conduct their business. Ibn Adret stated that even if such an area was completely enclosed and did not have six hundred thousand people in it each day, it had the status of a public domain.[92] According to the rule proposed by Ibn Adret, an eruv could not be created around Manhattan or any other large city. However, Rabbi Eisenstadt quoted Hakham Ashkenazi, who wrote that no rabbinic authority followed the

89 Feinstein, *Iggerot Mosheh*, Oraḥ ḥayyim, vol. 1, no. 139.
90 Eisenstadt, *Minḥat Ẓevi*, 32.
91 Moskowitz, *Sefer tikkun eruvin*, 54–56.
92 Shlomo Ibn Adret, *Avodat ha-kodesh* (Warsaw, 1876), *sha'ar* 3, no. 1.

opinion of Ibn Adret.[93] Rabbi Eisenstadt added that the *Shulḥan arukh* did not include this opinion and that the tradition for centuries had been to build eruvin around cities with areas defined as a "public squares."[94]

Rabbi Steif claimed that his suggestion to construct neighborhood eruvin in Manhattan would avoid the problem of the "public square," as most neighborhoods did not have large marketplaces, and if a neighborhood did have such an area, the local rabbis would be able to avoid including the marketplace in the eruv.[95]

Rabbi Feinstein, however, maintained that the halakhah followed Ibn Adret's opinion. Therefore, an eruv could not be built around Manhattan, since it contained "public squares" that would be considered public domains even when enclosed. He explained that rabbis built eruvin in European cities even though they contained public squares because the custom was to define a *pelatya* as a marketplace that had six hundred thousand passing through it. Since no city in Eastern Europe had such a large population, they were able to construct eruvin. However, Manhattan, which contained public squares and had a population exceeding six hundred thousand, was still a public domain. At the conclusion of the responsum, Rabbi Feinstein wrote that even though some rabbinic authorities disagreed with Ibn Adret, the combination of the problem created by the bridges and the issue of public squares rendered it impossible to create an eruv around Manhattan.[96]

Leasing of the City

At the end of his letter, Rabbi Eisenstadt explained that after all the eruv walls were in place, bread must be kept in Manhattan, and the city must be leased from one of the government officials for ninety-nine years.[97] Rabbi Steif agreed that the city could be leased from government officials and quoted examples from Poland as precedent.[98] Finally, he quoted Hakham Ashkenazi, who argued that the lease should be renewed every year or two, and Rabbi Solomon Tabak,

---

93 Tzvi Hirsch ben Yaakov Ashkenazi, *She'elot u-teshuvot Ḥakham Ẓevi* (Jerusalem, 1995), no. 37.

94 Eisenstadt, *Minḥat Ẓevi*, 35–36.

95 Ibid., 41–42.

96 Feinstein, *Iggerot Mosheh*, Oraḥ ḥayyim, vol. 1, no. 139, 5–6.

97 Eisenstadt, *Minhat Ẓevi*, 37.

98 See Samuel Ha-Kohen Borstein, *Sefer minḥat Shabbat* (Tel Aviv, 1964), *hasmatot le-simman* 94, who explains the tradition in Poland to lease the city from the local governmental authority. Rabbi Borstein quotes several different views on whether leasing from a Jewish governmental authority would be sufficient.

who argued that the lease could extend for either ten or twenty years.[99] Rabbi Steif concluded that each local rabbi could arrange the proper length of lease.[100]

Rabbi Moskowitz traced the history of leasing the city for the sake of creating an eruv, quoting the sources that had been utilized by Rabbis Eisenstadt and Steif. Rabbi Moskowitz concluded that it was permissible to rent the city from government officials or their agents, even if the agent was Jewish. At the end of his discussion on this topic, he quoted the argument of *Ḥazon ish* that the city should be leased from a local policeman based on the principle that the local policeman is the "tenant or agent" of governmental officials to enter houses.[101]

Rabbi Pirutinsky quoted an unnamed prominent rabbi who opposed the Manhattan eruv because he claimed that the government did not have the right to enter people's homes without their permission in America. Rabbi Pirutinsky responded that, according to the Rivash, the right to rent was based on the government officials' ability to place items in houses during times of war.[102] That right, Rabbi Pirutinsky argued, applied in America. Furthermore, he argued that the police and fire departments had the right to enter people's homes in the case of an emergency.[103]

Conclusion

In many respects, the debate over the Manhattan eruv in the years after World War II followed the pattern of other North American eruv debates. Although the debate revolved around halakhic principles and precedent, social concerns also played a critical role. The issue of public domain, which was addressed regarding the St. Louis eruv and the East Side of Manhattan eruv, was once again explored by the rabbinic leaders. The question of utilizing bridges as eruv boundaries and the potential problem of public traffic over the boundaries were also addressed, as was the proper manner of leasing the city. The only issue that was not brought up was the utilization of telegraph poles and wires as eruv boundaries, as the Manhattan eruv relied on river walls and piers to create its eruv walls.

---

99 Ashkenazi, *She'elot u-teshuvot Ḥakham Ẓevi*, no. 30; Solomon Leib Tabak, *Sefer she'elot u-teshuvot teshurat shai* (Bnei Brak, 1990), no. 357.

100 Steif, *Minḥat Ẓevi*, 42–43; and Steif, "Kuntres tikkun eruvin," *Ohr Yisro'el* 9, no. 1 (Tishrei 5764 [2003]): 15.

101 Abraham Yeshayahu Karelitz, *Sefer ḥazon ish* (Jerusalem, 1955), Hilkhot eruvin, 18:9.

102 Ben Sheshet, *She'elot u-teshuvot Rivash*, no. 405.

103 Pirutinsky, "Haẓa'ah le-tikkun eruv be-Manhattan," 13.

There was, however, a critical difference between this eruv debate and the previous ones in North America. From the beginning of the initiative in 1949, rabbis who led the initiative attempted to gain rabbinic consensus concerning the eruv. Letters were sent to the rabbis of New York soliciting their reactions and their criticisms. Even the opponents of the eruv led by Rabbi Feinstein were respectful of the supporters of the project and did not question their motives or declare their conclusions wrong.

There are several explanations for this attempt at consensus. First, in the years following World War II, the Jewish community, and especially the rabbinic community, felt vulnerable and weakened. There was a desire to create rabbinic unity rather than rabbinic strife. Rabbi Steif, in his initial letter to Rabbi Eisenstadt, suggested that each rabbi should build an eruv in his community to avoid the conflict that might ensue from the creation of a citywide eruv.[104]

Second, in Manhattan at the time, Rabbis Feinstein and Henkin were the two leading halakhic authorities. If the eruv were to gain acceptance, it was critical that these two rabbis be included in the process and that the eruv receive their acceptance, if not their approval. The fact that Rabbis Feinstein and Henkin both participated in the process, offered their encouragement, and did not openly oppose the eruv points to the successful process that was undertaken first by Rabbi Eisenstadt and then with the partnership of Rabbis Moskowitz and Kasher.

Finally, the Manhattan eruv was the first North American eruv that affected many different subcommunities. Rabbi Schwab wrote in strong opposition to the Manhattan eruv not as an outsider but as the rabbi of a community that would be included within this eruv. The eruv also included the Lower East Side, which was the community of Rabbis Feinstein, Henkin, and Moskowitz, and the Upper West Side, with its combination of Modern Orthodox rabbis and a Hasidic community of which Rabbi Kasher was a leading member. These communities all interacted with one another in multiple ways, and a rabbinic consensus had the potential to prevent tension and controversy.

However, perhaps the most important difference between the Manhattan eruv and the previous North American eruvin was that the Manhattan eruv was the first to rely heavily on the precedent of an earlier North American eruv, in this case, the 1905 eruv created by Rabbi Seigel on the East Side of Manhattan. In

---

104 Steif, "Kuntres tikkun eruvin," *Ohr Yisro'el* 9, no. 1 (Tishrei 5764 [2003]): 15. For a discussion of the decline of the "non-observant Orthodox Jews" and the rise of "observant Orthodox Jews" during this period, see Charles Liebman, "Orthodoxy in American Jewish Life," *AJYB* (1966): 21–92.

fact, the project of the Manhattan eruv began in 1936, when Rabbi Henkin wrote that although many Jews relied on Rabbi Seigel's eruv, it was no longer valid. Rabbi Eisenstadt, in his initial treatise proposing the creation of the Manhattan eruv, included a list of volumes that he had consulted. He included Rabbi Seigel's *Eruv ve-hoẓa'ah* and Rabbi Bernstein's *Hilkhata rabbeta le-Shabbata* in this list of books.[105] Rabbi Steif, in his approbation to Rabbi Moskowitz's *Sefer tikkun eruvin,* listed the volumes that needed to be consulted regarding the creation of this new eruv, the first of which was *Eruv ve-hoẓa'ah.* He also mentioned Rabbi Bernstein's *Hilkhata rabbeta le-Shabbata.*[106] Rabbi Kasher, in the introduction to his eruv treatise "Tikkun eruvin," discussed the history of the eruv in Manhattan beginning with Rabbi Seigel's *Eruv ve-hoẓ'ah* and the fact that Rabbi Schwadron gave an approbation to the volume.[107] Rabbi Pirutinsky began his article with the history of the Manhattan eruv, and he credited Rabbi Seigel with initiating discussion about an eruv around Manhattan.[108] Rabbi Kroizer, in an article published in *No'am,* mentioned the eruv in St. Louis and then referred to Rabbi Seigel's volume and to the approbations that were included.[109]

Although each of these rabbinic authorities pointed out that Rabbi Seigel's eruv only encompassed the East Side of Manhattan, it is clear that they viewed his eruv as the beginning of the process that led to the creation of the Manhattan eruv. On the one hand, this is not surprising. Rabbi Seigel had created an eruv around a portion of the borough that was being addressed and had dealt with many of the halakhic issues that were relevant to the Manhattan eruv. On the other hand, Rabbi Seigel's eruv had either fallen into disuse or was being used without rabbinic sanction. Therefore, it would have been easy for the rabbis to create the impression that the Manhattan eruv had been their own innovation and not open themselves to criticism that they were relying on an eruv that was, at the very least, no longer valid.

The recognition that Rabbi Seigel's eruv began the process that led to the creation of the Manhattan eruv reflects a turning point in the history of American Orthodoxy. Following World War II, the American Orthodox rabbinate began to recognize the existence of a history of American Orthodoxy. In the first half of the twentieth century, when people such as Rabbi Seigel or Rabbi Graubart

---

105 This page listing the books that he used appears as Appendix 3 in the typewritten copy of Rabbi Eisenstadt's treatise. It was not republished in the later version of the treatise. See Yeshiva University Archives MS no.? 1/2.

106 Moskowitz, *Sefer tikkun eruvin,* 9.

107 Kasher, "Tikkun eruvin," 5.

108 Pirutinsky, "Haẓa'ah le-tikkun eruv be-Manhattan," 9.

109 Kroizer, "Tikkun eruvin be-Manhattan N.Y," *No'am* 1 (1958): 197.

created their eruvin, they were uninterested in the fact that other rabbis had previously addressed these issues in America, as they saw their communities as continuations of the communities of Eastern Europe. Even though most rabbis were still born and educated in Europe, by the second half of the century, they recognized that they were building on a preexisting history of Orthodoxy in America. Therefore, even though the rabbis involved in the Manhattan eruv did not rely on Rabbi Seigel for his halakhic expertise, these same rabbis felt that it was important to trace the history of the Manhattan eruv. They believed that this history gave the Manhattan eruv more credibility. At the same time, it is not surprising that these rabbis mentioned the approbations to Rabbi Seigel's responsum, especially the one by Rabbi Schwadron, in their discussion of the history of the eruv, as this gave the additional credibility of this Polish rabbinic sage to an American rabbinic initiative.

The realization that earlier eruvin in the history of American Orthodoxy were not merely isolated events but were the beginning of a pattern of eruvin in communities in North America helped create the self-confidence and self-awareness that allowed for the explosion of community eruvin in the last quarter of the twentieth century.

Conclusion

In his approbation to Rabbi Joseph Moskowitz's volume *Sefer tikkun eruvin*, which supported the creation of the Manhattan eruv, Rabbi Moshe Feinstein, a leading opponent of the Manhattan eruv, wrote, "I have seen [in this volume] many topics that follow the law as the truth of Torah. Even though there are other matters in which, according to my humble opinion, there are opposing views, it is the Torah tradition that God is happy when two scholars argue for the sake of heaven."[1] The history of the American city eruv is the story of rabbinic scholars who debated the laws and traditions of past generations and attempted to apply those laws and traditions to the realities of North America.

The rabbis who supported the early American eruvin did not have the political clout or influence to gain permission to construct symbolic doorways that would serve as eruv boundaries. Therefore, these eruvin, like many of the eruvin that preceded them throughout the Jewish world, relied on natural boundaries and preexisting constructed boundaries. In certain instances, the rabbis relied on minority opinions to uphold the acceptability of an eruv boundary that was necessary for the completion of the eruv. However, not all rabbis were willing to rely on leniencies, which often led to fierce debates. While these debates took place in the cities of North America, they reflected a direct continuation of

1 Joseph David Moskowitz, *Sefer tikkun eruvin be-ir Manhattan* (New York, 1959), 8.

similar debates that had divided the rabbinic world as long as city eruvin existed. The American rabbis' reliance on these earlier authorities reflects a halakhic continuity that had followed the Jews from the talmudic period to the eruvin of medieval and early modern Europe and throughout the Jewish world wherever eruvin were created.

There were also other ways in which the North American eruv debates reflected a continuation of the challenges that the halakhah posed for Jewish communities living as a minority in foreign and sometimes hostile countries. Beginning in the late medieval period, rabbis discussed the possibility of leasing cities from a lesser authority than the king or mayor due to the insecurity of the Jewish community. Both Rabbis Rosenfeld and Seigel leased the areas encompassed by their eruvin from local police officers. They both justified this decision on the basis of halakhic sources, but their reliance on this mechanism reflects their inability to approach the mayor or other local authorities and request the leasing of the city for the purpose of the eruv.

By the 1950s, however, this situation had begun to change. In both Toronto and Manhattan, rabbis were now able to build new eruv structures, and in 1959, the rabbis in Manhattan were even able to lease the city from Mayor Wagner. The following decades saw a proliferation of eruvin throughout American cities and towns. While prior to 1970 there were only four community eruvin in North America, in 2021 there were over two hundred.[2]

Several factors contributed to the explosion in the number of eruvin being built in American cities and towns. First, by the 1970s, there emerged a movement within the Orthodox Jewish community towards a stricter level of practice and observance. In 1971, only 11 percent of Jewish males identified as Orthodox.[3] Yet, in that same year, Jewish sociologist Marshall Sklare wrote, "Orthodoxy has transformed its image from that of a dying movement to one whose strength and opinions must be reckoned with in any realistic appraisal of the Jewish community."[4] The gradual strengthening of the Orthodox community was reflected in stricter observance and increased attendance in Orthodox day

---

2 For a list of eruvin in North America, see "List of Eruvin," Wikipedia, http://en.wikipedia.org/wiki/List_of_eruvin. This list includes only eruvin that have websites. It is impossible to estimate the total number of smaller neighborhood eruvin in North America. One of the first of these post-1970 eruvin was built in Kew Gardens Hills, Queens. See Moshe Feinstein, *Iggerot Mosheh*, Oraḥ ḥayyim, 4:86, in which Rabbi Moshe Feinstein expresses support for the creation of this eruv in a letter written to Rabbi Peretz Steinberg of Queens on April 1, 1974.

3 Bernard Lazerwitz and Michael Harrison, "American Jewish Denominations: A Social and Religious Profile," *American Sociological Review* (August 1979): 659–661. See also Gurock, *Orthodox Jews in America*, 209–210.

4 Marshall Sklare, *America's Jews* (New York, 1971), 40.

schools. In addition, the Orthodox began to create vibrant communities. Already in 1960, Far Rockaway, Queens, was called "Torah Suburb by the Sea."[5] This increased level of observance and the creation of Orthodox communities led the rabbis to initiate the building of more community eruvin, and the communites supported these efforts.[6]

Another factor that allowed for the creation of eruvin was the increased involvement of Orthodox Jews in the political sphere. When *The New York Times* described the growing influence of local religious groups in a 1974 article, it quoted Rabbi Moshe Sherer, President of the Orthodox organization Agudath Israel: "There is hardly a legislator from any Jewish neighborhood in the city who does not know how we stand on issues that concern us and how thorough we are about informing our constituents about positions the legislators take on these issues."[7] Chaim Waxman, a sociologist who has studied the Orthodox community in America, argues that this approach toward involvement in government and civil matters was a reflection of the fact that Jews felt both more secure and more religiously autonomous in America. Therefore, they believed that it was their right to make their opinions known in matters of concern to the Jewish community, both nationally and locally.[8] This sentiment of feeling at home in America was reflected in a sense of gratitude toward the United States government and its policies. In 1982, Rabbi Menachem Mendel Schneerson, the Lubavitcher Rebbe, said of the United States government, "By the grace of God, we are in a country which is a benevolent polity."[9]

The fact that the creation of eruvin took place at the same time as Orthodox Jews were becoming more involved with local governments is no coincidence. The ability to approach the local authorities to request permission to erect

---

5 Michael Kaufman, "Far Rockaway: Torah Suburb by the Sea," *Jewish Life* (August 1960): 20.

6 Personal conversation with Rabbi Mordechai Willig, Rabbi of Young Israel of Riverdale, December 29, 2010. Rabbi Willig described the increased observance of the Orthodox Jews in Riverdale, New York in the early 1970s, which led to the building of the Riverdale eruv in 1975, which was funded and supported by the Riverdale community.

7 *New York Times*, May 19, 1998, B11.

8 Chaim I. Waxman, "From Treifene Medina to Goldene Medina: Changing Perspectives on the United States among American Haredi," in *Why is America Different? American Jewry on Its 350th Anniversary*, ed. Steven T. Katz (Lanham, MD, 2009), 119–123. This feeling of religious entitlement is evident, for example, in the celebrated case of the "Yale Five," in which five Orthodox students at Yale brought a lawsuit against the university asking that they be exempt from the school policy that they must live on campus. See Samuel G. Freedman, "Yeshivish at Yale," *The New York Times Magazine*, May 24, 1998.

9 Menachem Mendel Schneerson, *Likutei siḥot al parshiyot ha-shavua ḥagim u-mo'adim*, vol. 25, *Breishit*, second ed. (New York, 1972), 419. This is quoted in Waxman, "Treifene Medina," 126, n. 36.

poles and strings, thereby creating symbolic doorways around a neighborhood, required both access to these officials and a sense of privilege to ask for such permission. For the first time in modern history, Jews were able to construct their own communal eruvin without relying on natural or preexisting man-made boundaries. This meant that eruvin no longer needed to rely on many of the halakhic leniencies that were previously necessary. In addition, an eruv could now be built around any neighborhood, regardless of its geographic location or physical boundaries. Finally, the ability of members of the Orthodox community to approach government officials allowed the leasing of the city to be done directly from the mayor or governor. Once again, there was no longer a need to rely on the halakhic leniencies that had been necessary at the end of the nineteenth and beginning of the twentieth centuries.[10]

Even so, eruvin in North American cities continued to face challenges, from both within and outside the Orthodox Jewish community. When an eruv was built in Flatbush, Brooklyn, in 1978, Rabbi Moshe Feinstein wrote to the rabbis in Flatbush and explained that he had not wanted to get involved in the dispute over the validity of the Flatbush eruv but that he had decided to address the issue due to the fact that rumors had spread that he had permitted the eruv. Rabbi Feinstein clarified that he had already discussed many of the issues regarding the Flatbush eruv in his responsum regarding the Manhattan eruv that he wrote to Rabbi Eisenstadt in 1952; he also elaborated on several reasons to allow the eruv and several reasons to prohibit it.[11] In a subsequent responsum written by Rabbi Feinstein to the Flatbush rabbis in 1979, he concluded that it was unacceptable to build an eruv anywhere in Brooklyn, since Brooklyn had the status of a public domain. He explained that because Brooklyn did not have natural or man-made eruv walls, an eruv in Brooklyn would not be acceptable.[12]

---

10 A wonderful example of the comfort level of the American Orthodox community regarding eruvin is evident in the fact that the lease agreement between the Jewish communities of Boston, Brookline, and Newton and the Governor of Massachusetts was posted on the Internet. See "Kinyan Kesef," Boston Eruv, http://www.bostoneruv.org/kinyan_kesef.htm. For a recent discussion of the importance of political clout and sophistication among the Orthodox and its role in allowing the Orthodox to create communities that serve their needs, see Nomi M. Stolzenberg and David N. Myers, *American Shtetl: The Making of Kiryas Yoel, A Hasidic Village in Upstate New York* (Princeton, 2021).

11 Feinstein, *Iggerot Mosheh*, Oraḥ ḥayyim, vol. 4, no. 87. The responsa regarding the Manhattan eruv can be found in *Iggerot Mosheh*, Oraḥ ḥayyim, vol. 1, no. 138–139. Rabbi Feinstein began his responsum to Rabbi Eisenstadt on his request to build an eruv in Brooklyn and Manhattan in 1952, but in the end, the initiative was limited to the Manhattan eruv. For a discussion of the eruvin in Brooklyn and the controversies surrounding them, see Adam Mintz, "A Chapter in American Orthodoxy: The Eruvin in Brooklyn," *Hakirah* 14 (Winter 2012): 21–59.

12 Feinstien, *Iggerot Mosheh*, Oraḥ ḥayyim, vol. 4, no. 88.

In 1981, Rabbi Feinstein wrote a lengthy responsum explaining his rationale for prohibiting the building of an eruv in any community in Brooklyn. He wrote:

> In spite of the fact that I wrote that it is prohibited to build an eruv in Brooklyn even in one section in Flatbush and that it is likewise prohibited to build an eruv in Boro Park, several rabbis have gone and built eruvin in both Flatbush and Boro Park. . . . Therefore, I am required to clarify the matter so that there will not be a stumbling block for the hundreds and thousands [of Jews].[13]

Rabbi Feinstein proceeded to discuss many of the issues that he had already addressed with regard to the Manhattan eruv, and he once again made reference to his responsum on the Manhattan eruv. There was significant debate surrounding the eruvin in Brooklyn, especially the Boro Park eruv. The main proponent of the Boro Park eruv to whom Rabbi Feinstein's responsum was addressed was Rabbi Menashe Klein, head of the Ungvar Hasidic community in Boro Park.[14] The halakhic discussion utilized the precedents of the Eastern European eruvin. However, the rabbis also incorporated many of the issues that had been addressed by Rabbi Seigel and the rabbis who debated the validity of the Manhattan eruv, quoting their opinions and utilizing them in support of and in opposition to the eruvin in Brooklyn. The willingness of these rabbis to rely on the rabbinic views regarding these two earlier American eruvin reflects the recognition on the part of these late twentieth-century Orthodox rabbis of the halakhic credibility of their American rabbinic predecessors.[15]

The last decade of the twentieth century and the beginning of the twenty-first century also saw a new type of dispute regarding eruvin. Both Jews and non-Jews in several communities have opposed eruvin and brought legal action against them based on concerns that they reflected the influence of Orthodox Jews on the community and the demands they made on the entire community and that they would lead more Orthodox Jews to move into their neighborhoods.[16] The

13 Ibid., vol. 5, no. 28, 93. This responsum is addressed to Rabbi Feinstein's grandson, Rabbi Mordechai Tendler.

14 See Menashe Klein, *Om ani ḥomah: Mishneh halakhot* (Jerusalem, 2000).

15 See especially the discussion in *Ohr Yisro'el* 5, no. 2 (Tevet 5760). There was also a debate regarding the eruv in Williamsburg, which began with the construction of an eruv there in 1973. Rabbi Feinstein did not address this eruv specifically. However, much of the halakhic discussion on this eruv is included in *Sefer al miẓvat eruv* (New York, 2000), 15.

16 For a broader discussion of the issue of debates and controversies within the Jewish community, see Samuel G. Freedman, *Jew vs. Jew: The Struggle for the Soul of American Jewry*

eruv in Tenafly, New Jersey, for example, was the subject of a bitter legal battle between Jewish groups in this affluent suburb.[17] A letter sent to the mayor of Tenafly outlined the attitude of some of the eruv's opponents. It read: "The eruv will also be the beginning of many more demands the Orthodox people will impose on the town of Tenafly and its non-Orthodox residents."[18] In June 2003, the United States Supreme Court declined to hear the case, thereby bringing the legal battle to a close, and the eruv was built. This legal decision, however, failed to resolve the tensions within the community.[19] The eruv in Palo Alto, California, was only approved by the local authorities in 2007, seven years after the initial request was made to build it, due to legal challenges brought by residents.[20] The eruv controversy in Westhampton Beach, Long Island, pitted the Orthodox Jewish community against the secular Jewish and non-Jewish members of this upscale summer resort. In 2008, a full-page newspaper advertisement read: "Is Westhampton Beach an Orthodox Jewish Community? No it's a secular, open village with a proud history of welcoming all faiths. The erection of an eruv will proclaim us as an Orthodox Jewish community for all time. Don't let it happen."[21] In the end, the construction of the eruv was supported by the courts, and an eruv was built in eastern Long Island.

As the American Orthodox community enters the second decade of the twenty-first century, it continues to bind its halakhic roots to the traditions and precedents of the past. At the same time, it has forged a new legal tradition that may be called "American halakhah," which is influenced by the realities of Jewish life in America. These realities include growth and increased flourishing on

---

(New York, 2000); Mintz, "The Community Eruv," 211–230.

17 For a comprehensive study of the Tenafly eruv controversy, see Susan H. Lees, "Jewish Space in Suburbia: Interpreting the Eruv Conflict in Tenafly, New Jersey," *Contemporary Jewry* 27, no. 1 (October 2007): 42–79.

18 Lees, "Jewish Space in Suburbia," 55.

19 The London eruv debate reached the newspapers with a photograph published in the *Daily Mail* in 1994, which was borrowed from Stephen Spielberg's *Schindler's List* and printed above the headline "The danger of creating your own ghettoes." In reaction to this photograph, Holocaust survivors wrote statements about how, for them, the poles and wires of the eruv invoked visions of concentration camp fences. Although the London eruv was completed in 2003, the anti-eruv sentiment did not disappear. For a study of the London eruv controversy, see Jennifer Cousineau, "Rabbinic Urbanism in London: Rituals and the Material Culture of the Sabbath," *Jewish Social Studies* 11, no. 3 (Spring–Summer 2005): 36–57.

20 For a discussion of the Palo Alto eruv controversy, see John Mandsager, "The Eruv: A Space for Negotiating Identity" (master's thesis, Stanford University, Stanford, 2003) and Josh Richman, "New Eruv Reopens Old Church-State Debates in Palo Alto," *The Jewish Daily Forward*, July 20, 2007.

21 Joseph Berger, "Orthodox Jews Request Divides a Resort Village," *The New York Times*, June 22, 2008.

American soil. Yet the American Orthodox community has also faced backlash and been forced to address opposition from both non-Orthodox Jews and non-Jews within their communities. Both of these aspects of American Orthodoxy have continued to be factors in the construction of city eruvin in America.

Bibliography

Aboab, Samuel. *Sefer devar Shemu'el.* Venice, 1702.

Abraham of Narbonne. *Sefer ha-eshkol.* Halberstadt, 1868.

Albeck, Chanoch. *Shishah sidrei Mishnah: Mo'ed.* Jerusalem, 1958.

Algazi, Hayim. *Sefer banei ḥayyei.* Constantinople, 1707.

Angel, Marc D. *The Jews of Rhodes: The History of a Sephardic Community.* New York, 1978.

Ashkenazi, Zevi. *She'elot u-teshuvot Ḥakham Ẓevi.* Jerusalem, 2004.

Assaf, Simhah. *Tekufat ha-ge'onim ve-sifrutah: Harẓa'ot ve-shiurim.* Jerusalem, 1955.

Baker, Cynthia M. *Rebuilding the House of Israel: Architectures of Gender in Jewish Antiquity.* Stanford, CA, 2002.

Bartal, Israel. "Amerika shel ma'alah: Arẓot ha-Berit ke-idi'al u-khe-mofet le-Yehudei mizraḥ Eiropah be-me'ah ha-19." In *Be-ikvot Kolumbus: Amerikah, 1492–1992,* edited by Miri Eliav-Feldon, 511–522. Jerusalem, 1996.

Bechhofer, Yosef Gavriel. *The Contemporary Eruv: Eruvin in Metropolitan Areas.* Jerusalem, 1998.

Bender, Averam B. "*History of the Beth Hamedrosh Hagodol Congregation of St. Louis,* 1879–1969." *Bulletin of the Missouri Historical Society* (October 1970).

Ben Meshullam, Yeruham. *Sefer toledot Adam ve-Ḥavvah.* Jerusalem, 1974.

Ben Nahman, Moshe. *Hiddushei ha-Ramban,* edited by Moshe Hirschler. Jerusalem, 1973.

Ben Sheshet, Isaac. *She'elot u-teshuvot Rivash.* New York, 1974.

Berger, Joseph. "Orthodox Jews Request Divides a Resort Village." *The New York Times,* June 22, 2008.

Berlin, Hayim. *Sefer nishmat ḥayyim.* Jerusalem, 2008.

Berlin, Noah Zevi Hayyim. *Sefer aẓei almogim.* New York, 1977.

Bloch, Eliyahu Meir. "Mikhtav be-inyan eruvin be-Manhattan." Yeshiva University Archives MS 1300 1/7. Reprinted in *Kol ẓevi,* edited by Ari Zahtz and Michoel Zylberman, vol. 7, 15–22. New York, 2005.

Bernstein, Yehudah David. *Hilkhata rabbeta le-Shabbata.* New York, 1910.

Blondheim, Menahem. "Ha-rabbanut ha-Ortodoksi megaleh et Amerikah: Ha-ge'ografia shel ha-ruaḥ be-mitavim shel tikshoret." In *Be-ikvot Kolumbus: Amerikah, 1492–1992,* edited by Miri Eliav-Feldon, 483–510. Jerusalem, 1996.

Borstein, Samuel Ha-Kohen. *Sefer minḥat Shabbat.* Tel Aviv, 1964.

Breuer, Mordechai. *Modernity within Tradition: The Social History of Orthodox Jewry in Imperial Germany.* New York, 1992.

Brody, Robert. *The Geonim of Babylonia and the Shaping of Medieval Jewish Culture.* New Haven, 1998.

Brukhin, Jacob. *Mishkenot Ya'akov.* Jerusalem, 1960.

Caplan, Kimmy. "There is No Interest in Precious Stones in a Vegetable Market: The Life and Sermons of Rabbi Jacob Gordon of Toronto." *Jewish History* 23 (2009): 149–155.

———. "Ortodokẓia ba-olam he-ḥadash: Rabbanim u-derashot be-Amerikah, 1881–1924." *American Jewish History* 90, no. 1 (2002): 74–76.

———. "Rabbi Jacob Joseph, New York's Chief Rabbi: New Perspectives." *Hebrew Union College Annual* (1996): 1–43.

Compton, Richard J., and Camille N. Dry. *Pictorial St. Louis, the Great Metropolis of the Mississippi Valley: A Topographical Survey Drawn in Perspective A.D. 1875. St. Louis, 1876.*

Cousineau, Jennifer. "Rabbinic Urbanism in London: Rituals and the Material Culture of the Sabbath." *Jewish Social Studies* 11, no. 3 (Spring–Summer 2005): 36–57.

Danzig, Neil. *Mavo le-sefer halakhot pesukot im tashlum halakhot pesukut.* New York, 1999.

Deinard, Ephraim. *Sifrut Yisra'el be-Amerikah. Jaffa, 1913.*

———. *Kohelet Amerikah.* St. Louis, 1926.

Diner, Hasia R. *A Time for Gathering: The Second Migration 1820–1880.* Baltimore, 1992.

———. *Lower East Side Memories: A Jewish Place in America.* Princeton, NJ, 2000.

Ehrlich, Walter. *Zion in the Valley: The Jewish Community of St. Louis.* Columbia, MI, 1997.

Eisenstadt, Benzion. *Le-toeldot Yisra'el be-Amerikah.* New York, 1917.

Eisenstadt, Menahem Tzvi. *Sefer minḥat Ẓevi.* New York, 2003.

Eisenstein, Judah David. *Oẓar zikhronotai.* New York, 1930.

Elman, Yaakov. "Ma'aseh bi-shtei ayyarot: Maḥoza u-Pumbedita ke-meyaẓgot shtei tarbuyot hilkhatiyot." In *Torah li-shmah: meḥkarim be-mada'ei ha-Yahadut likhvod Professor Shama Yehudah Friedman,* edited by David Golinkin et al., 3–38. Jerusalem, 2007.

———. "Middle Persian Culture and Babylonian Sages: Accommodation and Resistance in the Shaping of Rabbinic Legal Tradition." In *The Cambridge Companion to the Talmud and Rabbinic Literature,* edited by Charlotte Elisheva Fonrobert and Martin S. Jaffee, 165–197. New York, 2007.

———. "The Socioeconomics of Babylonian Heresy," in *Jewish Law Association Studies* 17 (2007): *Studies in Mediaeval Halakhah in Honor of Stephen M. Passamaneck,* ed. Alyssa Gray and Bernard Jackson, 94–96.

Even, Isaac. "Chassidism in the New World." In *The Jewish Communal Register of New York City 1917–1918,* 341–346. New York, 1918.

Elyashar, Jacob Saul. *She'elot u-teshuvot simḥah le-ish.* Jerusalem, 1888.

Feingold, Avraham Eliyahu. *Tikkun eruvin.* Lublin, 1891.

Feinstein, Moshe. *Iggerot Mosheh.* New York, 1959.

———. *Darash Mosheh.* New York, 1988.

Felder, Gedaliah. *Yesodei Yeshurun.* Jerusalem, n.d.

Fonrobert, Charlotte Elisheva. "Neighborhood as Ritual Space: The Case of the Rabbinic Eruv." *Archiv für Religionsgeschichte* (2008): 252–257.

———. "From Separatism to Urbanism: The Dead Sea Scrolls and the Origins of the Rabbinic Eruv." *Dead Sea Dicoveries* 11, no. 1 (2004): 43–71.

Fradkin, Shnayer Zalman. *Torat ḥesed.* Warsaw, 1883.

Freedman, Samuel G. *Jew vs. Jew: The Struggle for the Soul of American Jewry.* New York, 2000.

———. "Yeshivish at Yale." *The New York Times Magazine.* May 24, 1998.

Goldman, Yosef. *Hebrew Printing in America 1735–1926: A History and Annotated Bibliography.* New York, 2006.

Gordon, Aharon. "Teshuvah be-niggud le-haẓa'ah le-tikkun eruvin be-ḥelek mi-mizraḥ New York." In *Kol ẓevi*, edited by Ari Zahtz and Michoel Zylberman, vol. 7, 37–48. New York, 2005.

Gordon, Jacob. "Zikhronos fun a Toronto'er rav." *Centennial Jubilee Edition Commemorating the Centenary of Jewish Emancipation in Canada and the Twenty-fifth Anniversary of the Jewish Daily Eagle.* Montreal, 1932.

Gottlieb, Samuel Noach. *Ohalei Shem.* Pinsk, 1912.

Graubart, Yehuda Leib. *A Sabbath Letter.* Toronto, 1922.

———. *Havalim ba-ne'imim.* Jerusalem, 1975.

———. *Sefer devarim ki-khtavam.* Toronto, 1932.

———. *Sefer zikaron.* Lodz, 1925.

Gurock, Jeffrey S. *Orthodox Jews in America.* Bloomington, 2009.

———. "Resisters and Accommodators: Varieites of Orthodox Rabbis in America, 1886–1983. *American Jewish Archives* (November 1983): 100–187. Reprinted in *The American Rabbinate: A Century of Continuity and Change, 1883–1983*, 10–97. New York, 1985.

———. *When Harlem Was Jewish, 1870–1930.* New York, 1979.

Ha-Kohen, Yisrael Meir. *Nidḥei Yisra'el.* Warsaw, 1893.

Henkin, Yosef Eliyahu. *Edut le-Yisra'el.* New York, 1949.

———. *Luaḥ ha-yovel shel Ezrat Torah.* New York, 1936.

Herman, Azriel. *Sefer mayyim ḥayyim.* In *Kovez̦ shut be-inyanei eruvin be-Arẓot ha-Berit.* n.p, n.d.

Hertzberg, Arthur. "'Treifene Medina': Learned Opposition to Emigration to the United States." In *Proceedings of the Eighth World Congress of Jewish Studies: Panel Sessions Jewish History*, 1–30. Jerusalem, 1984.

Hildesheimer, Esriel, ed. *Halakhot gedolot.* Berlin, 1888.

———. *Halakhot gedolot.* Jerusalem, 1972.

Hirschfeld, Yizhar. *The Palestinian Dwelling in the Roman Byzantine Period.* Jerusalem, 1995.

Hirschenson, Chaim. *Sefer malki ba-kodesh*, edited by David Zohar. Jerusalem, 2006.

Hutterer, Boaz. "Eruv ḥazerot be-merḥav ha-eroni: Hishtasheluto ha-hilkhatit mi-tekufat ha-Mishnah ve-ha-Talmud ve-ad teḥilat ha-me'ah ha-20" ("'The 'Courtyard Eruv' in the Urban Space: Its Development from the Time of the

Mishnah and the Talmud to the Twentieth Century"). PhD diss., Bar-Ilan University, Tel Aviv, 2013.

Ibn Adret, Shlomo. *Avodat ha-kodesh.* Warsaw, 1876.

Ibn Lev, Joseph. *She'elot u-teshuvot Mahari ibn Lev.* Frankfurt, 1726.

Jaffe, Shalom Elchanan. *Sho'el ka-inyan.* Jerusalem, 1895.

———. *Teshuvah ka-halakhah ve-divrei shalom.* Jerusalem, 1896.

Joselit, Jenna Weissman. *New York's Jewish Jews: The Orthodox Community in the Interwar Years.* Bloomington, IN, 1990.

Karelitz, Abraham Yeshayahu. *Sefer ḥazon ish,* Hilkhot eruvin. Jerusalem, 1955.

Karp, Abraham. "The Ridwas: Rabbi Jacob David Wilowsky; 1845–1913." In *Perspectives on Jews and Judaism: Essays in Honor of Wolfe Kelman,* 215–237. New York, 1978.

Kasher, Menachem Mendel. "Tikkun eruvin be-Manhattan New York." In his *Divrei Menaḥem.* Jerusalem, 1980.

———. *Torah sheleimah.* New York, 1953.

Katzenellenbogen, Ezekiel. *She'elot u-teshuvot kenesset Yeḥezkel.* Warsaw, 1883.

Kaufman, Michael. "Far Rockaway: Torah Suburb by the Sea." *Jewish Life* (August 1960): 20–33.

Kayfetz, Ben. "The Toronto Jewish Press." *Canadian Jewish Historical Society Journal* 7, no. 1 (Spring 1983): 40–42.

Klein, Menashe. *Om ani ḥomah: Mishneh halakhot.* Jerusalem, 2000.

Kotler, Aharon. *Mishnat Rabbi Aharon.* Jerusalem, 1985.

Kroizer, D. M. "Tikkun eruvin be-Manhattan N.Y." *No'am* 1 (1958): 193–244.

Lange, Elimelekh. *Hilkhot eruvin.* Jerusalem, 1973.

Lazerwitz, Bernard, and Michael Harrison. "American Jewish Denominations: A Social and Religious Profile." *American Sociological Review* (August 1979): 659–661.

Landau, Ezekiel. *Nodah bi-Yehudah.* 2nd ed. Jerusalem, 1990.

Lange, Elimelekh. *Hilkhot eruvin.* Jerusalem, 1973.

Lederhendler, Eli. *Jewish Responses to Modernity: New Voices in America and Eastern Europe.* New York, 1994.

Lees, Susan H. "Jewish Space in Suburbia: Interpreting the Eruv Conflict in Teaneck, New Jersey." *Contemporary Jewry* 27, no. 1 (October 2007): 42–79.

Lieberman, Saul. *Tosefta ki-feshutah.* New York, 1962.

Mandsager, John. "The Eruv: A Space for Negotiating Identity." Master's thesis, Stanford University, Stanford, 2003.

Margolioth, Ephraim Zalman. *She'elot u-teshuvot beit Efraim*. Warsaw, 1884.

Miller, Yoel Ha-Kohen, ed. *Teshuvot ge'onei mizraḥ u-ma'arav*. Berlin, 1888.

Mintz, Adam, ed. *It's a Thin Line: Eruv from Talmudic to Modern Culture*. New York, 2014.

———. "The Community Eruv and the American Public Square." *Dine Israel: Studies in Halakha and Jewish Law* 31 (2017): 211–230.

———. "A Chapter in American Orthodoxy: The Eruvin in Brooklyn." *Hakirah* 14 (Winter 2012): 21–59.

———. "Is Coca-Cola Kosher? Rabbi Tobias Geffen and the History of American Orthodoxy. In *Rav Chesed: Essays in Honor of Rabbi Dr. Haskel Lookstein*. Edited by Rafael Medoff. Jersey City, 2009.

Moore, Deborah Dash. *At Home in America: Second-Generation New York Jews*. New York, 1981.

Moskowitz, Joseph David. *Sefer tikkun eruvin be-ir Manhattan*. New York, 1959.

———. "Tikkun eruvin be-Manhattan Nu York," *Ha-Maor* 5, no. 8 (October 1954): 11–14.

Nathanson, Joseph. *Sho'el u-meshiv*. New York, 1980.

Pirutinsky, Moshe Bunim. "Haẓa'ah le-tikkun eruv be-Manhattan." *Ha-Pardes* 33, no. 9 (June 1959): 10.

Pollak, Menahem Seigel. "Kuntres be-inyan tikkun eruvin be-manhattan." *Kol Ẓevi* 7 (2005): 67–82.

Price, Avraham Aharon. "Tikkun eruvin." *Ha-Pardes* (1951): 11–38.

———. *Tikkun eruvin he-ḥadash be-ir Toronto Canada*. Toronto, 1987.

Pultman, Shmuel. *Me-az u-mi-kedem*. New York, 2008.

Rabinowitz-Teomim, Eliyahu David. *Seder Eliyahu*. Jerusalem, 1983.

Raphael, Yitzchak. *Enẓiklopedyah shel ha-Ẓionut ha-datit*. Jerusalem, 1958.

Reischer, Jacob. *Sefer shevut Ya'akov*. New York, 1961.

Richman, Josh. "New Eruv Reopens Old Church-State Debates in Palo Alto." *The Jewish Daily Forward*, July 20, 2007.

Rischin, Moses. *The Promised City: New York Jews, 1870–1914*. Cambridge, MA, 1962.

Robinson, Ira. "The First Hasidic Rabbis in North America." *American Jewish Archives* 44, no. 2 (1992): 501–517.

———. "Anshe Sfard: The Creation of the First Hasidic Congregations in North America." *American Jewish Archives* 62, no. 1–2 (2005): 53–66.

Rosenfeld, Zekhariah. *Tikvat Zekhariah*. Chicago, 1896.

Rothkoff, Aaron, "The American Sojourns of Ridbaz: Religious Problems within the Immigrant Community." *American Jewish Historical Quarterly* 57, no. 4 (June 1968): 557–572.

Schwab, Simon. "Mikhtav be-inyan tikkun eruvin be-Manhattan." *Ha-Pardes* 36, no. 5 (February 1962): 26.

Schwadron, Mordechai. *She'elot u-teshuvot Maharsham*. Jerusalem, 1958.

Sack, B. G. *Canadian Jews Early in This Century*. Montreal, 1975.

Safrai, Shmuel, and Zeev Safrai. *Mishnat Ereẓ Yisra'el: Massekhet Eruvin*. Jerusalem, 2009.

Sasportas, Jacob. *Ohel Ya'akov*. Amsterdam, 1737.

Schweid, Eliezer. *Democracy and Halakhah*. Lanham, MD, 1994.

Sefer ḥai anokhi le-olam. New York, 2003.

Seigel, Joshua. *Eruv ve-hoẓa'ah*. New York, 1907.

———. *Oznei Yehoshua*. Jerusalem, 1914.

Shapiro, Marc. "Another Example of Minhag in America." *Judaism* 39, no. 2 (Spring 1990): 148–154.

Shemen, Nachman. "Rabbeinu Yehudah Leib Graubart" [Yiddish]. In *Yovel-buch, Talmud Torah Eẓ Ḥayyim*, edited by N. Shemen and L. J. Zuker, 13–45. Toronto, 1943.

———. "Orthodoxy in Toronto." In *Sefer ha-yovel shel Talmud Torah Eẓ Ḥayyim*. Toronto, 1943.

Sherman, Moshe D. *Orthodox Judaism in America: A Biographical Dictionary and Sourcebook*. Westport, CT, 1996.

Sklare, Marshall. *America's Jews*. New York, 1971.

Sofer, Moses. *She'elot u-teshuvot Ḥatam Sofer*. Bratislava, 1841.

Sorin, Gerald. *A Time for Building: The Third Migration 1880–1920*. Baltimore, 1992.

Speisman, Stephen A. "Orthodox Rabbinate Updates Toronto Eruv." *Canadian Jewish News*, January 11, 1996.

———. "St. John's Shtetl: The Ward in 1911." In *Gathering Place: Peoples and Neighbourhoods of Toronto, 1834–1945*, edited by R. F. Harney. Toronto, 1985.

———. *The Jews of Toronto: A History to 1937*. Toronto, 1979.

Sperber, Daniel. *The City in Roman Palestine*. New York, 1998.

Stampfer, Shaul. "The Geographic Background of East European Jewish Migration to the United States before World War I." In *Migration across Time and Nations: Population Mobility in Historical Contexts,* edited by Ira A. Glazier and Luigi De Rosa, 220–230. New York, 1986.

Standage, Tom. *The Victorian Internet: The Remarkable Story of the Telegraph and the Nineteenth Century On-Line Pioneers.* New York, 1998.

Steif, Yonatan. "Kuntres tikkun eruvin." *Ohr Yisro'el* 9, no. 1 (2003): 6–15.

———. "Kuntres tikkun eruvin." *Ohr Yisro'el* 8, no. 4 (2003): 6–9.

———. *Sefer she'elot u-teshuvot ve-ḥiddushei Mahari Steif.* New York, 1968.

Stern, S. M. "The Constitution of the Islamic City." In *The Islamic City: A Colloquium,* edited by A. H. Hourani and S. M. Stern. Philadelphia, 1970.

Stetler, Lawrence. *By the El: Third Avenue and Its El at Mid-Century.* New York, 1995.

Stillman, Noam. "Ha-Yehudim be-historiyah ha-ironot shel ha-Islam bi-ymei ha-beinayim." In *Masa'it Mosheh: Mekhkarim be-tarbut Yisra'el ve-arav mugashim le-Mosheh Gil,* edited by Ezra Fleisher, Mordekhai Akiva Friedman, and Yoel Kramer, 246–255. Jerusalem, 1998.

Tabak, Solomon Leib. *Sefer she'elot u-teshuvot teshurat shai.* Bnei Brak, 1990.

Tamar, David. *Jewish Commitment in a Modern World: Rabbi Hayyim Hirschensohn and His Attitude to Modernity* [Hebrew]. Jerusalem: Shalom Hartman Institute, 2003. Reviewed by Marc Shapiro, *Edah Journal* 5, no. 1 (Tamuz 5765).

Ta-Shma, Israel. *Halakhah, minhag u-meẓi'ut be-Ashkenaz 1100–1350.* Jerusalem, 1996.

Teitelbaum, Yekutiel Yehudah. *Sefer gedulat Yehoshua,* edited by Moshe Arye Low. New York, 1986.

Teomim, Joseph ben Meir. *Peri megadim.* New York, 2006.

Troyb, Avrohom Shimon, ed. *Halakhot gedolot.* Warsaw, 1974.

Trunk, Israel. *She'elot u-teshuvot yeshu'ot malko.* Petrokow, 1927.

Tulchinsky, Gerald. *Taking Root: The Origins of the Canadian Jewish Community.* Hanover, NH, 1993.

Wachs, Hayyim Elazar. *Sefer nefesh ḥayyah.* Pietrokov, 1876.

Walfish, Yisrael Yaakov. *Maḥshevot Yisra'el.* Warsaw, 1900.

Waxman, Chaim I. "From Treifene Medina to Goldene Medina: Changing Perspectives on the United States among American Haredim." In *Why is America Different? American Jewry on Its 350th Anniversary,* edited by Steven T. Katz. Lanham, MD, 2009.

Weinberg, Refael Shmuel Ha-Kohen, ed. *Teshuvot Rav Sar Shalom Gaon.* Jerusalem, 1975.

Weissmandel, Michael Dov. *Torat ḥemed.* Mt. Kisco, New York, 1958.
Whaley, Joachim. *Religious Toleration and Social Change in Hamburg, 1529–1819.* Cambridge, MA, 1985.
Wunder, Meir. *Me'orei Galiẓyah: Enẓiklopedyah le-ḥakhamei Galiẓya.* Jerusalem, 1997.
Yudelovitz, Abraham. *She'elot u-teshuvot beit av.* 2nd ed. New York, 1929.
Zahalon, Yom Tov ben Moses. *She'elot u-teshuvot Mahariẓ.* Venice, 1694.

Index

Printed in the USA
CPSIA information can be obtained
at www.ICGtesting.com
JSHW011807120224
57180JS00007B/75

9 798887 190839